A HISTORY OF THE
THEATRE IN AMERICA

TRAINING FOR THE STAGE

By ARTHUR HORNBLOW

Foreword by DAVID BELASCO

EIGHT ILLUSTRATIONS   *$1.50 NET*

"I have read 'Training for the Stage' for the second time, and must say that it contains much of great interest to the professional. It should also be of great value to the novice. The author's treatment of his subject is very unusual and most skillfully handled. A really brilliant book."

DAVID BELASCO.

"It is so true and sensible and competent that it is one of the most valuable additions to my rather large collection of books on topics of the theatre. I wish I might have written it."

LOUIS DE FOE,
Dramatic Critic, *New York World.*

"Invaluable to those who seek the stage as a profession. It will also benefit the playgoer in that it will assist in forming a more accurate estimate of the player." — *Dramatic Mirror.*

A HISTORY OF THE THEATRE IN AMERICA

FROM ITS BEGINNINGS TO THE PRESENT TIME

BY

ARTHUR HORNBLOW

FOR NINETEEN YEARS EDITOR OF "THE THEATRE MAGAZINE"
AUTHOR OF "TRAINING FOR THE STAGE," ETC.

WITH PHOTOGRAVURE FRONTISPIECES AND
188 ILLUSTRATIONS IN DOUBLETONE

VOLUME I

PHILADELPHIA AND LONDON
J. B. LIPPINCOTT COMPANY
1919

TO
MY TWO SONS

PREFACE

FOR nearly two hundred years the theatre in America has been without a historian. Of books on plays and playacting there has been no end. We have also several histories of the stage, but practically all of them are limited to the chronicling of theatrical happenings in certain localities, such as Blake's "History of the Providence Stage," Clapp's "Record of the Boston Stage," Ireland's " Records of the New York Stage," etc. Until now no attempt has been made to produce a work embracing the entire field of American theatrical activity, from the earliest beginnings in Colonial days down to the present time.

Thirty years ago George O. Seilhamer began the publication of his " History of the American Theatre," perhaps the best, because the most complete, chronicle of the American stage up to the time of the Revolution that we have. Unfortunately, Mr. Seilhamer died when his history reached the year 1797, so that his splendidly conceived work remained unfinished. The three large volumes that did appear constitute, however, a monument of patient research, and I wish to acknowledge indebtedness to their interesting pages for much valuable information and data regarding the earlier period of our stage.

Of William Dunlap's better-known work " A History of the American Theatre "—now a classic of our literature—almost everything can be said in praise except that it is not history. The book, which might properly be classed as an autobiography, seeing that the author writes mostly of his own experiences in theatrical authorship and management, is a series of charming pen pictures of old-time players and theatres by one who was contemporaneous with them. The work has little value as history. It goes back only a few years earlier than Dunlap's own life, it completely ignores important events that had already made theatrical history before he was born, and the book ends with his own retirement from management. Wholly delightful as a piece of literature, full of piquant observation and amusing anecdote, Dunlap's book, bristling as it is with errors of dates and facts, must be regarded as a volume of amiable personal impressions rather than as a serious contribution to theatrical history.

In Joseph N. Ireland we have a historian of far greater competence. His work is precisely what it purports to be—a record of the New York stage from 1750 to 1859, and for the period it covers, it is the most complete, the most accurate, the most authoritative of all the histories of the New York theatres. It does not chronicle the earliest beginnings of our stage, for even Mr. Ireland, well-informed and accurate as he was, did not know that professional players acted Farquhar's farce " The Recruiting Officer " in New York City as early as 1732. Ireland mentions the performance, but merely as an unconfirmed report, the accuracy of which he is inclined to doubt. There exists, he says, no record of what play was performed, or who the players were. In this, the usually careful and accurate historian erred. The record does exist. To-day it is no longer a matter of speculation. The Ireland history continues down to the year 1859 and there the record stops, long before the most brilliant period of the American stage had been reached. In 1859 Edwin Booth was only at the outset of his remarkable career, Joseph Jefferson's " Rip Van Winkle " had not yet added to that comedian's fame, Lester Wallack had still to reëstablish his brilliant stock company at Thirteenth Street and Broadway, Augustin Daly, then an obscure playwright, had not yet entered the managerial field, A. M. Palmer and the glorious days of the Union Square Theatre still belonged to the future, Charles Frohman and David Belasco were not yet born!

(Obviously there was room for a history of the American stage which should start at the beginning and continue to the end, a work not confined to any one locality but which should show the growth and progress of the drama in Boston, Philadelphia, Chicago, San Francisco, and other cities as well as New York, a complete chronological narrative of the growth and development of the theatre in this country, showing how the drama first took root in North America, how the players, then regarded as little better than social outcasts, slowly overcame Puritanical intolerance, and a chain of theatres was gradually built, first along the Atlantic seaboard, and then through the great, sparsely settled West, the courageous thespians pressing their way through the still virgin forests, braving the perils of the great American desert, until they reached the Pacific Ocean. Surely a more fascinating story has never been told!)

It is not known definitely where the first company of professional actors seen in this country originally came from. They probably hailed from the West

Indies, being part of that little band of English
players who in 1746 crossed the Atlantic under the
leadership of John Moody, the adventurous barber
who later became a popular London comedian.
That there was acting here of a sort long before these
professional English players put in an appearance is
hardly to be doubted. That interesting English adventurer, Anthony Aston, says he acted in New York
about the years 1702–1703. No record exists, as far
as is known, of dramatic performances in New York
at that early date, but it is not unreasonable to believe
that, with the exception of Puritanical New England
where the extremely severe laws against play acting
proved for many years an effective barrier against
the incursions of enterprising thespians, theatrical
entertainment was everywhere, then as now, a favorite
form of public amusement.

It was, however, in Virginia that the drama first
took root. There arose the first theatre built in
America—the playhouse erected by William Levingston for the Staggs in Williamsburg in 1716—and
there, almost from the time of the settling of the
colony late in the Sixteenth Century, the mummer,
as opportunity allowed, assumed the motley, entirely
free from the vexatious restrictions which barred him
from the less hospitable North. It is likely that most
of the acting at this early period, even in Virginia
and Maryland where there were no laws against
plays, was almost entirely undertaken by amateurs
and college students. We know, for instance, that it
was Harvard students and not professionals who in
1690 appeared in " Gustavus Vasa," the first play
written by an American to be acted in this country,

and instances of other college performances are frequent, especially in pre-Revolutionary days when pieces of a polemical nature, most of them in support of British power in the Colonies, were presented by college students as part of the political propaganda of the day.

In a work of this kind, in which an attempt has been made to cover the whole field of theatrical activity in America, it is evident that it has been impossible to enter as fully into detail as in a history limited to only one locality. It would have been an impossible feat even if ten volumes had been devoted to it instead of two and it has not been attempted. The plan followed has been to present a plain narrative of the principal events connected with the development of the drama in this country, following as closely as possible the chronological order, describing the theatres built as well as the principal plays performed, and bringing back to life the great actors and actresses of the past—John Hodgkinson, Thomas Abthorpe Cooper, Mrs. Merry, George Frederick Cooke, Edmund Kean, Junius Brutus Booth, William Macready, James W. Wallack, Charlotte Cushman, J. H. Hackett, Edwin Forrest, E. L. Davenport, John Gilbert, John Brougham, W. E. Burton, William Warren, Joseph Jefferson, Clara Morris, Edwin Booth, Lawrence Barrett and many others—a truly brilliant company as they pass, one after the other, in stately procession across our stage. The later history of the theatre and the players of to-day have also not been neglected.

In estimating the ability and true rank of players, the author has not attempted to give his own judgment: first, because he could hardly have witnessed performances given a hundred years ago; secondly, because in the case of players of a later period there is so much diversity of opinion that any one man's judgment cannot be accepted as final. The method pursued, therefore, has been to present the views of leading contemporary critics. Although the judgment of these critics regarding the merits of the same actor may be diametrically opposed, as, for instance, it was in the case of Edwin Forrest, the reader will thus be better able to form an opinion of his own.

Thanks are due Jefferson Winter, Esq., for according permission to use for this purpose excerpts from William Winter's writings; and I am also indebted for the same reason to John Ranken Towse, Esq., the distinguished dramatic critic of the New York *Evening Post,* as well as to the Century Company of New York, and the Houghton, Mifflin Company, of Boston, for permission to quote respectively from the " Autobiography of Joseph Jefferson," and the writings of the late Henry Austin Clapp, for many years dramatic critic of the Boston *Daily Advertiser.*

Grateful acknowledgment is also made of the generous assistance rendered by Professor Frederick W. Atkinson, President of the Polytechnic Institute of Brooklyn, N. Y., who not only put his valuable and unique theatrical library at my disposition, but also loaned many of the rare portraits with which these volumes are illustrated.

Kind co-operation was also given by Dr. Lyon G. Tyler, President of William and Mary College, who furnished important information regarding the early Virginia theatres; by Professor Arthur Hobson

PREFACE

Quinn, Dean of the University of Pennsylvania, whose special knowledge of the early American dramatists proved invaluable; and by Brander Matthews, Professor of Dramatic Literature at Columbia University, New York.

For the many unusual theatrical portraits which illustrate this work, I am indebted to some of the best-known collectors in the country. Robert Gould Shaw, curator of the Theatre Collection at Harvard University, gave the use of his magnificent collection, and I am also indebted for many interesting portraits to William Seymour, the well-known stage director so long with the Boston Museum. My thanks go also to Charles Burnham, the prominent theatre manager, to the publishers of the *Theatre Magazine* and to Mr. Patrick F. Madigan.

I am likewise grateful to David Belasco for information regarding the early theatres in California, and to Mr. Frank Chouteau Brown, Miss Lucy France Pierce, Miss Clare P. Peeler, Mr. Richard Spamer and Miss Rozel Gotthold for data concerning respectively Boston, Chicago, Philadelphia, St. Louis and New Orleans.

I must also acknowledge courtesy extended by the archivist of the New York Historical Society, the secretary of the Virginia Historical Society, Mr. Guy Nichols, the amiable librarian of The Players, New York, Mr. J. I. C. Clarke, president of the Society of American Dramatists and Composers, Mr. Montrose J. Moses and Mr. Frank J. Wilstach.

ARTHUR HORNBLOW

NEW YORK, AUGUST, 1919

CONTENTS

CONTENTS

CONTENTS

ILLUSTRATIONS

VOLUME I

ILLUSTRATIONS

A HISTORY OF THE THEATRE IN AMERICA

CHAPTER I

THE FIRST AMERICAN THEATRE

BITTER PURITANICAL OPPOSITION TO PLAYS AND PLAY-ACTING.
SEVERE LAWS PASSED PROHIBITING STAGE ENTERTAINMENT OF
ANY KIND. EARLIEST RECORDS OF THEATRICAL PERFORMANCES
IN AMERICA. TONY ASTON, THE FIRST ACTOR TO APPEAR IN
NEW YORK. PERFORMANCE IN BOSTON CAUSES A RIOT. FIRST
THEATRE IN AMERICA BUILT IN WILLIAMSBURG, VA.

THE history of the theatre in America begins
early in the Eighteenth Century, about the time the
first rumblings were heard of the storm which was to
break the ties still holding the Colonies to the mother
country.

William Dunlap, the earliest historian of the
American stage, tells us that the drama was first introduced in this country by the Hallams in the year 1752
when they brought over a company from London
and presented " The Merchant of Venice " at Williamsburg, then the capital of Virginia, in a building
arranged for that purpose. " This," says Dunlap,
" was the first theatre opened in America by a company of regular comedians." This singularly mis-
leading statement is perhaps the most conspicuous of
a number of similar erroneous assertions which mar
an otherwise valuable and interesting work.[1] Dunlap

---

[1] A History of the American Theatre. By William Dunlap, New York, 1832.

21

ignored or was uninformed of a number of well authenticated dramatic performances which had been given in different parts of the Colonies many years before the arrival of the Hallams. Apparently, he knew nothing of the theatre built in Williamsburg, Va., in 1716. He had no knowledge of the theatre opened in New York in 1732. He makes no mention of the opening of the Playhouse in Dock Street, Charleston, S. C., in 1736.[2] He had never heard of Thomas Kean who acted Richard III at the First Nassau Street Theatre, New York, March 5, 1750.

Even so careful an historian as Joseph N. Ireland falls into the error of taking it for granted that no earlier records existed because he had not happened to stumble upon them. In his " Records of the New York Stage," [3] referring to an advertisement in *Bradford's Gazette* of October, 1733, which mentions George Talbot's store as being " next door to the Playhouse," he says, " No other reference has been found respecting it (the Playhouse) and any conjecture as to its proprietors, its performers, or the plays presented therein would be vain and fruitless."

How little " vain and fruitless " may be judged from the fact that to-day we not only know what play was performed in this New York theatre of 1732, but also who some of the players were.

Virginia has some claim to be considered the cradle of the native American theatre, but 1752 was not the date of the drama's birth in this country.

---

[2] George O. Seilhamer, another historian of the American Theatre, also appears to have been unaware of the existence of Charleston's earliest playhouse.

[3] Records of the New York Stage. By Joseph N. Ireland, vol. 1, page 2.

THE FIRST AMERICAN THEATRE

There were theatrical performances in Williamsburg and acting in New York by professional players many years earlier than that. We know that a regular theatre was built in Williamsburg and performances given as early as 1716. We also know that Murray and Kean's troupe of professional players acted "Richard III" in Williamsburg some time before the Hallams arrived and presented "The Merchant of Venice." In fact, the Hallams used the same theatre that the Murray-Kean company had recently occupied.

In view of the more than scant information regarding plays and players in the pre-Revolutionary newspapers and chronicles of the time, it would be an impossible task to attempt to ascertain when or where the first theatrical performance took place on the North American continent. It is likely that there were scattered dramatic performances of a sort in all the Colonies many years before we have any records of them, particularly in the South where the prejudice against the stage was less violent than in the North, but singularly enough it is in the Puritanical New England provinces that we find the first actual records of public theatricals, and in Quaker Philadelphia that the drama first found a permanent home.

That so little should be known of the early beginnings of the acted drama in America is not surprising when one considers the intolerance of the age against the theatre and the player. In face of the almost general condemnation of the playhouse the journals of the day were not encouraged to give much, if any, space in their slender columns to the doings of player-folk. It was also the custom at that time for the actors themselves to distribute handbills at the houses of prospective theatre goers, and thus stir up interest in the coming performance, instead of depending solely on newspaper advertising as is the modern practice. These reasons, perhaps, sufficiently explain the almost total absence of theatrical news in the pre-Revolutionary newspapers, a fact which has rendered exceedingly difficult the researches of the historian.

In the South the Colonists had imported a taste for the drama together with their other English customs, but in the North the playhouse was still considered the highway to hell and was everywhere fiercely condemned if not actually forbidden under the severest penalties. In 1750 the General Court of Massachusetts passed an act prohibiting stage plays and theatrical entertainments of any kind. On May 31, 1759, the House of Representatives in the Colony of Pennsylvania passed a law forbidding the showing and acting of plays under a penalty of £500. In 1761 Rhode Island passed " an act to Prevent Stage Plays and other Theatrical Entertainments within this Colony," and the following year the New Hampshire House of Representatives refused a troupe of actors admission to Portsmouth on the ground that plays had a " peculiar influence on the minds of young people and greatly endanger their morals by giving them a taste for intriguing, amusement and pleasure." In 1824 President Dwight of Yale College in his " Essay on the Stage " declared that " to indulge a taste for playgoing means nothing more or less than the loss of that most valuable treasure the immortal soul." Even as late as 1856, when the city of Brooklyn could boast of only one theatre and the citizens were gravely contemplating the erection of another, there was considerable opposition to the word "theatre," a compromise being finally reached by calling it an Academy of Music. Judge Daly [4] tells an amusing anecdote connected with the preliminary planning of this new house. There was a warm argument among the building committee over the questions of stage and scenery, a determined stand being taken against a curtain. "A curtain," exclaimed one solemn-faced objector, "is intended to conceal something and concealment suggests impropriety." So little versed in the lore of the theatre was this worthy city father that it was necessary to explain to him that stage plays were usually divided into sections, commonly called "acts," and that the curtain was lowered simply to mark the intervals.

Yet in spite of this hostile and uncompromising attitude toward the theatre, stage performances were occasionally, if not frequently, given, usually by special permission of the local authorities. The probability is that the laws forbidding play-acting remained a dead letter in many of the large towns at least, the regulations governing the players being introduced more to placate public opinion at the moment than with any serious intention of suppressing the player altogether as a public nuisance. How else can we account for the theatrical performances in New York in 1702 and again in 1732 or for the performances given in 1714 and in 1749 in Boston and Philadelphia?

It must not be forgotten that while the great

---

[4] Life of Augustin Daly. By Joseph Francis Daly. Macmillan.

majority of the Northern Colonists were bitterly opposed to the playhouse on religious and moral grounds, there was a large and growing class in the important centres who were burdened with no such scruples—people of means and leisure who had only recently crossed the Atlantic and who, when seeking recreation, naturally turned to a form of amusement highly popular at home. It is not unreasonable, then, to presume that as the Colonies grew in importance, and communication between America and Europe became more frequent, the old spirit of irreconcilable intolerance which put a ban on all secular amusements, was considerably modified, especially in the important towns. The citizens of these communities, in their moments of leisure, no doubt often longed for the pleasures of the theatre, glowing accounts of which arrived from London by every ship.

The drama in England had gradually risen from the depths into which it had sunk after the Restoration. Under the leadership of Addison, Pope, Steele and Swift began the so-called "Augustan age" of English literature. Dryden, hailed as a new Shakespeare, had already given the stage the vigor and brilliancy of his genius, while· Thomas Otway's tragedy "Venice Preserved" had earned for him the title of "Euripides of the English Stage." Addison, producing his "Cato," the finest English example of classical tragedy, at a moment of great political excitement, met with extraordinary success, calling forth praise even from the cynical Voltaire. Wycherley had made all London laugh with his masterpieces "The Country Wife" and "The Plain

Dealer "; Congreve, the greatest English master of
pure comedy, had produced his crowning triumph
"Love for Love." Colley Cibber had written his
best play, "The Careless Husband," and adapted
Shakespeare. George Farquhar, leader among the
comic dramatists, amused thousands with his
sprightly farces "The Recruiting Sergeant" and
"The Beaux' Stratagem." Sir Richard Steele, cater-
ing to the new public taste for sentimental comedy,
had won immediate success with "The Conscious
Lovers." The most famous men in England wrote
plays and attended their performance. The pit of
the theatre was the resort of wit and learning; while
fashion, beauty, taste and refinement, the proud and
exclusive aristocracy of the land, took their places in
the boxes, surrounding the assemblage of poets and
critics below.

The acting of the day was of the finest. Thomas
Betterton, the great Shakespearean actor, and all the
famous players of the Restoration were long past their
maturity, but a new generation—Wilks, Cibber,
Mrs. Porter, Peg Woffington and others, equally as
celebrated—was rising to take their places. Barton
Booth, the tragedian of the day, was so popular that
he had been admitted to the Patent, while Ann Oldfield, the barmaid who became the associate of duch-
esses, was the reigning attraction at Drury Lane.
Macklin, departing from tradition, had thrilled London by playing Shylock for the first time as a tragic
character. In the same year David Garrick, the fore-
most actor of his age, made his début in Goodman's
Fields as Richard III.

While the American Colonies were growing in

wealth and energy, the times were not without their anxieties. There was increasing unrest at the burdens and vexations put on the provinces by the English Parliament and threats of the Colonists to throw off the yoke of the mother country were heard on every hand. The encroachments of the French on the Ohio also created concern, and two years after the Hallams landed in America and made their first bow to Williamsburg audiences Governor Dinwiddie of Virginia despatched a young officer to the nearest posts to find out what the French were doing. The name of the young officer was George Washington. The French proving obstinate in their claims, the squabble was followed by the Fourth Intercolonial war, which was ended by the taking of Quebec and the conquest of Canada by the British.

The population of the Colonies, at the beginning of the Eighteenth Century, was about six hundred and fifty thousand. Newport, the metropolis of Rhode Island, had a population of five thousand, including Indians and negroes. Virginia had a population of sixty thousand, of whom about one-half were slaves. Massachusetts mustered about seventy or eighty thousand.

Means of travel in those days were so few and difficult that the cities were practically isolated. Coaches were slow and uncertain. It took a day to go from Philadelphia to New York and three days to go from New York to Boston. The great West was still an unexplored wilderness inhabited by marauding savages. The most popular mode of travel was by water. Hallam and his players selected the ocean route when they went North from Virginia in 1753. As an instance of the difficulties of communication between American cities, even as late as the year 1823, manager W. B. Wood [5] relates how the celebrated star Thomas Abthorpe Cooper one wintry night was unable to fill an important theatre engagement in Philadelphia because he found it impossible to reach that city from New York owing to an ice jam in the Hudson!

New York in 1700 had thirty thousand inhabitants, including seven thousand slaves. By 1732 the population had more than doubled, and it was rapidly becoming a gay and cosmopolitan town. Although not so important as Philadelphia, it grew larger and more prosperous year by year. Commerce thrived, stately ships left its docks for all the ports of the world, beautiful homes rose on each side of "Hudson's River." The people were industrious and sociable. There still remained among them some influence of the old Dutch burghers' manners and habits, but the predominating tastes were English and French. There were weekly evening clubs and in the winter balls and concerts under the patronage of the governor. It is only reasonable to presume that among these diversions theatre-going formed a part. The governor, almost invariably a member of the English aristocracy, was usually a man of culture whose taste for literature and art would naturally incline him to encourage rather than frown upon any attempt made to present plays in his jurisdiction, no matter what the local ordinances said to the contrary.

Exactly when the first dramatic performance was given in America it is, of course, impossible to say.

---

[5] Personal Recollections of the Stage. By William B. Wood.

There are records in Virginia of a play being acted in that colony [6] and the players summoned to court in consequence as early as 1665, but this was evidently only an amateur effort and need not detain us here. In 1690 Harvard students gave a performance at Cambridge, Mass., of Benjamin Colman's tragedy "Gustavus Vasa," the first play written by an American acted in America, of which we have any knowledge. We also know that there were dramatic performances by professional actors in New York at the opening of, if not before, the Eighteenth Century. Anthony Aston, a well-known English actor-adventurer, says he acted in New York about 1702, and there is no reason to doubt his word. What he acted or where we do not know. But the fact that he was able to follow his profession at all, would seem to indicate not only that theatrical performances at the time of his visit were not taboo, but that they were already a popular feature of New York life.

Anthony Aston, sometimes known as "Mat Medley," was born in England and educated as an attorney. He became an actor towards the end of the reign of William III, presenting a musical and dramatic entertainment written by himself entitled "The Medley." In this he toured the English provinces and in 1717 performed at the Globe and Marlborough taverns in Fleet Street, London. Chetwood in his history (1749) speaks of Aston as "travelling still and as well known as the post horse that carries the mail." He was the author of a Supplement to the "Apology" of Colley Cibber and of several plays, including "The Fool's Opera." This piece, printed in London about the year 1731, is prefaced by "a

---

[6] Early History of the Eastern Shore of Virginia. By J. C. Wise.

sketch of the author's life and a frontispiece giving a scene from the play." A bad wood-cut portrait of Aston himself is in the upper left-hand corner. The title page runs as follows:

"The Fool's Opera, or the Taste of the Age. Written by Mat Medley and Performed by his Company at Oxford: to which is prefixed a Sketch of the Author's Life Written by Himself. London (Circa 1731)."

In the quaintly worded preface Aston speaks of his voyage to America many years earlier (1701 is believed to be the exact date) and his acting in New York. He begins thus:

My merry hearts, you are to know me as a gentleman, lawyer, poet, actor, soldier, sailor, exciseman, publican, in England, Scotland, Ireland, New York, East and West Jersey, Maryland, Virginia (on both sides Cheesapeek), North and South Carolina, South Florida, Bahamas, Jamaica, Hispaniola, and often a coaster by all the same. . . . After many vicissitudes I arrived at Charles Towne (Charleston, S. C.) full of lice, shame, poverty, nakedness and hunger—turned player and poet and *wrote one play* on the subject of the country.

After leaving Charleston, Aston proceeded North by ship. When nearly at the mouth of New York harbor the ship was blown to the Virginia Capes. After some delay he arrived in New York by way of Elizabeth. He continues:

There I lighted on my old acquaintance, Jack Charlton, Fencing Master and Counsellor Reignieur, sometime of Lincoln's Inn (who) supply'd me with business (work?) till I had the honour of being acquainted with that brave, honest, unfortunate gentleman, Capt. Henry Pullein, whose ship (The Fame) was burnt in the Bermudas; he (to the best of his ability) assisted me, so that after acting, writing, courting, fighting that winter (1702?) my kind Captain Davies, in his sloop built at Rhode, gave me free passage for Virginia.

31

There is nothing in this account to warrant Mr. Oscar Wegelin's [7] assumption that Aston was the first professional player to act in New York. The very fact that the English adventurer makes nothing of his appearance, but announces the fact in the most commonplace way, would seem to indicate that he found other actors here when he reached New York. Otherwise, if acting had been unknown here, he would surely have had something to say of the sensation which such a novelty must have been to New Yorkers, unaccustomed to anything of the sort. The chief interest in Aston's sketch is the positive statement that there was acting in New York at the time of his visit. This being the very earliest information we have regarding theatricals in New York, the account of his visit is of great historic interest and value.

It is to be surmised from Aston's own statement that wherever he acted or in whatever play he acted, the occasion did not bring him much remuneration, or he would not have had to apply to his friend, the captain, to assist him with a free passage. After leaving New York, he went to London where he married and we hear no more of him.

After Aston's departure there was no mention of theatricals in the Colonies for many years. The first American newspaper had not yet made its appearance (the earliest public journal, the Boston *News Letter,* was not published until 1704) nor did any of the correspondence of the time, until 1714, make the slightest reference to plays or players. In that year,

---

7. "The Beginning of the Drama in America." By Oscar L. Wegelin.

however, Justice Samuel Sewall,[8] of Massachusetts, wrote a letter in which he protests against the acting of a play in the Council Chamber of Boston, affirming that even the Romans, fond as they were of plays, were not " so far set upon them as to turn their Senate House into a Playhouse." " Let not Christian Boston," he continues, " goe beyond Heathen Rome in the practice of Shamefull vanities."

There is no further trace of the proposed performance. Owing to the judge's protest, it probably was not given in the Council Chamber. Possibly the promoters found some other quarters more suitable, for it will be noted that Judge Sewall merely protests. He does not invoke the law to prohibit the performance altogether.

A couple of decades later—1750 to be exact—a performance of Thomas Otway's tragedy " The Orphan "[9] was given in a coffee house in State Street, Boston, by local amateurs, assisted by two professional players recently arrived from England. The affair was such a novelty and the curiosity of the Boston public to see the play so keen, that the doors of the coffee house were besieged and an incipient riot took place. This disturbance caused such a

---

[8] "This early opponent of the American drama," says Judge Charles P. Daly in his 'First Theatre in America,' "was an interesting character. As a judge he took part in the Salem Witchcraft Trials and is said to have been the only one of the judges who publicly confessed his error. In 1697, five years after these trials, he prepared a written confession which was read to the congregation of the old South Church in Boston by the minister, the judge, during the reading, standing up in his place."

[9] This piece, which later became immensely popular with early American theatregoers, was founded on a novel called English Adventures. It was one of the two plays (the other being " Venice Preserved ") which gained for Thomas Otway the high rank he holds among the tragic poets of the Restoration. Notwithstanding his success, the author ended his days in the most abject poverty. The story goes that he almost choked to death while ravenously swallowing a crust of bread thrown to him by a passing stranger.

scandal that the authorities were compelled to take notice, and the General Court at once enacted a law, not only forbidding acting within the Commonwealth, but even rendering the spectators liable to a fine.

Yet Boston, early in the Eighteenth Century, was not quite such a place of gloom and solemn visages as New England tradition would lead us to think. This one can readily believe after reading a description, recorded by Spencer, of one of the principal residences in that town:

There was a great hall ornamented with pictures and a great lantern and a velvet cushion in the window-seat that looked into the garden. In the hall was placed a large bowl of punch from which visitors might help themselves as they entered. On either side was a large parlor, a little parlor or study. These were furnished with mirrors, oriental rugs, window curtains and valance, pictures, a brass clock, red leather back chair, and a pair of huge brass andirons. The bedrooms were well supplied with feather beds, warming pans and every other article that would now be thought necessary for comfort or display. The pantry was well filled with substantial fare and delicacies. Silver tankards, wine cups and other articles were not uncommon. Very many families employed servants, and in one we see a Scotch boy valued among the property and invoiced at £14.[10]

Even before this period in the matter of dress certain of the ladies were eager to copy the London and Paris fashions, so much so that a writer of the time complained, " Methinks it should break the heart of Englishmen to see so many goodly English women imprisoned in French cages peering out of their hood holes for some men of mercy to help them with a litle wit."

The distinction of having erected what is believed

---

[10] History of the United States. By J. A. Spencer.

to be the first theatre in America belongs to Williamsburg, Va. Research has not brought to light any playhouse in the Colonies of earlier origin than the one built in the then capital of Virginia in 1716, the year that Governor Spotswood crossed the Blue Ridge, the first white man, as far as known, to enter the Great Valley.

The theatre was erected by one William Levingston, who " for some time previous," says Dr. Tyler in his interesting book on Williamsburg,[11] " had been managing in New Kent County a peripatetic dancing school, in which the star dancers were Charles Stagg and his wife Mary. There is a contract recorded at Yorktown dated July 11, 1716, by which William Levingston, merchant, agrees with Charles and Mary Stagg, his wife, actors, to build a theatre in Williamsburg and to provide actors, scenery and music out of England for the enacting of comedies and tragedies in the said city. On November 21, 1716, Mr. Levingston purchased three and one-half acre lots and erected thereon a dwelling house, kitchen and stable. He laid out also a bowling alley and built a theatre."

That this is the same " Playhouse " mentioned by Hugh Jones in his now very scarce work " The Present State of Virginia,"[12] published in London in 1724, there can be little doubt. It is also probable

---

[11] "Williamsburg, the old Virginia Capital," by Lyon G. Tyler.

[12] One of the rarest books relating to Virginia published in the eighteenth century. The author was a Professor at William and Mary College, Williamsburg. After describing the situation and plan of Williamsburg college, the State house, the church, he continues: "Next there is a large octagon Tower which is the Magazine or Repositary of Arms and Ammunition, standing far from any house except Jamestown Court House, for the town is half in Jamestown County and half in York County. Not far from hence is a large area for a Market Place, near which is a *Play House*, and good Bowling Green."

that on the stage of this theatre was acted the play
mentioned by Governor Spotswood in a letter written June 24, 1718. In this letter the governor refers
to eight members of the House of Assembly who
slighted an invitation to his house to witness a play.
He writes:

> In order to the solemnizing His Majesty's birthday, I gave a
> public entertainment at my home and all gentlemen that would
> come were admitted. These eight committeemen would neither
> come to my house nor go to the play which was acted on the occa-
> sion, but, on the contrary, these eight committeemen got together all
> the turbulent and disappointed burghers to an entertainment of their
> own in the House of Burgesses and invited the mob and plentifully
> supplied it with liquor to drink the same health as was drunk in the
> governor's house, taking no more notice of the government than if
> there had been none in the place.[13]

No records exist as to what plays were presented
at this theatre built by William Levingston in 1716.
There was no newspaper in Virginia until 1732 when
the *Virginia Gazette* first made its appearance. The
house does not appear to have prospered, for in 1723
its mortgage was foreclosed and Dr. Archibald
Blair, the mortgagee, took possession of the property.
Charles Stagg died in Williamsburg in 1735, and
after his death Mary Stagg earned a living holding
" dancing assemblies."

In 1735 and 1736 the theatre was utilized for
amateur productions, the students of William and
Mary College giving performances. It is also believed that a company of professional players acted
regularly there. The *Virginia Gazette* for September 10, 1736, contained this advertisement:

[13] Spotswood's Letters. Collections of the Virginia Historical Society, vol. ii,
p. 284.

THE FIRST AMERICAN THEATRE

This evening will be performed at the Theatre by the young gentlemen of the College the Tragedy of " Cato," and on Monday, Wednesday and Friday will be acted the following comedies by the young Gentlemen and Ladies of the country—" The Busybody,"[14] and " The Recruiting Officer " and " The Beaux' Stratagem." [15]

There is some doubt as to the exact meaning of this announcement. Some writers believe that it refers only to amateur performances. It is quite plain that it was the students who were to present " Cato," but it is not equally certain that amateurs were to appear in the comedies mentioned. The expression " young Gentlemen and Ladies of the country " might well mean persons of both sexes belonging to the Colony who had organized themselves into a company of professional players. Some authorities give it this interpretation. The students were to perform " Cato " on that particular night, and on other nights the comedies would be presented by the organized theatrical company then performing regularly in the theatre.

A contemporary letter written September 17, 1736, only a week after the above advertisement appeared in the *Virginia Gazette* seems to point conclusively to this being the case. One Colonel Thomas Jones [16] writes to his wife in the country:

You may tell Betty Pratt there has been but two plays acted since she went, which is " Cato," by the Young Gentlemen of the

---

[14] Comedy by Susanna Centlivre (1667–1723), an English writer who married Queen Anne's cook. She was the author of many popular pieces, each noted for its liveliness. Other plays by this dramatist, seen on the American stage, are "The Wonder" and "A Bold Stroke for a Wife."

[15] Farce by Farquhar, author of "The Recruiting Officer." This piece, which long held its place on our boards, is said to have been written in six weeks while the author lay on his death bed.

[16] "Colonial Virginia. Its People and Customs," by Mary Newton Standard.

College, as they call themselves, and " The Busybody," by *the Company* on Wednesday night last, and I believe there will be another to Night. . . .

Additional color to the belief that competent players were acting in Williamsburg at that time, is given by a letter written by Colonel William Byrd of " Westover " to his good friend Sir John Randolph of Williamsburg. The colonel, evidently familiar with " The Busybody " (presented for the first time in London in 1709 with Ann Oldfield as Isabinda), is interested to learn how the play was received in Williamsburg. He writes:

Which of your actors shone most in the play, next Isabinda who, I take it for granted, is the Oldfield of the theatre? How came Squire Marplot off? With many a clap, I suppose, though I fancy he would have acted more to the life in the comedy called " The Sham Doctor." But not a word of this for fear in case of sickness he might poison you.[17]

This last bit of facetiousness evidently points to the rôle of Marplot being played by the Colonel's physician, which again would give support to the amateur theory.

That the drama should have taken root in Virginia earlier than anywhere else in America is not surprising. The Virginians, a gay, pleasure-loving people, had nothing in common with the more sober Puritans of New England. " They were," says Bancroft, " a continuation of English society, who were attached to the monarchy, with a deep reverence for the English church, and a love for England and English institutions." Descendants of the old cavaliers, their philosophy was to enjoy life while they could, rather than spend their days making gloomy prepara-

[17] Va. Mag. Hist. Biog., 240, 241.

tions for death. Far from having prejudices against play-acting, they welcomed the thespian with open arms. Virginia and Maryland are, in fact, the only American colonies which never had laws prohibiting play-acting.

Williamsburg about that period was the most aristocratic and prosperous town on the continent. It was the seat of the Upper House and the House of Burgesses and the governor's official residence. The Law Courts were there; and the public buildings, chief of which was the College, were as fine as any in England. The women dressed fashionably and most of the leading families kept their coach. The shops were stocked with rich merchandise and it was the custom of the wealthy plantation owners and country gentry to run into the town for their shopping and amusements. Cooke, in his " History of the People of Virginia," gives an interesting description of Williamsburg in those early days:

It was the habit of the planters to go there with their families at this season to enjoy the pleasures of the capital and one of the highways, Gloucester, was an animated spectacle of coaches and four containing the nabobs and their dames, Maidens in silk and lace, with high-heeled shoes and clocked stockings. All these people were engaged in attending the assemblies at the Palace, in dancing at the Apollo, in snatching the pleasures of the moment and enjoying life under a regime that seemed mad for enjoyment. The violins seemed to be ever playing for the diversion of the youths and maidens; cocks were fighting, horsemen riding, students mingled in the throng in their academic dress, and his Serene Excellency went to open the House of Burgesses in his coach drawn by six milk-white horses. It was a scene full of gaiety and abandon.

Just the place, it might seem, to support a theatre, yet in Williamsburg, as elsewhere, it was not the wealthy who were the best patrons of the drama. "The Virginia planter," Seilhamer reminds us, "was a fox hunting squire with the airs of an English duke. In the cities the first families were scarcely less haughty than royalty itself. The rich were too mighty to patronize the theatre at home." Support of the playhouse came not from the class which could best afford the luxury, but from that large and ever-growing intelligent middle class which was quick to demand all the intellectual pleasures the Old World was enjoying—the same citizens to whose devotion and patriotism was due a little later the establishment of the Republic and who still to-day remain the principal factors in the development of our national drama.

After 1736 the theatre in Williamsburg seems to have languished, for we do not hear of any more performances. In 1745 the playhouse, which had not been put to any use for several years, was bought by a number of prominent men of the Colony and presented to Williamsburg as a town hall.

This ended the career, and is all we know, of the first theatre in America.

CHAPTER II

THE FIRST PLAY ACTED IN NEW YORK

FARQUHAR'S "RECRUITING OFFICER" SEEN AT THE NEW THEATRE.
EARLY AMERICAN PLAYHOUSES. CANDLES FOR FOOTLIGHTS.
THE DRAMA IN CHARLESTON. EARLIEST KNOWN THEATRICAL
PERFORMANCE IN PHILADELPHIA. JOHN MOODY, THE BARBER
ACTOR. THE MURRAY-KEAN TROUPE IN NEW YORK. THOMAS
KEAN IN SHAKESPEARIAN REPERTOIRE.

WHAT was the first play acted in North America
by professional players?

Dunlap, in his History, says that the earliest play
seen in New York was Sir Richard Steele's comedy
"The Conscious Lovers," performed at the Nassau
Street Theatre, September 17, 1753, by the Hallam
company. But, as we shall see, Dunlap is again in
error. The first play presented in New York of
which we have actual record was George Farquhar's
comedy "The Recruiting Officer." This, the earliest
play known to have been acted in North America by
professional players, was seen at what was described
as the "New" Theatre on December 6, 1732, or
twenty years earlier than the date which Dunlap
gives as the first performance in America by regular
performers.

The "New Theatre"[1]—the first playhouse in New
York of which we have any knowledge—was in a

---

[1] The word "New" as applied to the early American theatres was not intended to be a distinctive or permanent name, although usage sometimes made
it such. The most recently opened playhouse everywhere was usually known
as the "New" Theatre. For instance, the first Park Theatre, opened in 1798,
was originally called the New Theatre. From the fact that there was a "New"
Theatre in New York in 1732 one must infer that there had been at least one
playhouse there before that date.

building belonging to the Hon. Rip Van Dam, then acting governor of the city. The opening of the theatre was noted by the New York correspondent of the *New England and Boston Gazette* who contributes to the issue of that journal of December 11, 1732, under the heading "New York News," the following:

On the 6th instant, the New Theatre, in the building of the Hon. Rip Van Dam Esq, was opened with the comedy of "The Recruiting Officer," the part of Worthy acted by the ingenious Mr Thomas Heady, barber and Peruque maker[1a] to his Honour.

No further details were given and the complete list of the company is not known, but the names of Messrs. R. Bessel, Drown, Eastlake, Cone, Mesdames Drown, Chase, Cantour and Miss Brennan were advertised as taking part in the performance. Where these players came from or what their standing was is not known. Their names do not appear again in theatrical history. Brown in his History describes them as " a company of professional actors from London." He does not give his authority for this statement, but, after having related that they arrived in New York in September, 1732, goes on to say: " They secured a large room in the upper part of a building near the junction of Pearl Street and Maiden Lane, which was fitted up with a platform stage and raised seats, capable of seating about four hundred persons. They continued their performances for one month, acting three times a week. Early in December of the same year they resumed, having made several additions to their party. This company continued

---

[1a] In colonial society, where so much depended upon manners, well arranged apparel and a flowing wig, a peruke maker was a person of consequence, as appears from the manner in which Mr. Heady is referred to.

(playing in New York) until February, 1734; it was then disbanded."[2]

It has been suggested that those taking part were not professional actors but merely amateurs. There is nothing either in the newspaper announcement or in the circumstances to warrant any such assumption. If there was acting in New York by professional actors as early as 1702, the year of Anthony Aston's visit, there is no reason why the strolling mummer should not have plied his calling there thirty years later. Moreover, in an age when acting was looked down upon as a hardly avowable occupation, it is far more probable that professional players should be found braving public scorn than young people of standing in the community. Because Mr. Heady, "his honour's barber," was in the cast, it does not necessarily follow that he and his associates were amateurs. It was not uncommon in those days to find actors officiating with the razor when a dull theatrical season or some other reason prompted a change of occupation. John Moody, the English actor-manager, who was the first to cross the Atlantic with a theatrical troupe, was a barber by profession, and Mr. Huggins,[3] a well-known member of Harper's Rhode Island Company in 1793, left the stage to become one of the most famous barbers New York ever had.

Farquhar's witty comedy, written during Marlborough's victories, at a time when all England

---

[2] A History of the New York Stage, by T. Allston Brown. Dodd, Mead & Co.

[3] Mr. Huggins, after a brief and uneventful stage career, became a noted barber in New York. His tonsorial advertisements in the *Evening Post*, written by Anthony Bleecker and other wits of the town among his customers, which were afterwards gathered into a volume under the title "Hugginiana," placed him among the literati that were then a feature of New York.

blazed with the martial spirit and the recruiting officer was busy in every town, was a very popular play
throughout the Eighteenth Century and continued to
be acted up to about thirty years ago.⁴ Some of the
lines border closely on indecency and the jests are
broader than modern audiences are accustomed to,
but the gaiety and good humor of the piece make
ample amends for what may be lacking in propriety.
Leigh Hunt considered it one of the best of Farquhar's plays. It was revived at the Park Theatre,
New York, in 1843 and again by Augustin Daly in
1885 when John Drew was seen as the dashing Captain Plume, a rôle originated by the celebrated Wilks,
and Ada Rehan played Sylvia, a part originally acted
by the famous Mrs. Oldfield.

No newspaper comment on this New York performance of 1732, other than the paragraph from the
Boston journal quoted above, has come to light, but
incontestable corroboration of the fact that there did
exist a theatre in New York about that date we find
in an advertisement which appeared a few months
later in the *New York Gazette,* which refers to the
New Theatre as if it were an established institution,
the location of which was known to all. The advertisement appeared in the issue of October 15, 1733,
and runs as follows:

To be sold at reasonable rates. All sorts of Household Goods
viz., Beds, Chairs, Tables, Chest of Drawers, Looking Glasses,
Andirons and Pictures, as also several sorts of Druggs and Mede-
cines, also a Negro Girl about 16 years of age has had the small pox

---

⁴ George Farquhar (1678-1707), one of the most successful of the comic
dramatists of the 18th century, was the son of a clergyman and born in Londonderry, Ireland. His best known comedies are "The Recruiting Officer" and
"The Beaux' Stratagem."

and is fit for Town or Country. Enquire of George Talbot. Next door to *the Play-house.*[5]

The governor of the colony from 1720 to 1728 was Governor Burnet, who is described by Smith,[6] the first historian of New York, " as a man of sense and of polite breeding, a well read scholar, sprightly and of a social disposition." Such a man would probably have looked with favor on the drama and it is more than likely that, during the eight years of his administration, dramatic performances were given in New York with some degree of regularity. Rip Van Dam, owner of the building in which the New Theatre was situated, was acting governor from the time of Burnet's departure until the arrival of Governor Cosby in 1732, a few months before the New Theatre was opened.

There is considerable confusion as to the exact location of the 1732 players owing to the statement in the *New England and Boston Gazette* that the New Theatre, where they acted, was in a building belonging to the Hon. Rip Van Dam. When, eighteen years later, the Murray and Kean Company arrived from Philadelphia, they also took a large room in a building owned by Rip Van Dam and converted it into a theatre. Are we to conclude that Rip Van Dam owned several large lofts suitable for dramatic performances and rented a different one to each troupe, or is it not more probable that the newcomers from Philadelphia would in preference choose a room that had already been used for the same purpose? Judge Daly[7] leans to this view: " The two

[5] See files *New York Gazette*, New York Public Library.
[6] Smith's History of New York, Albany, 1814.
[7] First Theatre in America. By Charles P. Daly.

theatres," he says, " were probably in the same building now generally referred to as the Nassau Street
Theatre." On the other hand, Brown, in his " History of the New York Stage," makes a wide distinction between the two theatres. " The 1732 company,"
he says, " was located near the junction of Pearl Street
and Maiden Lane, while the First Nassau Street
Theatre, where Murray and Kean and later the
Hallams appeared, was located on the east side of
Kip (now Nassau) Street, between John Street and
Maiden Lane." Yet it is significant that Dunlap
refers to the Hallams as appearing " at the *New
Theatre* in Nassau Street." The New Theatre, it
will be recalled, was the name of the house where the
1732 players were first seen. The weight of evidence,
therefore, would seem to point to the Nassau Street
Theatre being the cradle of the earliest known theatrical performances in New York.

What did this early American playhouse look
like? Brown gives this description of it:

It was a two-storied house with high gables. The stage was
raised five feet from the floor. The scenes, curtains and wings
were all carried by the managers in their " property " trunks. A
green curtain was suspended from the ceiling. A pair of paper
screens were erected upon the right and left hand sides for wings.
Six wax lights were in front of the stage. The orchestra consisted of a German flute, horn and drum players. Suspended from
the ceiling was the chandelier, made of a barrel hoop, through which
were driven half a dozen nails into which were stuck so many
candles. Two drop scenes representing a castle and a wood, bits
of landscape river and mountain comprised the scenery.[a]

Theatres in the early days of the drama in this
country were, as a rule, little more than large rooms
with a crudely arranged stage, rough benches for

seats and a few boxes on either side. Built entirely
of wood and invariably painted red, they were of the
flimsiest construction and could be put up or pulled
down in very short order. The Beekman Street
Theatre, the fourth playhouse erected in New York,
cost only $1625. There was no attempt to erect more
substantial theatres until the American public had
given unmistakable proof of its ability and desire to
support the drama as a permanent institution. Philadelphia claims the honor of having erected the first
permanent temple of Thespis—the old Southwark
Theatre, a brick building opened in 1766 and partly
destroyed by fire in 1821. Annapolis comes next
with a brick theatre erected in 1771. But playhouses
really worthy of the art they served were not seen
until the approach of the Nineteenth Century when
four theatres, as finely and elaborately equipped as
any in Europe, were opened to the public—the Chestnut Street Theatre, Philadelphia (1794), the Federal Street and Haymarket theatres, Boston (1794-
96), and the Park Theatre, New York (1798).

The seating capacity of the earliest theatres was
about three hundred and performances were given
every second or third night. The heating and lighting arrangements were of the most primitive order.
There was, of course, no general steam heating plant.
Usually, there was one large stove in the centre of the
foyer, near the street entrance, and round this, during
each entr'acte, the chilled spectators would crowd to
thaw themselves out. Notices posted conspicuously
in the lobbies " respectfully requested the audience
not to spit on the stove." Notices also appeared in
the house bills requesting " ladies and gentlemen to
bring their own charcoal foot warmers." These were

small square boxes with perforated lids and metal receptacles inside for hot embers, such as were commonly used in the pews of churches. When Allen played with his company in Albany in the winter of 1785–6, as an extra inducement to those seeking comfort as well as pleasure, this announcement was made: " An additional stove is provided and the floor of the boxes lined in order to make the theatre as warm and comfortable as possible." Even as late as 1830 there were posted conspicuously in the fashionable St. Charles Theatre, New Orleans, such notices as this: " It is particularly requested that dogs will not be brought to the theatre, as they cannot be admitted." Another house rule read: " Peanuts are proscribed."

Candles and, later, oil were the methods of lighting. Candles did service everywhere until oil lamps came into favor. The picture of Thomas Wignell, the manager, carrying a pair of silver candlesticks as he lighted President Washington to his box is familiar to all. Candles were also used for the footlights and it was nothing unusual during a tender love scene or moment of tense tragedy for a stage hand to come down and snuff the smoking candle wicks. " Sconces with candles," says Frank Chouteau Brown,[*] " were used along the walls or projecting from balconies or boxes as these could easily be trimmed when necessity required by an usher or any individual seated near by, who felt so disposed." He continues:

A little later the footlights were arranged on a separate wooden strip or on a long platform which could be lowered into or below the front edge of the stage, thus reducing the illumination on the scene (and also giving a chance to trim the wicks when that was

---

[*] Theatre Magazine, July, 1918.

necessary). This same crude method of controlling the footlights was continued for a number of years, and used with both the sperm and oil lighting, and from this came the origin of the word " float," as applied to the footlights.

Joe Cowell, the English comedian, who came to New York in 1821, gives this description of the lighting arrangements at the then highly fashionable Park Theatre:

> The house was excessively dark; oil, of course, then was used, in common brass Liverpool lamps, ten or twelve of which were placed in a large sheet-iron hoop, painted green, hanging from the ceiling in the centre, and one, half the size, on each side of the stage. . . . Later, glass chandeliers were purchased to supply the place of the iron hoops.[10]

That the players of 1732 continued giving performances at the " New Theatre " is proved by subsequent announcements that appeared in the *New York Gazette*. Some time after the opening of " The Recruiting Officer," this advertisement appeared:

> This evening will be performed the tragedy of " Cato," and for three evenings next week the following comedies will be acted Viz: " The Recruiting Officer," " The Beaux' Stratagem " and " The Busybody."

It will be noted that this bill is identical with that of the 1736 performance in the Playhouse at Williamsburg already referred to. Unless we are satisfied beyond doubt that the latter was nothing but an amateur enterprise, one is irresistibly carried along to the only alternative conclusion, that the company of players who appeared in New York in 1732 and the players who acted in Williamsburg in 1736 were

---

[10] Thirty Years among the Players, by Joe Cowell, New York, 1844.

one and the same troupe. They continued playing in New York until 1734.

The next we hear of play-acting is in the South. The scene shifts from New York to Charleston, S. C., where, it is not unlikely, the New York company proceeded after leaving the New Theatre.

Charleston (or Charles Towne as it was then spelled) was a rapidly growing community and for many years enjoyed with New York, Philadelphia and Williamsburg, Va., the distinction of being one of the most active theatrical centres in America.

The town did not boast of a theatre in time for the earliest performance of which we have any record, Otway's tragedy, " The Orphan," which was given in the " Court Room " on January 24, 1735. This play was followed by others, all presented in the same place. The patronage received was probably so satisfactory that before the next season came round a regular theatre was built in Dock Street, or Queen Street as it was renamed later. A map of Charleston dated 1738 shows the site of the theatre on the south side of Queen Street, a little west of Church Street, on the lot of land now occupied by the rear portion of the old Planters' Hotel, within less than a hundred yards of the Huguenot and St. Philip's churches.

On January 24, 1736, the *South Carolina Gazette* contained the following announcement:

On Thursday, the 12th of February, will be opened the new theatre in Dock Street, in which will be performed the comedy called " The Recruiting Officer." Tickets for the pitt and boxes will be delivered at Mr. Charles Shepherd's on Thursday, the 5th of February. Boxes 30s. Pitt 20s, gallery 15s.[11]

---

[11] These prices for Colonial theatre-going seem extraordinarily high, and probably indicate that, owing to the smallness of the theatre, the seating capacity was extremely limited. Three dollars for the gallery and four dollars

FIRST PLAY ACTED IN NEW YORK

There is no mention of the opening of the theatre in the news columns of the *Gazette,* but on February 23 is advertised a performance of Otway's " Orphan," followed later by advertisements announcing " The Recruiting Officer " and " George Barnwell," [12] a very popular melodrama of the Eighteenth and early Nineteenth Century.

The season closed with the ever' popular " Orphan " on March 23, 1736. After this, things appear to have gone badly with the enterprise, for the *Gazette* for May 23 contains the following:

ON THE SALE OF THE THEATRE

How cruel Fortune, and how fickle, too,
To crop the Method made for making you!
Changes tho' common, yet when great they prove,
Make men distrust the care of Mighty Jove.
Half made in thought (though not in fact) we find
You bought and sold, but left poor H. behind.
P. S.—Since so it is ne'er mind the silly trick.
The pair will please, when Pierrot makes you sick.

It is not known who sold or who acquired the property, but later advertisements show that its general character remained unchanged, plays, balls and concerts continuing to be given.

There is no further mention of plays in Charleston for several years and to find the players again we must retrace our steps to New York.

for a seat in the pit (or orchestra) is unheard of even in our own extravagant day. The greater purchasing value of money in those times makes them even higher, almost double in fact. For the Nassau Street performances in New York the prices were $1.25 in the orchestra, 75 cents in the gallery, $2 for box seats.

[12] This play, by Lillo, is famous for having been praised by Diderot and Lessing as a model of its kind. Like "The Gamester," it was written with a moral purpose. The piece depicts the danger a young man runs of being tempted to steal and murder by infatuation for an unscrupulous woman and was intended as an argument in favor of opening the eyes of youth to the perils incurred from such associations.

51

The 1732 company, as we have said, had discontinued their performances at the New Theatre in 1734 and left for parts unknown, possibly Williamsburg or Charleston. But the drama in New York was by no means dead. There is no mention to be found in the public prints of further theatrical activity for some time after the departure of the earlier players, but that the stage of the New Theatre again became active five years later seems to be proved by a volume of poems now in the possession of Mr. William Nelson, of New Jersey. The book is entitled "Poems on Several Occasions," one of the poems being headed:

PROLOGUE.
Intended for the second opening of ..e Theatre
at New York. Anno 1739.

Nothing more is known about it, and the theatrical history of New York goes unrecorded until the arrival of the Murray and Kean company from Philadelphia in 1750.

Meantime the drama had taken a timid hold in the city of Penn. Destined to play a few decades later such a brilliant part in the annals of our stage, the birthplace of Joseph Jefferson, the town where Edwin Forrest grew to manhood, lived and died, Philadelphia was, at that period, the leading city on the American continent, and up to the beginning of the Nineteenth Century the most important theatrical town in the United States. Its citizens were wealthy and enterprising and more public spirited than the people of any of the sister colonies. Yet, notwithstanding its ever growing importance and the fact that the founder had opened Pennsylvania as a land of refuge for liberty of conscience, there was the most determined opposition on the part of the Quakers to any attempt to introduce play-acting. While the players had many warm friends and supporters in Philadelphia the anti-theatrical party was in the majority. This hostile element did everything possible to check and harass the players, invoking the existing statutes, causing new and more severe laws to be passed, and organizing meetings of protest.

There was still another barrier to the success of any theatrical enterprises. This was the fact that Philadelphia was proud of its scientific and literary eminence in the Colonies. "The golden youth of the metropolis," says Seilhamer, emulating the solid attainments of Dr. Franklin, "affected to regard the lectures of Professor Kinnersly on electricity and his practical experiments at the Academy as more instructive and entertaining than the exhibition of stage plays by a company of strolling players."

Yet plays were acted in Philadelphia as early as 1749. To that fact a MS. journal kept by John Smith, a son-in-law of James Logan, bears witness. An entry in the journal is as follows:

August 22, 1749. Joseph Morris and I happened in at Peacock Bigger's and drank tea there and his daughter being one of the company who were going to hear the tragedy of "Cato" acted, it occasioned some conversation in which I expressed my sorrow that anything of the kind was encouraged.

Some historians believe this was only an amateur performance. Dunlap says, "It is on record that the magistracy of the city had been disturbed by some idle young men perpetrating the murder of sundry plays in the skirts of the town; but the culprits had been arrested and bound over to their good behavior after confessing their crime and promising to spare the poor poets in future." Other authorities give these Philadelphia theatricals far greater importance. Seilhamer sees in them the " real beginning of the drama in America." He goes on to say:

There is no reason to doubt that the company of comedians from Philadelphia which appeared in New York for the first time on March 5, 1750, was substantially the same that Dunlap describes as " Some idle young men perpetrating the murder of sundry plays." The managers were the same Messrs. Kean and Murray, and in both cities Thomas Kean played the leading role, both in tragedy and comedy.

Robert Venable, an old negro who was still alive in 1844, told John F. Watson [13] that he went to the first play at Plumstead's store and that " many fell out " with Nancy George because she went there to play. Nancy George, as is well known, was one of the principal actresses of the Murray and Kean company in New York.

The theatre used in Philadelphia in 1749, and in which the Hallams appeared later, was in a warehouse belonging to William Plumstead,[14] situated on the corner of the first alley above Pine Street. This building remained standing until 1849. It was used as a sail loft for many years, and Dunlap said in 1832 that " the remains or traces of scenic decoration were to be seen in it within forty years."

[13] Watson's "Annals of Philadelphia."

[14] William Plumstead, a prominent Philadelphian of his day, was noted for his liberal views and his generous attitude toward the players. Originally a Quaker, he abandoned the principles of the Society of Friends early in life. He became mayor of Philadelphia in 1750, was several times Justice of the Peace, represented Northampton County in the General Assembly of the Province, and was Register General of Pennsylvania at the time of his death.

FIRST PLAY ACTED IN NEW YORK

While these Philadelphia theatricals of 1749 hardly mark the " real beginning of the drama in America " as Seilhamer suggests, seeing that there had already been professional performances both in New York and Williamsburg at least fifteen years previously, they are certainly of great importance because it was the first heard of the Murray-Kean company, an organization which, from that time on and until the arrival of the Hallams, was practically the only professional dramatic organization on the American continent. As an organization, it kept intact for twenty years, presenting most, if not all, the plays of the Hallam repertoire and proving a serious competitor of the Hallams, as the latter discovered on their arrival.

Where the Murray-Kean company came from originally we do not know. Probably they were English actors from the West Indies, many of whom had been acting regularly in Jamaica and Barbadoes. Perhaps they were that band of players which John Moody, an English theatrical celebrity well known in the West Indies, is said to have recruited in London and brought to America three years before the Hallams crossed the ocean.

John Moody, an actor of Drury Lane and regarded by some historians as the real founder of the American stage, was originally a barber. Abandoning the tonsorial profession. for the theatre, and possessing a rich brogue, he acquired some reputation playing Irish parts. Aspiring to be a tragedian, although the London managers insisted he was only a comedian, he became disgusted with England and sailed for the West Indies, reaching Jamaica in 1745.

There he found an amateur company giving performances in a ball room. He proposed to them the opening of a regular theatre with a company which he offered to bring out from England. The suggestion was accepted, subscriptions were opened and Moody re-appeared the following year with a company. The success of the venture was such that Moody made a fortune in four years. At the end of that time, however, the ranks of his players had been so thinned by illness that he found himself compelled to return to England to obtain new recruits. When he arrived in London such inducements were made to him by Garrick to return to the stage that he gave up all idea of the Jamaica enterprise and sold out his interest to the company he had already gathered, the chief members of which were Messrs. Douglass,[15] Kershaw, Smith, Daniels, Morris and their wives and a Miss Hamilton, the principal actress. This little band of players set sail, reaching Jamaica in 1751, " the first dramatic company," says John Bernard,[16] " that crossed the Atlantic of which there exists any personal record."

But if the Plumstead warehouse players were part of the Moody organization, which is doubtful, why was Philadelphia, of all places, selected for the opening engagement—Philadelphia the stronghold of Quakerism, with its hidebound prejudice against everything pertaining to the stage—when Virginia and the pleasure loving descendants of the gay cavaliers offered an altogether different kind of welcome?

[15] This undoubtedly is the David Douglass whom Mrs. Hallam married after the death of Lewis Hallam in Jamaica in 1755.

[16] Early Days of the American Stage, by John Bernard.

Or are we to come to the conclusion that it was the Murray-Kean company we found acting " Cato " and " The Busybody " in Williamsburg, Va., in 1736? If so, what were they doing during those thirteen years that elapsed between 1736 and 1749 when they first appeared in Philadelphia? Again, if they were the John Moody players, the Hallams must have known of their presence in America before they themselves left England. In that case, why was Lewis Hallam silent concerning them? Puzzling questions these, that may remain forever unanswered.

In February, 1750, the Philadelphia company, still under the joint management of Walter Murray and Thomas Kean, arrived in New York and applied to Governor Clinton [17] for permission to act. The *New York Weekly Postboy* for February 26, 1750, contains this reference to the new arrivals:

Last week arrived here a company of comedians from Philadelphia, who we hear have taken a convenient Room for their Purpose in one of the buildings lately belonging to the Hon. Rip Van Dam Esq., deceased, in Nassau Street, where they intend to perform as long as the season lasts, provided they meet with suitable encouragement.

The theatre secured by the Murray-Kean company is believed to have been the same used by the actors who gave the performance of " The Recruiting Officer " eighteen years earlier. It is to be noted that Rip Van Dam had died since he last rented his property to a troupe of players. If the new arrivals

[17] Admiral George Clinton was the son of an earl, and had previously held a distinguished position as commander of the English fleet in the Mediterranean. His wife Lady Clinton was a woman of great personal charm who had moved in the best circles of London society. Persons of this kind were doubtless more than ready to encourage early attempts to introduce the drama in the New World.

were occupying the same premises, the publisher of the *Postboy* did not recall that fact for he makes no mention of it. The same issue of the newspaper contained this advertisement:

By his Excellency's Permission
at the Theatre in Nassau Street.
On Monday the 5th day of March next
will be presented The Historical Tragedy of
" King Richard III."
Wrote originally by Shakespeare
and altered by Colly Cibber, Esq.

In this play is contained The Death of King Henry 6th, the artful acquisition of the Crown by King Richard, the Murder of the Princes in the Tower. The Landing of the Earl of Richmond and the Battle of Bosworth Field.

Tickets will be ready to be delivered by Thursday next, and to be had of the Printer thereof.

Pitt 5/. Gallery 3/.

To begin precisely at half an hour after 6 o'clock and no Person to be admitted behind the Scenes.

The company consisted of Messrs. Murray and Kean, joint managers, and Messrs. Jago, Scott, Leigh, Marks, Smith, Woodham, Moore, Tremain, Master Dickey Murray, the manager's son, and Mesdames Nancy George, Mrs. Taylor, Mrs. Davis, Mrs. Leigh, Mrs. and Miss Osborne. Kean, Tremain and Jago played in tragic parts. Murray was a comedian. Miss Nancy George and Miss Osborne were the chief ladies in comedy and tragedy.

Very little is known about Thomas Kean, either as a man or as an actor. He is not believed to be any relation to the Keans who became celebrated half a century later, although Seilhamer thinks it barely possible that he was a brother or other relation of Aaron, the reputed father of Edmund Kean. In any case, his career has gone practically unrecorded in the annals of theatrical history. He is believed to have been originally a writer or writing master who, having some talent for the stage, adopted it temporarily as a profession, for, at the close of the 1750–51 engagement in New York, when the tragedian took a benefit,[18] it was for the alleged purpose of retiring permanently from the actors' profession to take up his former work as a writer.

That he must have had considerable acting ability, one is compelled to believe. He selected for his first New York appearance one of the most difficult and ambitious rôles in the whole range of the drama—that of the hump-backed Richard, and gave so creditable a performance that the theatre was crowded and the play repeated the following week.

"Richard III" was acted for the last time on March 12, after which Dryden's "Spanish Friar" was put in the bill. For April 2 "The Orphan," "wrote by the ingenious Mr. Otway," was announced. Performances took place only twice a week, the company continuing to play regularly on

---

[18] The origin of theatrical benefits is interesting. Colley Cibber, in his "Apology," gives this explanation concerning them: "During the reign of King Charles (Charles II) an actor's benefit had never been heard of. The first indulgence of this kind was given to Mrs. Barry in King James' time, in consideration of the extraordinary applause that had followed her performance. But there this favour rested, to her alone, till after the division of the only company in 1695, at which time the patentees were soon reduced to pay their actors half in good words and half in ready money. In this precarious condition, some particular actors (however binding their agreements might be) were too poor or too wise to go to law with a lawyer, and therefore rather chose to compound their arrears, for their being admitted to the chance of having them made up by the profits of a benefit play. This expedient had this consequence: that the patentees, tho' their daily audiences might and did sometimes mend, still kept the short subsistence of their actors at a stand, and grew more steady in their resolution so to keep them, as they found them less apt to mutiny while their hopes of being cleared off by a benefit was depending. In a year or two these benefits grew so advantageous that they became at last the chief article in every actor's agreement."

Mondays and Thursdays from March 5 to April 30, when the absence of further announcements led Judge Charles P. Daly and other investigators to infer that the season closed. But on July 16 the following appeared in the *Postboy:*

> The heat having prevented the play last Thursday night, it is designed to be presented this evening, as it has the appearance of being moderate weather.

On the 23rd was announced: "The last night of playing this season, ' Love for Love ' and ' The Stage Coach.' "

That this company was successful may be inferred from the fact that they re-opened the following season, on September 13, with " The Recruiting Officer," followed the next week by a performance of Addison's " Cato." On the 24th the *Postboy* had this to say about the performance of " Cato ":

> Thursday evening the tragedy of " Cato " was played at the Theatre in this city before a very numerous audience, the greater part of whom were of opinion that it was pretty well performed. As it was the fullest assembly that ever appeared in that house,[19] it may serve to prove that the taste of this place is not so much vitiated or lost to a sense of liberty but that they can prefer a representation of virtue to one of loose character.

This editorial comment would seem to indicate that the plays previously seen on the local boards had not been of a very high standard and that criticism had been aroused by the low character of the theatrical entertainment then most popular with the New York theatregoer—a condition of affairs with which we

---

[19] This phrase does not mean much as far as mere numbers are concerned. When Kean took his benefit at the close of the second season the house was also "crowded to capacity," and we have the authority of Mr. Parker, who printed the tickets, that there were exactly 292 persons in the house on that occasion.

are unfortunately only too familiar ourselves at the present day.

During the two seasons in New York, the following plays were given: "Richard III," Otway's "Orphan," Dryden's "Spanish Friar," Farquhar's "Sir Harry Wildair," "The Recruiting Officer," "Beaux' Stratagem," "George Barnwell," "The Beggar's Opera," [20] "The Distressed Mother," [21] Congreve's "Love for Love" and Mrs. Centlivre's "A Bold Stroke for a Wife," with the following farces: "The Beau in the Suds," "The Mock Doctor," "The Devil to Pay," "The Walking Statue," "The Old Man Taught Wisdom," "Damon and Phillida," "Hob in the Well" and "Miss in Her Teens." They continued to act twice a week until June 17, 1751, closing with a succession of benefits, when the company went to Williamsburg, Va.

The various benefits brought forth some curious announcements. Mrs. Davis' benefit, it was stated, was for the purpose of enabling her to "buy off her time." In those days it was the custom of masters of vessels to book passengers for New York on the understanding that they were to be sold as servants immediately upon arrival to any person who would pay their passage money. They were sold for a definite period of time and were called "Redemptioners." Mrs.

[20] John Gay's burlesque farce "The Beggar's Opera," the most popular musical piece of the Eighteenth Century, first took London by storm in 1727 when Lavinia Fenton turned the heads of the beaux as Polly Peachum, won a ducal lover and ultimately the coronet of a duchess. It is said that Dean Swift first suggested the idea of the piece which Congreve said would "either take greatly or be damned confoundedly." How far right he was may be inferred from the fact that the piece remained popular for over half a century. Its first production here by the Murray-Kean company marks the introduction of light musical comedy in this country.

[21] An English version of Racine's "Andromaque."

Davis apparently belonged to this class, " of whom," Ireland reminds us, " many became the parents of aristocratic families, north and south."

Mr. Jago, in an ingenuous appeal, " humbly hopes that all ladies and gentlemen will be so kind as to favour him with their company, as he never had a benefit before, and is *just out of prison."*

The advertisement of the widow Osborne, who appropriately selected for her bill " The Distressed Mother," is a gem. Her announcement read:

> On Monday next will be presented for the Benefit of the widow Osborne " The Distrest Mother," with several Entertainments to which will be added " The Beau in the Suds." As 'tis the first time this poor widow has had a benefit, and having met with divers late Hardships and Misfortunes, 'tis hoped all Charitable, Benevolent Ladies *and others* will favour her with their company.

Before the close of the second season, Kean announced in the *Postboy* that he had resolved to quit the stage and follow his former vocation of writing, and that he would on the following Monday evening, enact the part of Richard III for his benefit, it being the last time of his appearance on the stage. For some unknown reason this program was changed as shown by the later announcement in the *Postboy,* April 29, 1751:

> By advice of his friends, Mr. Kean causes to be presented this evening, for his Benefit, a Comedy called " The Busybody," with the " Virgin Unmask'd," with singing by Mr. Woodham, particularly the celebrated Ode called *" Britain's Charter."*
>
> As this will positively be the last time of Mr. Kean's appearing on the stage, he honestly hopes all Gentlemen, Ladies, *and others,* who are his Well-wishers, will be so kind as to favour him with their Company. Tickets to be had at the Theatre, and at the New Printing Office in Bever Street.

But notwithstanding this formal farewell, Mr. Kean did not leave the stage. As will be seen later, he continued to head the company wherever it appeared.

The *Postboy* made no editorial or critical comment on these New York performances, with the exception of the brief notice already quoted, but the issue of March 19, two weeks after the players' arrival, contained a leading article, warmly defending the stage and upholding the character of the actor. This probably is the earliest public championship of the drama in the Colonies. While one cannot resist the thought that possibly the money spent by the actors for advertising space may have had something to do with inspiring the writer, the mere fact that such a defense should appear as the leading article, at a time of bitter religious and social prejudice, is of great interest, marking as it does the entering wedge of a determined effort made by the more liberal minded citizens to encourage the drama as a legitimate form of public amusement. The article is too long to quote here in full, but, in part, the writer says:

As we cannot always apply ourselves to Contemplation or Business, she (Religion) sometimes indulges us in Recreation and Amusement and even prompts us to relax the Mind and by innocent Diversions to prepare our Selves for the more serious Employment of our respective Stations. But of all Amusements methinks the noblest and most elevated are those intellectual Enjoyments which improve and divert the Mind without straining the rational Faculties. Of this species is the Diversion of the Stage. . . . "But Plays have been perverted to mischievous Purpose!" And what is free from the same imputation? Because a profligate Fellow takes the Gown and preaches Heresy, is it criminal to hear an orthodox sermon? Can the Bee suck no honey from a Flower because the gloomy Spider only extracts its Poison? There is no doubt but the stage may be improved to good as well as perverted to all Purposes. " But do not Plays put the Town to a needless expense and carry off large sums of money?" Nothing like it. On the contrary, the Actors promote the Circulation of Cash by employing Masons, Carpenters, Taylors, Painters, etc., and generally leave their money where they got it. For my own part, methinks 'tis a Pity that the Stage is not held in greater Repute so that the young Gentlemen of the Town might Act without any Prejudice to their character. Sure I am that the Advantages of learning to Act well would richly compensate their trouble and be found an Acquisition of singular Service in the Conduct of Life.

That there was everywhere in the Colonies a steadily growing interest in the acted drama was evinced not only by the new laws constantly being enacted against the player, but by the openness and candor with which the things of the theatre were discussed in polite circles. New York, especially, was noted for its fondness for the playhouse. " People," says Esther Singleton,[22] "read plays as literature." The libretto (printed book) of the most recent stage success,[23] was bought as eagerly as the latest novel. If the company wished to produce a play of which they had no libretto they could be reasonably sure that they could borrow it from somebody in town. They advertised in May, 1751: " If any gentleman or lady has the farce called ' The Intriguing Chambermaid ' and will lend it awhile to the players, it will be thankfully acknowledged."

The fascination which the stage had for young

---

[22] "Social New York under the Georges," by Esther Singleton.

[23] That printed plays were common at that time is shown by an advertisement in Gaine's *Mercury*, when "Macbeth" was presented at the John Street Theatre, New York, March 3, 1768, announcing that copies of the tragedy might be had at the Bible and Crown, in Hanover Square.

people was also a favorite subject for criticism with contemporary quidnuncs. A writer in 1739 complained that New York society was going to the dogs. After showing how a young girl was pampered and spoiled from childhood, he went on to say:

She is now ten years of age, her mind is ripe for plays. Here is again a noble field of vanity presented to Madam, her mind is wholly taken up with the pleasure it affords and an actress' part, repeated by heart, yields greater joy to her parents than if she knew the whole Catechism.

CHAPTER III

THE COMING OF THE HALLAMS

THEIR ORIGIN AND PROFESSIONAL STANDING. PREPARATIONS FOR
AN AMERICAN TOUR. ROBERT UPTON. THE MURRAY-KEAN
TROUPE IN ANNAPOLIS. ARRIVAL OF LEWIS HALLAM AND HIS
COMPANY AT YORKTOWN, VA. FIRST PERFORMANCE OF THE
COMPANY AT WILLIAMSBURG. A VIRGINIA THEATRE AUDIENCE.
THE FIRST THEATRICAL PROLOGUE SPOKEN IN AMERICA.

MEANTIME the eyes of shrewd English theatre
managers and actors turned longingly in the direction of America. Glowing, if not altogether truth-
ful, accounts of the success of John Moody's company
of players in the West Indies had circulated along
London's Rialto. The Colonies were well populated,
highly prosperous, and growing rapidly in importance. Such a country might well become the players'
Eldorado!

William Hallam, a London actor-manager, conceived the bold idea of organizing a completely
equipped company of players and sending it across
the Atlantic. With a view to preparing the way he
entrusted one Robert Upton with the mission of proceeding to America to find what could be done about
securing or erecting theatres, and advanced him a
considerable sum of money for that purpose. Upton
may be regarded, therefore, as the first of that long
line of genial press gentry who have added, and continue to add, to the gaiety of theatricals in these parts.
But Upton did not prove a faithful ambassador. Instead of working in Hallam's interests, he sought

66

only to serve himself. " On his arrival," complains Hallam in an open letter of protest, " Upton found here that sett of pretenders with whom he joined and, unhappily for us, quite neglected the business he was sent about from England. For we never heard of him after."

This " set of pretenders " was undoubtedly the Murray and Kean company which Upton found acting here on his arrival. There had been dissensions in the ranks of the organization, and Upton, evidently none too scrupulous in the matter of business ethics, easily prevailed on some of the Kean players to join forces with him, among them being the widow Osborne, Mr. Leigh or Lee and Mr. Tremain.

Upton went to New York at the head of the company thus organized and opened at the Nassau Street Theatre December 26, 1751, with " Othello," Upton himself appearing in the title role. The tragedy was followed by Garrick's farce " Lethe." [1] Later bills included " The Fair Penitent," [2] " The Honest Yorkshireman," " Tunbridge Walks," " Venice Preserved," " Richard III," " The Lying Valet," " The Provoked Husband."

But the engagement did not prove a success and after the third week Upton came out with a card, announcing that owing to lack of public support he would bring the season to a close by giving a few benefits, beginning with his own. At that period, it was usual for the actor taking a benefit to make a

---

[1] At that time it was customary for a serious piece to be followed by a light one, reversing the more modern custom of a curtain raiser.

[2] Tragedy by Nicholas Rowe (1674-1718). It was owing to the success of this piece that the name of the principal character, Lothario, became significant of the manners and morals of the fashionable rake.

personal call on the leading citizens and solicit their patronage. To encourage a good attendance, Upton begged the public to remember that he was an absolute stranger and " if in his application he should have omitted any Gentleman or Lady's House or Lodging, he humbly hopes they'll impute it to want of information, not of respect."

On February 20 what was announced as " absolutely the last performance " took place, the bill being " Venice Preserved," but on March 2 and 4 the theatre was again opened, the last bill consisting of " The Fair Penitent " and " Honest Yorkshireman," followed by a farewell epilogue by Mr. Upton. A few days later, Mr. and Mrs. Upton sailed for England.

We must now go back twelve months and return to William Hallam who was still in London awaiting word from Upton. None being forthcoming, Hallam determined, nevertheless, to go on with his proposed venture and he made his final preparations to cross the Atlantic with a dramatic company.

The historian Dunlap, wedded to the erroneous notion that the Hallams were the first professional players to act in the Colonies, has conferred upon William Hallam the title " Father of the American Stage." To that honor William Hallam is not entitled, for, as we have seen, he did not introduce the drama in this country. But his name deserves to be perpetuated in American theatrical annals as the first theatrical manager who had the courage and ability to organize and equip a company and send it all the way from England to America, an undertaking which in those days was of no mean proportions.

68

THE COMING OF THE HALLAMS

The players that we have seen already acting here were either recruited in this country or came from the West Indies, a comparatively short journey. To come all the way from England in those days of precarious shipping facilities, on a venture of the success of which was problematical, was a very different matter. It needed the courage of a gambler. But Hallam saw or thought he saw an opportunity not to be neglected and he seized it.

The coming of the Hallams is an episode of great importance in the history of the American theatre, not because they were the first professional players to appear in this country (which they were not) but because the manner of their organization, the extent and quality of their repertoire, the general excellence of the company marked the first attempt to put the drama in this country on a dignified and permanent footing. In this sense the Hallams may be said to have been "the first to introduce the drama in America." Lewis and Mrs. Hallam were players of ability and standing in London, each individual member of the troupe was a capable, well disciplined player, and the organization formed a homogeneous whole. The plays presented included practically everything that London was applauding at the time, from the stately tragedies of Shakespeare, Addison and Rowe, to the brilliant comedies of Congreve, Farquhar and Steele. The repertoire, which might well put that of any mo'ern stock company to shame, comprised "not only the best works in a dramatic sense," says Seilhamer, "but the purest plays the English stage had produced up to that time. The dramatists were men with a few exceptions whose fame will form a part of the glory of English dramatic literature until the world ceases to prize English letters." [3]

It is indisputable that no matter how well other players had previously filled the bill, it was not until the advent of the Hallams that the drama received that impetus and public recognition which allowed of its fullest and best development in new and almost virgin territory.

Hallam's company was far superior to any that had preceded it. "Mrs. Hallam," says Judge Daly, " was not only a beautiful woman but an actress of no ordinary merit." He continues:

Hallam was himself an excellent comedian, and two other members of the company, Rigby and Malone, were actors of established reputation upon the London boards. The arrival of a complete company like this, who were not only practised in their art, but amply provided before their departuure with dresses and all that was necessary for effective dramatic representation, was something too formidable to contend against. They seem, therefore, to have entirely supplanted the early pioneers of whom nothing further is known except that some of their number, Murray, Tremain, Scott and Miss Osborne played in Hallam's original company afterward when it was under the management of Douglass. [4]

Who were the Hallams? Their name does not loom large in the annals of the English theatre. Genest, in his very complete " History of the London Stage," makes only casual reference to them, and H. Barton Baker, a more recent historian, does not mention them at all, which might indicate that they were players of only second or even third-rate importance.

Adam Hallam, the father of William, was an actor at Covent Garden. His second wife, Anne Hal-

---

[3] "History of the American Theatre," by George O. Seilhamer.
[4] First Theatre in America, by Charles P. Daly.

lam, was a relative of Rich, the manager of Covent Garden, and it is hinted that Adam Hallam obtained his engagement at that house only through his wife's influence. He never attained any particular prominence as an actor, but played acceptably such rôles as Worthy in " The Recruiting Officer," Malcolm in " Macbeth," Laertes in " Hamlet," etc. Finally, he became a pensioner on the managers, taking a benefit in 1746. He had five sons, William, Lewis, George and Thomas, all actors, and another son, a naval officer. Thomas Hallam was accidentally killed by the celebrated Charles Macklin. The two actors were friends, but had a dispute one night over a wig which Macklin had worn the previous evening. In his excitement Macklin ran a stick into Hallam's eye and the actor died the next day. Macklin was convicted of manslaughter, but evidently escaped with light punishment for shortly afterward, in 1741, he made himself famous by playing Shylock for the first time as a serious character.

While it is on record that William Hallam acted occasionally, he was known as a manager rather than as an actor. The story told regarding him by Dunlap has been discredited by more recent investigators, but it is worth giving here not only because it sounds plausible, but because Dunlap is supposed to have obtained his information from Lewis Hallam the second, a nephew of William Hallam, who was living in Dunlap's lifetime (1766–1839) and known to many as " old Mr. Hallam." The story, in Dunlap's own words, is as follows:

Garrick reached the summit of his fame about 1745. He had been rejected by Fleetwood and Rich, managers of Drury Lane and

Covent Garden, in 1741, and after a probation at Ipswich he was received and fostered at the theatre of Goodmans' Fields by his friend Giffard, the predecessor, as proprietor and manager of that place of entertainment, of William Hallam. In consequence of Garrick's success, Goodmans' Fields theatre became the centre of attraction. Drury Lane and Covent Garden were deserted. At the end of the season of 1742, Fleetwood was glad to engage both manager and actor. Giffard, now befriended by Garrick, was invited to Drury Lane, and William Hallam succeeded Giffard at Goodmans' Fields, becoming the proprietor of Garrick's cradle, rendered famous but unprofitable from the circumstance of having had such a nursling. Drury Lane flourished, but the successor of Giffard and Garrick became bankrupt in 1750. This event led to the voyage (to America) planned by the Manager (William Hallam) and executed by his brother Lewis, the father of that Lewis Hallam who is remembered still as " Old Mr. Hallam."

Seilhamer, a later historian than Dunlap, and one who has shown himself more reliable than his predecessor in the matter of dates, insists that there is no foundation for the story. He says: " After Giffard's retirement in 1742 the Goodman's Fields Theatre was closed and there is no record in Genest's remarkably full ' History of the London Stage ' of Hallam's management between that time and 1750." He continues:

It is not unlikely, however, that Mr. Hallam was in some sense the manager of another theatre in Goodman's Fields, described as " at the Wells " in Lemon Street. Giffards was in Ayliffe Street. Adam Hallam, father of William and Lewis Hallam, had a benefit at the Wells Theatre in March, 1746. A Mrs. Hallam played there in legitimate roles in the autumn and winter of 1746— Genest notes that at this time there were three Hallams engaged at the theatre in Goodman's Fields (which was not the Goodmans Fields theatre), Hallam, Sr., L. Hallam, and G. Hallam. There is no mention of W. Hallam, but he may have been the manager then, as he certainly was ten years later, as appears from a scrap record of the old Sadler's Wells Theatre. This is all the more probable since on the 5th of September, 1751, exactly one year before the first appearance of the Hallam company in America, Mrs. Hallam had a benefit at the Lemon Street house, appearing as Desdemona, while Lewis Hallam played Roderigo. This is clearly the Lewis Hallam who was soon to sail for America, and the Desdemona, it may be assumed with safety, was his wife.[5]

After sifting all the evidence available, one is inclined to conclude that the Hallams were players of experience and ability, but of no very conspicuous talent, who had not succeeded in making any great headway on the London stage and so eagerly welcomed the suggestion made by William Hallam, the shrewd backer of the enterprise, that they pool their interests and try their fortunes in America. Dunlap tells us how the company was organized, and, as he got his information from one of the Hallams, we can count on its being fairly accurate:

Lewis and his wife having consented to cross the Atlantic and seek their fortunes in what might then not improperly be called the western wilderness, the ex-manager's next step was to find suitable persons to fill up the *corps dramatique* and to induce them to join his brother and sister in this theatrical forlorn hope. He succeeded in enlisting a good and efficient company willing to leave their country (and perhaps their creditors) and fitted to ensure success to the perilous adventure. The emigrants were next assembled at the house of William Hallam; a list of stock plays produced by him, with attendant farces and the cast of the whole agreed upon in full assembly of the body politic, which appears to have been a well-organized republic, every member of which had his part assigned to him both private and public, behind and before the curtain. Lewis Hallam was appointed manager, chief magistrate or king, and William, who stayed at home, was to be "Viceroy over him." The brothers were to divide profits equally after deducting the expenses and shares. Thus William was entitled to half of such profits as projector and proprietor, and Lewis and the other half as manager.

---

[5] History of the American Theatre, by George O. Seilhamer.

The company consisted of twelve adult members and three children of Lewis Hallam—Lewis the second, Adam and a daughter. Lewis Hallam, who was a low comedian, headed the company. Mrs. Hallam was leading lady. Mr. Rigby played leading rôles in tragedy and comedy. Mrs. Rigby was of no great prominence in the company. Mr. and Mrs. Clarkeson played utility. Miss Palmer, Mr. Singleton, Mr. Herbert, Mr. Wynell, Mr. Adcock and Mr. Malone completed the organization.

The plays chosen for the repertoire were the most popular pieces on the London stage at the time. They included " Hamlet," " The Merchant of Venice," " Richard III," by Shakespeare; " The Beaux' Stratagem," " The Constant Couple," " Inconstant," " The Recruiting Officer " and " Twin Rivals," by Farquhar; " The Careless Husband," by Cibber; " Committee," by Howard; " The Conscious Lovers," by Steele; " The Fair Penitent," " Tamerlane " and " Jane Shore," by Rowe; " George Barnwell," by Lillo; " The Provoked Husband," by Vanbrugh; " Suspicious Husband," by Hoadly; " Theodosius," by Lee; " Woman's a Riddle," by Bullock; together with a number of farces including " Lethe," " Lying Valet," " Miss in Her Teens," by Garrick; " The Mock Doctor," by Fielding; " Damon and Phillida," by Cibber.

With this repertoire and one pantomime " Harlequin Collector or the Miller Deceived," the adven-

---

* This comedy by Sir John Vanbrugh, not quite completed when the author died and finished by Colley Cibber, presents a lively picture of fashionable life in London at the end of the seventeenth century. The principal woman character Lady Townly, a spoiled and heartless woman of fashion, only awakes to her duty as a wife when her husband is about to leave her.

turers set sail in the good ship *Charming Sally,* Captain Lee, master, early in May, 1752.

We must leave the Hallam company en route for the New World and return to the Murray-Kean troupe which, it will be remembered, closed their New York season on June 17, 1751.

On leaving New York, the company immediately made its way South, no doubt by pre-arrangement with Kean, who, as we have seen, had taken a benefit two months previously when he publicly announced his intention to leave the boards for good. In view of this formal adieu to the stage, and the fact that Kean was still with the company when it reached Virginia, we are perhaps justified in inferring that his " adieu " was not intended to be taken any more seriously than many of the " farewells " of our present day, and that the two months which intervened between the time the tragedian left his colleagues in New York and the appearance of the company in Williamsburg, Va., were spent by him in planning and promoting the Virginia tour.

Mr. Woodham, an actor of the company who, it will be recalled, sang an ode entitled *Britain's Charter* at Kean's benefit in New York, probably invested some money in the Virginia venture, for, directly the company reached Williamsburg, we find his name heading the managerial firm of Woodham, Murray and Kean.

In the *Virginia Gazette* for August 29, 1751, appeared the following announcement:

By permission of His Honour the President (of the Council, who was acting Governor), Whereas the Company of Comedians that are in New York intend performing in this City, but there being no Room suitable for a Play-House, tis propos'd that a Theatre shall be built by way of Subscription, each Subscriber advancing a Pistole[7] to be entitled to a Box Ticket for the first Night's Diversion.

Those Gentlemen and Ladies who are kind enough to favour this undertaking are desired to send their Subscription Money to Mr. Finnie's, at the Raleigh, where Tickets may be had.

N. B. The House to be completed by October Court.

The Finnie mentioned in the advertisement was probably Kean's backer, because when a year later the Hallams came to Williamsburg and secured the theatre it was one Alexander Finnie who transferred the property to them. The plot selected by Kean for his theatre was on " two lots on the Eastern side of Eastern Street (Waller Street) just back of the Capitol. On this the new playhouse was erected, the deed being dated September 2, 1751,"[8] the promoters promising to have the house ready by the October Court when the town would be crowded with visitors and generous patronage was assured.

On October 21, 1751, the *Gazette* contained this brief acount of the opening of the new playhouse:

On Monday a Company of Comedians opened at the New Theatre near the Capitol in Williamsburg with " King Richard III " and a tragic dance composed by Monsieur Denoier called " The Royal Captive."

This is all we know of that engagement. The company's stay in Williamsburg, like that of the Hallams a year later, was exceedingly brief. Although the capital of the Province, Williamsburg in those times was little bigger than a good sized village of our own day. The theatregoing population was nowhere large enough to warrant a prolonged stay.

---

[7] A Spanish coin then circulating in the Colony and worth about $3.80.
[8] Williamsburg, the old Virginia Capital. By Lyon G. Tyler.

After a few additional performances, the company announced its departure as follows:

> The Company of Comedians intend to be at Petersburg by the middle of next month and hope that the Gentlemen and Ladies who are Lovers of Theatrical Entertainment will favour them with their company.

Meantime dissension had arisen in the company which resulted in three members, the widow Osborne, Mr. Leigh and Mr. Tremain, leaving the organization to join Mr. Upton.

Later the Woodham, Murray, Kean company went to Norfolk, Va., and in the spring were back in Williamsburg, as may be seen from the following advertisement in the *Gazette* of April 17, 1752:

> By Permission of his Honour the Governor
> At the New Theatre in Williamsburg
> For the Benefit of Mrs Beccely.
> On Friday being the 24th of this Inst
> Will be performed a comedy called the
> " Constant Couple "
> or a
> " Trip to the Jubilee "
> The part of *Sir Harry Wildair* will be Performed
> by Mr Kean
> *Colonel Standard*
> by Mr Murray
> and the part of *Angelica* to be performed
> by Mrs Becceley
> With Entertainment of Singing between the Acts.

The company played at Hobb's Hole, as Tappahannock was then called, from May 10 to 24, and in Fredericksburg during the " June Fair." This was their final appearance in the Colony.

No doubt from a desire to avoid competition with

the new London company, which landed at Yorktown in June, 1752, and the coming of which had
already been heralded, Messrs. Murray and Kean
wisely decided to leave Virginia to the Hallams and
went to Annapolis, Md., where, under the high sound-
ing name " Company of Comedians from Virginia,"
they opened June 18, 1752, with " The Beggar's
Opera " and the farce " The Lying Valet."

The *Maryland Gazette* contained the following
announcement:

By Permission of his Honour the President
At the New Theatre in Annapolis
By the Company of Comedians
On Monday next, being the 13th of this inst. July
1752, will be performed a comedy called,
" The Beaux Stratagem."
Likewise a farce called
" The Virgin Unmasked."
To begin Precisely at 7 o'clock
Tickets: Box 10 shillings, Pit 7 and 6 pence, gallery 5/ –

Annapolis at that time was the capital of the
Colony and like Williamsburg, a busy, thriving town.
The leading officials of the Province resided there
and it was a popular resort with the wealthy planters.
As elsewhere in the South, there was no local prejudice against the drama. The inhabitants were people
of taste and culture. The theatre as a social institution became popular soon after the beginning of the
century and continued to thrive there for many years.

Kean still headed the company in Annapolis,
appearing in all his principal rôles. Others who still
remained were Messrs. Murray and Scott and Miss
Osborne. New names on the list were Mr. Ryanson

and Messrs. Wynell and Herbert. These last two were Hallam players who joined the company later. The repertoire was practically the same as in New York, including in addition to the opening bill "The Busybody," "The Beaux' Stratagem," "The Virgin Unmasked," "The Recruiting Officer" and "The Mock Doctor." This organization remained intact for over twenty years, changing its name as it moved from place to place. Thus, in New York it was known as the "Comedians from Philadelphia"; in Williamsburg as the "Comedians from New York." Later the company visited Upper Marlborough, Piscataway and Port Tobacco, then places of wealth and consequence in Maryland, where it was known as the "Comedians from Annapolis." On one occasion, it ventured to bill itself as the "New" American Company (in competition with the Hallams who styled themselves "the American Company"). "These facts not only prove," says Seilhamer, "that the Hallam company was not the first regularly organized theatrical company in this country, but that the American Company, so called, was never without a rival south of the Chesapeake."

Lewis Hallam and his company arrived safely at Yorktown, Va., early in June, 1752, after a six weeks' passage. The time spent on the water was not wasted, for the plays which had been selected, cast and put in study before embarkation were regularly rehearsed during the voyage. On reaching Yorktown, the players proceeded at once to Williamsburg where application was made to Governor Dinwiddie for permission to act. A few days before the arrival of the London thespians the Virginia planters were put on the tiptoe of expectation by the following announcement in the *Gazette:*

This is to inform the Public that Mr. Hallam, from the New Theatre in Goodmansfield, London, is daily expected here with a select Company of Comedians; the Scenes, Cloaths, and Decorations are entirely new, extremely rich, and finished in the highest taste; the Scenes, being painted by the best Hands in London, are excelled by none in Beauty and Elegance, so that the Ladies and Gentlemen may depend on being entertain'd in as polite a Manner as at the Theatres in London, the Company being perfect in all the best Plays, Operas, Farces and Pantomimes that have been exhibited in any of the Theatres for these ten years past.

On his arrival in Williamsburg, Hallam's first step was to secure a theatre. Dunlap tells us that he eventually found some sort of a storehouse in the suburbs and altered it to suit his purpose. But this is apparently another of the many statements from the same source for which there seems to be no foundation. The Woodham, Murray, Kean company, it will be recalled, had built a theatre in Williamsburg two years previously. It would have been strange if Hallam had overlooked this new house, ready made to his hand, or preferred to it an old storehouse involving considerable outlay for alterations. On this point we cannot ask for better testimony than that of the *Gazette.* Its issue of August 21, 1752, makes it quite plain that Hallam altered the existing playhouse. An announcement in the paper reads:

The Company lately from London have altered the Playhouse to a regular theatre fit for the reception of Ladies and Gentlemen and the execution of their own performance, and will open on the first Friday in September with a play called "The Merchant of Venice," written by Shakespeare. Ladies engaging seats in the boxes are advised to send their servants [9] early on the day of the performance to hold them and prevent trouble and disappointment.

The theatre was the same occupied by the Woodham, Murray, Kean company the previous year. This house, it will be remembered, was situated on the eastern side of Eastern Street (Waller Street) just back of the capitol. One Benjamin Waller owned the land originally on Eastern Street. He sold two lots to Alexander Finnie. On these lots Kean and his fellow managers had erected the Playhouse in 1751. After Kean's departure, the property continued in Finnie's name till its transfer to Lewis Hallam. But it appears that neither Finnie nor Kean nor Hallam paid for the lots, for in 1754 Benjamin Waller, who " has entered for default upon the property on East Street whereon the Playhouse stands," sold the same to John Stretch, printer.

On Lewis Hallam's arrival in Williamsburg he " obtained from Finnie a transfer of the lots on which the theatre stood and altered it at great expense " into a regular theatre. The building was a homely, wooden structure resembling a tobacco barn and stood on the edge of woods which, at that time, came up to Eastern or Waller Street.[10] The house was so near the woods, Dunlap tells us, that the manager could stand in the door and shoot pigeons for his dinner.

---

[9] A curious custom in vogue at that time. The performance usually began at six, and ticket holders were supposed to send substitutes as early as 4 o'clock, so for two hours and longer the front seats of the boxes were occupied by negroes and negresses, a motley crew of every age, waiting for their masters and mistresses. Early on the afternoon of the performance the servants could be seen making their way along the streets all bound in the direction of the playhouse, where they sat holding places for their respective masters. Not so far removed this from the telegraph boys of our own time who now stand in line before a theatre all night waiting for the opening of the box office.

[10] Williamsburg, the old Colonial Capital. By L. G. Tyler.

A week before the opening, the *Gazette* gave the complete program of the coming première, which in those days would naturally be a social event of considerable importance. It read as follows:

By permission of the Hon. Robert Dinwiddie, Esq., His
Majesty's Lieutenant Governor and Commander in
Chief of the Colony and Dominion of Virginia
By a Company of Comedians from London
At the Theatre in Williamsburg
On Friday next, being the 15th of September, will be
presented a Play Call'd
" The Merchant of Venice "
(Written by Shakespear)
The part of *Antonio* (the Merchant) to be perform'd
By Mr. Clarkson.
Gratiano, by Mr. Singleton.
Lorenzo (with songs in character) by Mr. Adcock.
The Part of *Bassanio* to be perform'd by Mr. Rigby.
Duke, by Mr. Wynell.
Salanio, by Mr. Herbert.
The Part of *Launcelot* by Mr. Hallam.
And the Part of *Shylock* (the Jew) to be perform'd by
Mr. Malone.
The Part of *Nerissa* by Mrs. Adcock,
Jessica, by Mrs. Rigby.
and the Part of *Portia* to be perform'd by Mrs. Hallam.
With a new occasional Prologue.
To which will be added a Farce, call'd
" The Anatomist,"
or
" Sham Doctor."
The Part of *Monsieur le Medecin* by Mr. Rigby.
And the Part of *Beatrice* by Mrs. Adcock.

No Persons whatsoever to be admitted behind the Scenes.
Boxes, 7s. 6d. Pit and Balconies, 5s. 9d. Gallery 3s. 9d. To
begin at Six o'Clock.   Vivat Rex!

THE COMING OF THE HALLAMS

It will be noted that the above bill, copied from the Williamsburg newspaper of the day, gives the date of the opening performance as September 15 and the title of the concluding farce as " The Anatomist." Dunlap, Seilhamer and other historians tell us that the date was September 5 and the concluding piece Garrick's " Lethe." Here we have another instance where assertions have been made without the correctness of the statements first being verified. There can be no question as to the exact date, nor as to the title of the afterpiece, since both are matters of public record. Such errors may appear trifling, but to the dramatic student, seeking only the facts regarding the early history of the theatre in this country, correctness in dates and titles is important.

The only account we have of the reception the English players received and the impression they made is the following brief mention in the *Virginia Gazette* of September 22, 1752:

> On *Friday* last the company of Comedians from *England* opened the theatre in this City, when " The Merchant of Venice " and " The Anatomist " were performed, before a numerous and polite audience, with great Applause.

Some idea of what house and audience looked like on the occasion of this memorable première may be had from the description given by John Esten Cooke in his novel " The Virginia Comedians." It is only fiction, but it serves as an acceptable pen picture of the actual scene and no doubt is pretty faithful to the original :

> Within, the playhouse presented a somewhat more attractive appearance. There was a " box," " pit," and " gallery," as in our own day; and the relative prices were arranged in much the same

manner. The common mortals—gentlemen and ladies—were forced to occupy the boxes, raised slightly above the level of the stage and hemmed in by velvet-cushioned railings—in front of a flower-decorated panel extending all around the house—and for this position they were moreover compelled to pay an admission fee of seven shillings and sixpence. The demigods—so to speak—occupied a more eligible position in the " pit," from which they could procure a highly excellent view of the actors' feet and ankles, just on a level with their noses; to conciliate the demigods this superior advantage had been offered, and the price for them was further still reduced to five shillings. But " the gods," in truth, were the real favorites of the manager. To attract them, he arranged the high upper " gallery," and left it untouched, unencumbered by railings, velvet cushions, or any other device; all was free space and liberal as the air; there were no troublesome seats for " the gods," and three shillings and ninepence all that the manager would demand. The honor of their presence was enough. . . . From the boxes a stairway led down to the stage, and some rude scenes, visible at the edges of the curtain, completed the outfit.

When Mr. Lee and his two daughters (characters in the novel) entered the box, which had been reserved for them next the stage, the house was nearly full and the neatness of the edifice was lost sight of in the sea of brilliant ladies' faces and showy forms of cavaliers which extended, like a sea of glittering foam, around the semi-circle of the boxes. The pit was occupied by well-dressed men of the lower class as the times had it, and from the gallery proceeded hoarse murmurs and the unforgotten slang of London. Many smiles and bows were interchanged between the parties in the different boxes, and the young gallants, following the fashion of the day, gathered at each end of the stage, and often walked across to exchange some polite speech with the smiling dames in the boxes nearest. After the orchestra, " consisting of three or four foreign-looking gentlemen, bearded and moustached," had done what they could in the way of preliminary entertainment, the manager came forward in the costume of Bassanio and recommended himself and his company to the " aristocracy of the great and noble colony of Virginia." The curtain slowly rolled aloft, and the young gallants scattered to the corners of the stage, seating themselves on stools or chairs, or standing.

THE COMING OF THE HALLAMS

For this memorable première Mr. Singleton, who played Gratiano and who, in addition to being a good actor, had considerable talent as a poet,[11] had written a prologue especially for the occasion, which was recited by Mr. Rigby. As the first prologue [12] spoken in America, it is worth reprinting here if only as a matter of record:

O For the tuneful Voice of Eloquence,
Whose Numbers flow with Harmony and Sense,
That I may soar above the common Wing,
In lively strains the grateful Subject sing;
To celebrate the laurel'd Poet's Fame,
And thro' the world the Stage's Use proclaim.
To charm the Fancy, and delight the Soul,
To deal Instruction, without harsh Controul,
To cultivate (by pleasing Arts) the Mind,
To win the Reason, and with Wit refin'd
To check each Error and reform Mankind.
For this the Bard, on *Athen's* Infant Stage,
At first produc'd the *Drama's* artful Page;
At once to please and Satyrize he knew,
And all his Characters from Nature drew;
Without Restriction then, as Nature taught,
The Player acted, and the Poet wrote;
The Tragic Muse did Honour to the State,
And in a Mirrour taught them to be great;
The Comick too, by gentle Means reprov'd;
Lash'd every Vice, and every Vice remov'd:
For tho' the Foible, or the Crime she blam'd,
Smil'd on the Man, and with a Smile reclaim'd.

---

[11] In 1767 Mr. Singleton published at Barbadoes "A General Description of the West Indian Islands" in blank verse. The poem was republished in London ten years later.

[12] William Dunlap, in his "History of the American Theatre," presents an entirely different Prologue which he says was dictated to him by "Old Mr. Hallam" himself. Ireland, Seilhamer and other historians have reprinted this Dunlap version, assuming it to be the correct one. We know now that the Dunlap Prologue was apocryphal. The real Prologue, as given above, was printed *in extenso* in the *Virginia Gazette* of September 22, 1752, a week after its delivery in the Williamsburg Theatre.

Thus was the *Grecian* Stage, the *Romans* too;
When e'er they wrote, had Virtue in their View:
In this politer age, on *British* ground,
The sprightly Scenes, with Wit and Sense abound,
The brilliant Stage with vast Applause is crown'd
And Shouts of Joy thro' the whole House resound;
Yet not content to bear so great a Name,
The Muse still labor'd to encrease her Fame;
Summ'd her Agents quickly to appear,
Haste to Virginia's *Plains, my Sons, repair,*
The Goddess said, *Go, confident to find*
An audience sensible, polite and kind.
We heard and strait obey'd; from *Britain's* shore
These unknown Climes advent'ring to explore:
For us then, and our Muse, thus low I bend,
Nor fear to find in each the warmest Friend;
Each smiling aspect dissipates our Fear,
We ne'er can fail of kind Protection here;
The Stage is ever Wisdom's fav'rite Care;
Accept our Labours then, approve our Pains,
Your smiles will please as equal to our Gains;
And as you all esteem the Darling Muse,
The gen'rous *Plaudit* you will not refuse.

Dunlap draws attention to the fact that the occasion marked the first appearance on any stage of the younger Lewis Hallam, then a boy of twelve. He played the servant to Portia and had only one line to speak but when he found himself in presence of the audience he became panic stricken. He stood motionless and speechless until, bursting into tears, he walked off the stage. This was the inglorious debut of an actor who was a great favorite in tragedy and comedy for nearly half a century.

It is not known how frequently performances were given during this first Williamsburg engagement or what the bills were. The only reference to the company, subsequent to the opening, to be found in the newspapers of the day, is in a Williamsburg letter to the *Maryland Gazette* of November 9, 1752. In this letter the correspondent describes the visit of a number of Indian chiefs to the theatre. He says:

The Emperor of the Cherokee nation with his Empress and their son, the young Prince, attended by several of his warriors and Great Men and their Ladies, were received at the Palace by his Honour the Governor, attended by such of the Council as were in Town, on Thursday, the 9th inst., with all the marks of Courtesy and Friendship, and were that evening entertained at the theatre with The Tragedy of " Othello " and a Pantomime Performance which gave them great surprise, as did the fighting with naked Swords on the Stage, which occasioned the Empress to order some about her to go and prevent them killing one another.

The Hallams remained in Virginia some eleven months and then went north, going directly to New York. Dunlap says that the company visited Upper Marlborough, Piscataway and Port Tobacco, but this is another of Dunlap's errors. This historian confused the Hallam company with the Woodham, Murray, Kean company which had already visited the towns mentioned and reaped such profits as were to be had. Realizing that the rival company had forestalled him, Hallam wisely decided to leave the province and make a bold bid for patronage in New York.

CHAPTER IV

LEWIS HALLAM IN NEW YORK AND PHILADELPHIA

DIFFICULTIES WITH THE AUTHORITIES. REMARKABLE REPERTOIRE. OPPOSITION OVERCOME IN THE QUAKER CITY. DEATH OF LEWIS HALLAM. RISE OF DAVID DOUGLASS. INVASION OF NEW ENGLAND. THE MORAL DIALOGUES. THOMSON'S EPILOGUE IN DEFENCE OF THE PLAYER.

LEWIS HALLAM arrived in New York with his company in June, 1753, bearing a certificate from Governor Dinwiddie recommending the comedians as actors and testifying to the correctness of their conduct as men. Armed with this testimonial, he at once applied to the authorities for permission to act, but the local magistrates, for some reason not easily understood, seeing that Kean had been allowed to act only twelve months before, withheld a license and Hallam was forced to remain idle until September. Meantime, to enlist public sympathy, he issued the following petition explaining his position:

As our expedition to New York seems likely to be attended with a very fatal Consequence, and ourselves haply censured for undertaking it without assurance of success, We beg leave humbly to lay a true state of our case before the worthy inhabitants of this city; if possible, endeavour to remove those great obstacles which at present lie before us, and give very sufficient reasons for our appearance in this part of the world, where we all had the most sanguine hopes of meeting a very different reception; little imagining that in a City—to all appearance so polite as this—the Muses would be banished, the works of the immortal Shakespeare and others, the greatest geniuses England ever produced, denied admittance among them, and the instructive and elegant entertainment of the Stage utterly protested against; when, without boasting, we may venture

88

to affirm that we are capable of supporting its dignity with proper decorum and regularity.

In the infancy of this scheme it was proposed to Mr. William Hallam, now of London, to collect a Company of Comedians and send them to New York and other colonies of America. Accordingly he assented, and was at vast expense to procure Scenes, Cloaths, People, etc., and in October, 1750, sent out to this place Mr. Robert Upton, in order to obtain permission to perform, erect a building, and settle everything against our arrival; for which service Mr. Hallam advanced no inconsiderable sum. But Mr. Upton, on his arrival, found here that sett of pretenders with whom he joined, and, unhappily for us, quite neglected the business he was sent about from England, for we never heard from him after.

Being thus deceived by him, the company was at a stand till April, 1752, when, by the persuasion of several gentlemen in London, and Virginia Captains, we set sail on board of Mr. William Lee (Master of the ship " Charming Sally "), and arrived, after a very expensive and tedious voyage, at York River, on the 28th of June following, where we obtained leave of His Excellency the Governor, and performed with universal applause, and met with the greatest encouragement; for which we are bound by the strongest obligations to acknowledge the many and repeated instances of their spirit and generosity.

We were there Eleven Months before we thought of moving, and then asking advice, we were again persuaded to come to New York by several gentlemen who told us we should not fail of a genteel and favorable reception; that the inhabitants were generous and polite, naturally fond of Diversions rational, particularly those of the Theatre: nay, they even told us that there was a very fine Play House building, and that we were really expected.

This was encouragement sufficient for us, as we thought, and we came firmly assured of success; but how far our expectations are answered we shall leave to the Candid to determine, and only beg leave to add, That, as we are People of no Estates, it cannot be supposed we have a Fund sufficient to bear up against such unexpected Repulses. A Journey by Sea and Land, Five Hundred Miles, is not undertaken without money. Therefore, if the worthy Magistrates would consider this in our Favor—that it would rather turn out a Public Advantage and Pleasure than a Private Injury, they would, we make no doubt, grant us permission and give us an opportunity to convince them that we are not cast in the same mould with our Theatrical Predecessors; or that in Private Life or Public Occupation we have the least affinity to them.

This tactful appeal had the desired effect. Permission was finally accorded and Hallam made his preparations to open. Finding Kean's old theatre on Nassau Street (between Maiden Lane and John Street) too small for his purpose, he pulled the building down and built upon the same spot what the *New York Gazette* of 1753 described as " a very fine, large and commodious new theatre," which he opened on September 17, 1753, with Steele's [1] comedy " The Conscious Lovers." The cast was as follows:

Young Bevil	Mr. Rigby	Tom	Mr. Singleton
Mr. Sealand	Mr. Malone	Phillis	Mrs. Becceley
Sir John	Mr. Bell	Mrs. Sealand	Mrs. Clarkson
Myrtle	Mr. Clarkson	Lucinda	Miss Hallam
Cimberton	Mr. Miller	Isabella	Mrs. Rigby
Humphrey	Mr. Adcock	Indiana	Mrs. Hallam
	Daniel	Master L. Hallam	

The comedy was followed by Cibber's ballad farce " Damon and Phillida."

The company gave performances only three times a week—Mondays, Wednesdays and Fridays. The prices charged for admission were: Boxes 8/–, Pit 6/–, Gallery 3/–. The season lasted from September 17, 1753, to March 18, 1754.

During these six months Hallam produced no

[1] Sir Richard Steele (1672–1729), one of England's most famous men of letters during the reign of Queen Anne. He wrote several plays, of which "The Conscious Lovers" is the best and most successful.

fewer than twenty-one plays, of which three were Shakespearean tragedies, and twelve comedies and farces. It would have been a remarkable achievement for a well equipped stock company long established in their home city with every facility at hand. Considering the handicap under which that little band of strolling players labored, acting in unfamiliar surroundings, with a large portion of the population indifferent or openly hostile to the things of the theatre, it was indeed a marvellous record. The repertoire comprised the cream of English dramatic literature at that time—Shakespeare's mighty tragedies, Congreve's and Steele's brilliant comedies, the masterpieces of Cibber, Lillo, Farquhar, Addison, Rowe, Fielding. New Yorkers were given an opportunity to see them all and, according to tradition, each play was adequately cast and acted. What manager of to-day could come anywhere near such a record as this, even with all the resources of the modern theatre at his command?[2]

In the Shakespeare plays Mr. Rigby alternated with Mr. Malone in playing the principal rôles. When Rigby played Richard III, Malone was content with the rôle of Buckingham. When Malone

---

[2] Compared with the famous American stock companies of a century later, this record was not, of course, extraordinary. At the Boston Museum as many as fourteen long plays were presented in two weeks and a season of six months would average eight or ten plays a month. The other Boston theatres of 40 years ago, Selwyn's, Howard Athenæum, the Boston and the old National, did as well if not better. The Philadelphia theatres, Mrs. John Drew's, the Walnut Street, and the Chestnut Street, did equally well. Our more recent stock companies (within 20 years) changed the bill every week and in a season of 30 or more weeks would give 30 or more plays. The legitimate stars of thirty years ago, Edwin Booth, Lawrence Barrett, E. L. Davenport, John McCullough, Joseph Jefferson, John E. Owens, Edwin Adams et al., would give six plays a week in the various stock theatres throughout the country.

played Lear, Mr. Rigby was willing to play the Usher, and so on. In Williamsburg, Malone played Othello and Mrs. Hallam was the Desdemona, a part which she had acted with success in England. Malone was probably the first actor to play Othello, Shylock and Lear on the American stage, as Thomas Kean was probably the first Richard. Mr. Hallam, a comedian, had no great ambition as an actor. He sometimes remained out of the cast altogether, and was often willing to surrender a good low comedy rôle to some other member of the company. These little details are interesting as showing the friendliness and good will that marked the personal and professional relations of this little band of players from England—something not always encountered in theatrical organizations.

New names appeared in the cast when the company opened in New York. Mr. Bell, Mr. Miller and Mrs. Becceley were not members of the company when it first reached Virginia. Mrs. Becceley, a singing soubrette, was seen later as Polly in " The Beggar's Opera." In addition to these newcomers, Mr. and Mrs. Love and Mr. Hulett were engaged as dancers. " Mr. Hulett," says Dunlap, " was for many years the only dancing master in New York. Some of us old fellows remember the steps taught by this worthy man whose sons were the teachers of succeeding generations."

The New York season closed March 18, 1754, with " The Beggar's Opera " and " The Devil to Pay," on which occasion the bill of the play contained this announcement:

LEWIS HALLAM IN NEW YORK

Lewis Hallam, comedian, intending for Philadelphia, begs the favour of those having any demands upon him to bring in their accounts and receive their money.

This notice is interesting as showing that the comedians had at least made enough money during the New York season to enable them to pay their debts. In those days, when the player was regarded as no better than a vagabond, the announcement that he was ready to discharge his obligations like other honorable men, must have been disconcerting to his defamers and done much to increase the community's respect for the dramatic profession.

Soon after his arrival in New York, Hallam turned his attention to Philadelphia as the company's next stand. The city of Penn held out many allurements. It was only a short distance to go. The population was large. The people, prosperous and cultured, had the taste and means to support a first class theatrical organization. Yet there were almost unsurmountable difficulties in the way. Although he had many sympathizers in the Quaker City, citizens who saw no offence to either religion or morality in dramatic performances conducted in a first class manner, the majority of the inhabitants were bitterly opposed to play-acting of any kind. Yet the more liberal minded minority resented being deprived of pleasures New York was enjoying, and a number of lovers of the drama communicated with Hallam, urging him to go to Philadelphia.

While the New York season was still young, therefore, Hallam decided to send Malone to Philadelphia to open the way, promising him that, if successful, he should have for his reward the parts of

Falstaff in " Henry IV " and " The Merry Wives," and Don Lewis in " Love Makes a Man." [3] Malone undertook the mission and went to Philadelphia, but met with so much opposition that he could accomplish nothing. In this dilemma, he sent word to Hallam to come to his assistance. The manager, on his arrival, found the town divided into two camps— those who favored permission being granted the players to open a theatre, and those uncompromisingly hostile to the proposed theatricals. A petition signed by a large number of citizens urged Governor Hamilton to prohibit the acting of profane stage plays. This move was met by a counter petition urging the Governor to do the exact opposite. The controversy raged furiously for a time, but finally the forces of reason prevailed, and manager Hallam was accorded permission to give twenty-four performances, provided that nothing " indecent or immoral " were presented. The manager also bound himself to give one performance for the benefit of the poor and security for all debts contracted on behalf of the company.

The Hallam players left New York immediately

---

[3] The established line of parts dates back to Shakespeare's time and continued until about twenty years ago. The lines of "business" for which actors were specifically engaged and which covered the several parts in the well known tragedies and comedies that were to be played throughout the season were, for example: Leading Man: Charles Surface, Richelieu, Orlando or Jaques, Brutus or Cassius. First Heavy Man: Joseph Surface. First Old Man: Sir Peter Teazle, etc. In those early days the "character" part (as now so termed) would fall to either the comedian, heavy man or first old man. The lines of "business" were punctiliously respected, but there have been cases where comradeship and courtesy have prompted the leading man to give up his leading rôle for a night to another actor, for his benefit. The custom had its drawbacks as well as its advantages, for, while it encouraged the actor to do his best, it also resulted in him retaining the rôle long after he was able to do it justice. For instance, an actor would continue to impersonate youthful lovers long after he had lost all virility and his face was criss-crossed with wrinkles. Within the last two decades the lines of "business" have passed away. It is now "catch on as catch can." Our actors today (1919) are all specialists.

after the closing of their season March 18, and, proceeding directly to Philadelphia, took possession of the same theatre used by the Murray-Kean company in 1749, situated in the warehouse owned by William Plumstead in King or Water Street, between Pine and Lombard Streets, and here they opened April 15, 1754, with Rowe's tragedy " The Fair Penitent " and " Miss in Her Teens " as the after-piece.

Having been so well advertised, there was naturally great curiosity to see the " players from London," and the house was crowded to the doors, many persons being unable to obtain admission. During the performance a spectator was recognized as one of the signers of the unfriendly petition, and being regarded as a spy, he was quickly hustled out. " The company," [4] says Dunlap, " gained money and reputation notwithstanding continued and vigorous opposition. Pamphlets were published and distributed gratis during the theatrical campaign and every effort made to show the evils attendant upon plays and players and playhouses, but Shakespeare and his followers prevailed. The tree was planted and could not be rooted out."

Two months was the length of the Hallams' stay in the Quaker City. Among the plays presented, in addition to the opening bill, were " The Gamester," by Moore; " Tamerlane," by Rowe; " The Provoked Husband," by Vanbrugh; " The Careless Husband," by Cibber, and probably several of the plays already seen in New York.

While the company was playing its Philadelphia engagement, William Hallam, the projector of the

---

[4] History of the American Theatre. By William Dunlap.

enterprise, arrived from England. He did not stay longer than the time necessary to settle accounts with his brother, after which he returned to London.

What profits the Hallams had to divide is not known. The *Thespian Dictionary,* published about 1808, declared that Lewis Hallam made $50,000 by his venture, but lost it all in the American war, a ridiculous assertion on its face, seeing that Hallam died in 1755. "It is not likely," says Seilhamer, "that Hallam did much more than make both ends meet between 1752 and 1754. . . . America in the middle of the Eighteenth Century was not a land of gold like California in 1849. As a rule, the people were poor, and even those who were richest[5] were not rich according to modern standards. America in the Hallam period was a rough land of earth and stone and tree, and even the theatrical towns—Williamsburg, Annapolis, New York and Philadelphia —were mere villages in comparison to what is called 'a good show town' in the theatrical slang of this age."

On the close of the season, the entire company went to Jamaica, West Indies, where Lewis Hallam, who had been ailing for some time, died. On his decease, the company disbanded and none of its mem-

[5] Some idea of a typical rich man's house in the American Colonies about the middle of the eighteenth century may be had from this description of the belongings of the Hon. Rip Van Dam, who held the office of President of the Council and acting governor of New York in 1732. "The house he lived in," says Esther Singleton in "Social New York under the Georges," "was worth about £500. It was of brick and was two stories high. The worth of his household furniture and negro slaves was estimated at from £250 to £300. Among his goods and chattels, he had a japanned chest of drawers valued at £3,. a black Walnut table, a looking glass, a desk and bookcase, ten chairs, and elbow chair (£4) a clock £9, a large table, a chest of drawers, twelve leather chairs, twelve black chairs, a mahogany table, a writing desk, a screen, two sconces and a backgammon table. He also owned a silver hilted sword and 12 gold rings. His negroes came to £50 and his silver to £90."

bers, with the exception of Mrs. Hallam, and her two sons Lewis and Adam Hallam, were seen again on the American stage.

Nothing more was heard of the Hallams until 1758 when David Douglass married Mrs. Hallam and reorganized the company.

David Douglass was one of the troupe of players that John Moody recruited in London and took out to the West Indies in 1751. He was not very conspicuous as an actor, but he showed himself a man of character and ability, and, according to Dunlap, " appeared to have been by descent and education a gentleman." As a manager he played a most important rôle in American theatricals. For thirty years he was virtually theatrical king of the western hemisphere. When, at the outbreak of the Revolution, he was compelled to cease his activities here, he returned to Jamaica, where he subsequently became one of his Majesty's printers, a master in chancery and a magistrate. He died at Spanish Town in 1786, having accumulated a fortune of £25,000.

In the new company as reorganized by Douglass, Mrs. Hallam was made the star. Mrs. Hallam was a woman of great beauty and elegance, still in the prime of life, and able to play effectively youthful heroines in both tragedy and comedy. " Far superior," says Ireland, " to any actress who had preceded her, she retained for many years all the kind feelings of the public, who regarded her with an admiration reaching almost to idolatry. She was the original actress in New York, as far as any printed records show, of Juliet, Cordelia, Portia, Jane Shore, Calista, Mrs. Beverly, Lady Betty Modish, Mrs. Sullen,

7 97

Bisarre and many other leading parts. In after life, she declined to such rôles as the Duchess of York, Mrs. Heidleberg and Deborah Woodcock." She died in Philadelphia in 1773.

Lewis Hallam, now eighteen years of age, was leading man, except in such heavy rôles as Richard III, Lear and Tamerlane. This was the same youth who, only a few years previously, had burst into tears and run off the stage in confusion when the company made its first appearance in Virginia. As he grew older, young Hallam acquired more confidence and gradually developed into a leading actor of great versatility and talent. During the fifty years he was on the stage, he was a great favorite both in tragedy and comedy, and he played almost every rôle of importance in the repertoire of the period. " In the prime of life," says Ireland, " he was slightly above the middle height, erect and thin, but strong, vigorous and graceful—being an accomplished fencer and dancer. A slight cast in one eye, resulting from an injury in his youth, although scarcely perceptible in characters of tragedy and high comedy, materially heightened the expression and effect of his features in humorous parts." He was twice married, once in early life to a lady in the West Indies and afterwards to Miss Tuke, a young and beautiful girl, who afterwards became well known on the American stage as Mrs. Hallam. He died in Philadelphia in 1808.

Adam, his younger brother, was also a member of the company, but seemingly he had no great talent, for his name soon disappeared from the bills. Helen Hallam had not yet joined the company, but Nancy Hallam was seen occasionally in children's parts.

98

LEWIS HALLAM IN PHILADELPHIA

Apart from the Hallams, Mrs. Love was the only member of the old company who had been retained. Mrs. Adcock's place had been taken by Mrs. Harman, a granddaughter of Colley Cibber and an excellent actress, who died in New York in 1773. Her husband, Mr. Harman, played leading heavies. Others in the company included Owen Morris, who made his first appearance as Polonius and, later, gained fame in "comic old men" parts, Mr. and Mrs. Allyn, Mr. and Mrs. Tomlinson, and Mr. Reed, who was Singleton's successor. To Mr. Hallam, of course, fell the rôles formerly played by Mr. Rigby.

Douglass had planned to open in New York in the fall of 1758 and, to that end, had made early preparations to secure a theatre. As Hallam's old theatre in Nassau Street had been torn down and a church erected on the site, he built a new playhouse on what was then known as Cruger's Wharf, near what is now called Old Slip. The theatre was soon ready and he arrived in New York with all his company for the intended opening. Unfortunately, in his calculations, he had quite overlooked one important detail, the conciliation of the City Fathers to the extent of obtaining their consent to his giving dramatic performances. At the eleventh hour, he sought to repair the omission, but too late. The magistrates, offended at his temerity in proceeding with his plans without their sanction, curtly refused his application. Thereupon, the manager came out with the following card in Gaine's *Mercury:*

Mr. Douglass, who came here with a Company of Comedians, having applied to the Gentlemen in Power for permission to play, has (to his great mortification) met with a positive and absolute denial. He has in vain represented that such are his circumstances and those of the other members of his company that it is impossible for them to move to another place; and tho', in the humblest manner, he begged the Magistrates would indulge him in acting as many Plays as would barely defray the expenses he and the Company have been at in coming to this city, and enable them to proceed to another, he has been unfortunate enough to be peremptorily refused it. As he has given over all thoughts of acting, he begs leave to inform the Public that in a few days he will open a Histrionic Academy, of which proper notice will be given in this paper.

But this appeal, instead of helping matters, had just the opposite effect. The magistrates thought they saw in the proposed " Histrionic Academy " ⁶ an attempt to get round their prohibition, and no doubt it was an attempt at subterfuge, just as to-day the Sunday laws are often evaded by advertising performances as " sacred concerts," for later, when the actor manager went to Rhode Island, where attempts to act plays of any kind met with the most determined opposition, he presented " Othello " in the guise of a " Moral Dialogue." In a further communication, Douglass denied any desire to resist authority and, finally, the city officials relented and he was allowed to open.

His season began December 28, 1758, with Rowe's tragedy " Jane Shore." The season lasted until February 7, 1759, during which time eighteen plays were

---

⁶ In England|the "Histrionic Academy" was a very common expedient to which players were driven to evade the law. Even the great Siddons on one occasion was forced to adopt the subterfuge. She and John Philip Kemble once gave a comic opera in Wolverhampton under that high sounding title. The bill stated that the performance would be given without "fee, gain, hire or reward" and "absolutely no tickets sold." On the other hand, no one would be admitted without a ticket, which could be had for the asking by applying to a certain person whose address was given and which person, the advertisement went on to say, had FOR SALE some excellent tooth powder just received from London neatly done up in packages at 2/–; 1/–; and 6d each!

presented. Among these were " The Inconstant,"
" The Recruiting Officer " and " The Stage Coach,"
by Farquhar; " The Orphan " and " Venice Pre-
served," by Otway; " Douglas," by Home; " The
Drummer," by Addison; " The Spanish Friar," by
Dryden, and " Richard III " and " Othello," by
Shakespeare.

More than ordinary interest is attached to the performance of " Douglas," which took place on January
24, in view of the fact that it was the first production
in America of the most famous tragedy of the
Eighteenth Century, and one which for a hundred
years retained a prominent place in the affections of
American theatregoers. Originally rejected by Garrick, but produced later at Edinburgh with great success, it represented five years' work of the Rev. John
Home, a Scotch Presbyterian minister who lost his
pulpit for having written " a profane stage play." A
human and powerful drama, based on the pathetic
Scotch ballad *Gil Morrice,* the leading part of young
Norval has always appealed strongly to handsome
young actors of the romantic type. Incidentally, it
may be recalled that it was in this part that Edwin
Forrest made his first appearance on the stage.

On the opening night of the new theatre, Mrs.
Douglass delivered the Epilogue written by Adam
Thomson,[7] a revised and improved version of that
originally delivered in Philadelphia by Mrs. Hal-

[7]Adam Thomson, a Scotchman of Philadelphia, whose lively newspaper
tilt with "Buckram" for his Parody on the Epilogue, furnished one of the
literary controversies of the day. Dunlap erroneously attributes the Thomson
Epilogue to the player-poet Singleton, an obvious blunder, as Seilhamer points
out, seeing that Singleton had been absent from the country five years at the
time of its delivery. The Dunlap Society, assuming the historian to be correct, unfortunately perpetuated the error by including the Epilogue among
its publications as Singleton's.

101

lam in 1754. As a spirited protest by the players at the intolerance of the time towards their calling, it made considerable impression and was often repeated later in other cities. It deserves preservation as an historical document:

> Much has been said at this unlucky time,
> To prove the treading of the stage a crime.
> Mistaken zeal, in terms oft not so civil,
> Consigns both play and players to the devil.
> Yet wise men own, a play well chose may teach
> Such useful moral truths as the parsons preach;
> May teach the heart another's grief to know,
> And melt the soul in tears of generous woe.
> So when the unhappy virtuous fair complains
> In Shakspere's, Lee's or Otway's moving strains,
> The narrowest hearts expanded wide appear,
> And soft compassion drops the pitying tear.
> Or would you warn the thoughtless youth to shun
> Such dangerous arts which numbers have undone,
> A Barnwell's fate can never fail to move,
> And strike with shame and terror lawless love.
> See, plunged in ruin, with a virtuous wife,
> The Gamester weeps, despairs and ends his life.
> When Cato bleeds he spends his latest breath,
> To teach the love of country strong in death.
> With such examples and a thousand more,
> Of godlike men who lived in times before,
> The tragic Muse renewing every age,
> Makes the dead heroes tread the living stage.
> But when to social gayety inclined
> Our comic Muse shall feast the cheerful mind,
> Fools of all sorts and fops a brainless crew,
> To raise your mirth we'll summon to your view;
> Make each pert coxcomb merry with his brother,
> Whilst knaves conceal'd shall grin at one another.
> 'Tis magic ground we tread, and at our call
> Those knights appear that represent you all.
> Yet, hold! methinks I hear some snarler cry,

" Pray, madam, why so partial—rat me—why
Don't you do justice to your own sweet sex?
Are there no prudes, coquettes or jilts to vex? "
'Tis granted; vice and folly's not confined
To man alone, but spreads to womankind.
We frankly own—we may indeed, as well—
For every fluttering beau we've an affected belle,
Nor has dramatic Satire's candid page
Failed to chastise them justly on the stage.
Thus human life's our theme—a spacious field
Which the soul's noblest entertainments yield.
By men of worth admired from time,
Who nature's picture never judged a crime;
And if the soul in nature's cause we move,
The friends of nature cannot disapprove.
We trust they do not by the splendid sight
Of sparkling eyes that grace our scenes to-night;
Then bravely dare to assert the taste you've shown,
Nor be ashamed so just a cause to own;
And tell our foes what Shakspere said of old—
Our former motto spoke it, I am told—
That here the world in miniature you see,
And all mankind are players as well as we.

The opposition and difficulties which Douglass
had met with from the outset of his New York season
might well have discouraged him from further
attempts in such inhospitable territory. In Philadelphia the prospects were no brighter. Feeling
against the stage ran high and continued to be bitterly hostile. But, undeterred, the energetic manager resolved, notwithstanding, to proceed there as
planned. He decided to build a new theatre in the
Quaker City, and, as this took time, five months at
least elapsed before the new house was ready. In the
meantime, it is believed that he and his company

103

played a short engagement at Perth Amboy, then a garrison town and the capital of the Province of New Jersey.

It was late in the spring of 1759 when Douglass and his players reached Philadelphia. The new theatre was situated at the southwest corner of Vernon and South Streets, on what was known as "Society Hill." It is believed that the manager preferred to put up a building in this locality instead of using the old theatre in Plumstead's warehouse, where Hallam had played, because Society Hill, being beyond the city limits, was out of the jurisdiction of the town authorities. This time he had taken the precaution to secure Governor Denny's sanction to perform. Permission was granted on condition that the company gave one performance for the benefit of the Pennsylvania Hospital. But in spite of this official support the hostility continued, the Quakers going so far as to apply to Judge Allen for an injunction against the players. The story goes that the judge not only dismissed the application, but retorted with a quiet chuckle that he had always got more moral virtue from plays than from sermons. Shortly after this, the judge's wife died and the " antis " were prompt to pronounce this domestic misfortune Heaven's judgment for having given encouragement to profane stage-plays.

Balked in one direction, the Quakers tried to stop the performances in another. On May 22, 1759, they presented an address to the House setting forth that " they have with real concern, heard that a company of stage players are preparing to erect a theatre and exhibit plays to the inhabitants of this city which they conceive, if permitted, will be subversive of the good order and morals which they desire may be preserved in this government." The elders of the Lutheran German Congregation of Philadelphia and the Presbyterian Synod of New York and Philadelphia presented similar petitions. The House could not ignore these representations and a bill against play-acting was presented May 28 and passed May 31. This put Governor Denny in a dilemma. He had given Douglass his permission and he wanted to keep faith with him. So he withheld the bill [8] until June 15 when he returned it with some amendments. The measure was finally passed but was set aside in the King's Council September 2, 1760.

Meantime, Douglass had not been slow to take advantage of the respite thus afforded. He began his season at the new theatre on Society Hill on June 25 and remained open until December 27. Among the plays presented during that time were Rowe's " Tamerlane " and " Fair Penitent," Fielding's " The Virgin Unmasked," Vanbrugh's " Provoked Hus-

---

[8] *Bill Against Players Passed by the House of Representatives of the Colony of Pennsylvania May 31, 1759.* And whereas several companies of idle persons and strollers have come into this Province from foreign parts in the characters of players, erected stages and theatres and thereon acted divers plays by which the weak, poor and necessitous have been prevailed on to neglect their labour and industry and to give extravagant prices for their tickets and great numbers of disorderly persons have been drawn together in the night to the great distress of many poor families, manifest injury of this young colony and grievous scandal of religion and the laws of this Government.

Be it therefore Enacted, that every person and persons whatsoever that from and after the First day of January which will be A.D. 1760, shall erect, build any playhouse, theatre, stage or scaffold for acting, showing or exhibiting any tragedy, comedy, tragi-comedy, farce, interlude or other play or part of a play whatsoever or shall act, shew or exhibit them or any of them or be in any ways concerned therein or in selling any of the tickets aforesaid in any city, town or place within this Province and be thereof legally convicted in manner aforesaid shall forfeit and pay the sum of five hundred pounds lawful money aforesaid.

band," Farquhar's " Recruiting Officer," Lillo's
" George Barnwell," Gay's " Beggar's Opera," etc.
The engagement was notable for the five Shake-
spearean plays presented, " Richard III," " Hamlet "
(believed to be the first time in America), " Lear,"
" Macbeth," " Romeo and Juliet." In " Richard
III," Mr. Harman played the humpbacked king,
Mr. Hallam was the Richmond, and Mr. Douglass
the King Henry. In " Hamlet " Mr. Hallam was
the melancholy Dane, Mr. Harman, Polonius, Mr.
Douglass the Ghost, and Mrs. Harman the Ophelia.
Mr. Harman played the title rôle in " Lear," Mr.
Hallam was seen as Macbeth, the first tragedian to
act the part on this continent. Later,[9] Hallam played
Romeo to his mother's Juliet—probably the first and
last time that a son has played the lover to his own
mother. The season closed with two benefits—
" George Barnwell," for a fund to purchase an organ
for the College, and " Hamlet " for the benefit of the
Pennsylvania Hospital in accordance with the agreement made with Governor Denny.[10]

After leaving Philadelphia, Douglass went to
Maryland where he visited several of the small towns
before proceeding to Annapolis. Here he also built
a theatre, beginning his season March 3 and continuing until May 12. The opening bill was Otway's
tragedy " The Orphan," followed by Garrick's farce
" Lethe."

The season was again remarkable both for the

---

[9] In New York, January 11, 1762.

[10] Later, the Hospital refused the money raised at this benefit on the
curious plea that "it was not in the power of the Treasurer to commit this act
of folly, notwithstanding it was raised by exhibiting a stage play near this
city which was done without the consent of the said managers in consequence
of the injunction of the late Governor Denny."

number and quality of the plays produced. It was not the custom of the pre-Revolutionary newspapers to make any comment on theatrical performances. Possibly they were afraid, in view of the general animosity against the stage, of losing some of their subscribers. But on March 6, three days following the opening, this review of the Douglass players appeared in the Maryland *Gazette:*

On Monday last the Theatre in this city was opened, when the tragedy of " Orphan " and " Lethe " (a dramatic satire) was performed in the presence of his Excellency the Governor to a polite and numerous audience, who all expressed their satisfaction. The principal characters both in the play and entertainment were performed with great justice, and the applause which attended the whole representation did no less honour to the abilities of the actors than to the taste of their auditors. For the amusement and emolument of such of our readers as were not present we here insert the Prologue and Epilogue, both written by a gentleman of this Province, whose poetical works have rendered him justly admired by all encouragers of the liberal arts.

This was the first time that laudatory mention had been made of their performances in any American newspaper, and it is not unlikely that Douglass paid for the insertion of the paragraph. On the other hand, it must not be overlooked that the players were now in more friendly territory. Indeed, an entirely different kind of welcome awaited them throughout Maryland.

The Annapolis casts are noteworthy for the changes that occurred in the organization. The names of several newcomers appear. Mr. Harman had retired, his place being taken by Mr. Palmer, who before then had played only at benefits. Mrs. Morris, wife of the comedian, we find taking Mrs.

Harman's rôles, while Allyn and Tomlinson and their wives were substituted by Mr. Murray, Mr. and Mrs. Dowthwaite and Miss Crane. Seilhamer is inclined to think that Mr. Murray may have been the same Murray who was Thomas Kean's partner in 1750. He says: " How came Mr. Douglass to secure these recruits and why were the members of his company, who were with him before and afterwards, absent from Annapolis? These questions are not easily answered, but the Annapolis season shows that even at that early period it was possible to reorganize a theatrical company in America at short notice."

On the other hand, Henry, Wignell, Hodgkinson and other managers of later date were compelled to make frequent trips to England in search of new players for their companies. Even fifty years later this dearth of actors continued, showing that the native supply was not as abundant as Seilhamer imagined. Joe Cowell, the English comedian, complains of the scarcity of actors. He writes: [11]

Performers and others employed in a theatre could not be obtained nor were there a sufficient number of American actors on the whole Continent to form a company. Fortunately for the young population of that day, they had something better to do. Out of the members at the Park Theatre all were English with the exception of Reed, Woodhull, Phillip, Barker and Nixon. All the females worth speaking of were English with the exception of Mrs. Wheatley, a native of New York, and a much better actress in my opinion than all of them put together.

From Annapolis the Douglass company went to Upper Marlborough, Va., and later to Williamsburg, Va., where they acted during the winter of 1760–61.

[11] "Thirty Years Among the Players," by Joe Cowell.

The following year (1761) they went to Rhode Island and acted at Newport that summer.

Newport was then one of the chief seaports of New England, the capital of Rhode Island, and a well populated, prosperous community. There is no record of any theatricals in the colony before the coming of the Douglass troupe. In fact, their visit was notable as marking the first appearance of actors in New England.

Although Douglass had taken the precaution to arm himself with a certificate from the Governor of Virginia testifying to the conduct and capacity of his players, he found himself facing a difficult situation. Throughout New England the attitude toward the stage was one of uncompromising hostility. There was no general statute in Rhode Island prohibiting stage plays, but the playhouse was everywhere denounced as the House of Satan, and play-actors as familiars of Beelzebub himself.

It must not be overlooked that there was some justification for the bitterness of the time toward the theatre. The settlers of the New England states were almost all descendants of those Puritans on whom the Seventeenth Century dramatists had heaped their coarsest taunts and ridicule. On the other hand, the moral defects, looseness of tone, mockery of the marital ties which the conduct of some players had made appear indispensable parts of theatrical life; also the libertinism of many of the plays of the period, nearly all of which were sensual and licentious in tone and treatment—all this gave offence. The plays of Mrs. Centlivre, Vanbrugh, Farquhar and other playwrights revelled in such indecencies as would not be tolerated even in our easy going day. Another ground of complaint was that when the actors came to town the community became demoralized. One petition begging that play acting be forbidden reads:

It is well known that on the nights of performance the theatre is surrounded by a large concourse of people, who resort there not to see the performance within, but to take part in the performance without. Riots, drunkenness, and obscenity are among the least of the evils nightly practised. While the audience within are strengthening their morals, and adding to the stock of their religious principles by listening to the precepts of the stage, the rabble without are drenching themselves in rum, and wallowing in open and public prostitution.

All this had intensified and fed the opposition to stage and player.

Anxious to avoid as much as possible giving offense to the powerful anti-theatrical element, and probably with a view to first feeling the pulse of the public in general before proceeding further with his plans for a long stay in the town, Douglass disguised his first bill " Othello " under the cloak of " A Series of Moral Dialogues." Instead of immediately building a theatre and openly labelling it such, as he had done in other places, he engaged a room at the King's Arms Tavern where, on June 10, he presented Shakespeare's tragedy in this novel form:

MORAL DIALOGUES,
IN FIVE PARTS,

Depicting the Evil Effects of Jealousy and other Bad Passions, and Proving that Happiness can only Spring from the Pursuit of Virtue.

Mr. DOUGLASS will represent a noble and magnanimous Moor named Othello, who loves a young lady named Desdemona, and after he has married her, harbors (as in too many cases) the dreadful passion of jealousy.

> 'Of jealousy, our being's bane,
> Mark the small cause and the most dreadful pain.

Mr. ALLYN will depict the character of a specious villain, in the regiment of Othello, who is so base as to hate his commander on mere suspicion, and to impose on his best friend. Of such characters, it is to be feared, there are thousands in the world, and the one in question may present to us a salutary warning.

> The man that wrongs his master and his friend,
> What can he come to but a shameful end?

Mr. HALLAM will delineate a young and thoughtless officer, who is traduced by Mr. ALLYN, and, getting drunk, loses his situation, and his general's esteem. All young men, whatsoever, take example from Cassio.

> The ill effects of drinking would you see,
> Be warned and keep from evil company.

Mr. MORRIS will represent an old gentleman, the father of Desdemona, who is not cruel or covetous, but is foolish enough to dislike the noble Moor, his son-in-law, because his face is not white, forgetting that we all spring from one root. Such prejudices are very numerous and very wrong.

> Fathers beware what sense and love ye lack,
> 'Tis crime, not color, makes the being black.

Mr. QUELCH will depict the fool, who wishes to become a knave, and trusting one gets killed by him. Such is the friendship of rogues—take heed.

> When fools would knaves become, how often you'll
> Perceive the knave not wiser than the fool.

Mrs. MORRIS will represent a young and virtuous wife, who, being wrongfully suspected, gets smothered (in an adjoining room) by her husband.

> Reader, attend; and ere thou goest hence
> Let fall a tear to hapless innocence.

Mrs. DOUGLASS will be her faithfull attendant, who will

hold out a good example to all servants, male and female, and to all people in subjection.

> *Obedience and gratitude*
> *Are things as rare as they are good.*

The Dialogues were so well received that Douglass was encouraged to stay on. Disregarding an adverse vote of the town he erected a theatre [12] at Easton's point, in the north part of the town, and here, on September 7, 1761, gave a performance of Vanbrugh's comedy " The Provoked Husband " for the benefit of the poor. " This," says Blake, " was the first dramatic performance given in New England by a regular company of professional actors." [13]

The 1761 season closed with the performance of the tragedy of " Douglas," the occasion being commented upon by the Newport correspondent of *Gaine's Mercury* in these terms:

Newport, Nov. 3.—On Friday evening last the company of comedians finished their performances in this town by enacting the tragedy of " Douglas " for the benefit of the poor. This second charity is undoubtedly meant as an expression of gratitude for the countenance and favor the town has shown them; and it cannot without an uncommon degree of malevolence be ascribed to an interested or selfish view, because it is given at a time when the company are just leaving the place, and consequently can have neither fear nor hope from the public. In return for this generosity, it ought in justice to be told that the behaviour of the company here has been irreproachable: and with regard to their skill as players the universal satisfaction they have given is their best and most honorable testimony. The character they brought from the Governor and gentlemen of Virginia has been fully verified, and therefore

---

[12] The theatre must have been of the flimsiest construction for the following year it is said to have been blown down in a gale, the company barely escaping with their lives.

[13] History of the Providence Stage, by Charles Blake.

we shall run no risk in pronouncing that they are capable of entertaining a sensible and polite audience.[14]

Encouraged by his success at Newport, Douglass took his company next year (1762) to Providence, R. I., where the opposition to the stage was even more pronounced. Building a theatre was out of the question in view of the public sentiment, so, as one way out of the difficulty, he built a " school house " in Meeting Street and here, as announced in an advertisement in the Newport *Mercury* of August 10, he gave performances for several weeks in defiance of the clamor against profane stage plays. " This," remarks Seilhamer, " is probably the only time in the history of the drama when a theatre was called a school house, but what seems humorous now must have been exceedingly serious in 1762. These two seasons at Newport and Providence were the first and last times that a company of comedians was able to gain a hearing in any part of New England before the Revolution."

In August, 1762, the Rhode Island Assembly passed an act forbidding the further building of theatres or any more acting under the severest penalties and the act was ordered to be proclaimed throughout the streets of Providence by beat of drum.

---

[14] This and other comment in the pre-Revolutionary newspapers smack somewhat of the perfunctory "reading notice" of our own time. Praise for the poor player was so scarce in those early days that no doubt Douglass was very willing on occasion to grease the accommodating palm of an impecunious printer.

CHAPTER V

DAVID DOUGLASS, THEATRE BUILDER

ERECTION OF THE BEEKMAN STREET HOUSE. MR. DOUGLASS THE FIRST AMERICAN FALSTAFF. RIOTOUS AUDIENCES. OPENING OF THE SOUTHWARK THEATRE, PHILADELPHIA. MISS CHEER MAKES HER FIRST APPEARANCE IN SHAKESPEARIAN REPERTOIRE. PRODUCTION OF "THE PRINCE OF PARTHIA." DÉBUT OF JOHN HENRY, AMERICA'S FIRST MATINEE IDOL. STAGE MORALS.

THE splendid repertoire and excellent performances of the Douglass company not only commanded attention and respect wherever it pitched its tent, but the shrewdness and capacity of the organizer was evident in all his undertakings. That Douglass succeeded in accumulating $125,000 before he died—a considerable fortune in those days—may be taken as some indication that his theatrical enterprises were financially successful. After his first *faux pas* with the New York officials, he grew more tactful and, by a conciliatory attitude, won the favor of many persons, even those prejudiced on general principles against the stage, who, otherwise, might have proved troublesome. His theatrical campaigns were skilfully planned and he allowed nothing to stand in his way. If not satisfied with the theatre he found in the town where he wished to play, he at once proceeded to build another. As there were no theatres anywhere, with the exception of the few already mentioned, he was always building theatres. He was, indeed, the pioneer of America's big theatre builders. Nowadays it is a theatrical commonplace for a manager, backed with unlimited capital, to throw a chain

114

of million dollar theatres across the continent, but in pre-Revolutionary times, when the actors were literally strolling players, when the drama, struggling for recognition, was beset on all sides by ignorance, bigotry and malevolence, it was a very different matter. The man's courage and energy were astonishing. While his company was still acting in Rhode Island and battling with local intolerance, Douglass was in New York making arrangements to build another theatre.

The theatre he had built three years previously on Cruger's Wharf he now judged unsuitable for his purpose, so he erected a new one on the southwest corner of Nassau and Chappel (now Beekman) Streets. This house, known as the Beekman Street Theatre, was the fourth playhouse built in New York.

The granting of permission to build was opposed in one quarter on the curious ground that the players would cost the city £6000. To this criticism, Douglass made reply, giving some interesting figures. The cost of the theatre he estimated at $1,625. The capacity of the house was only $450. For a season of sixteen nights—the official permit allowed him only two performances a week for two months—the receipts were calculated at $300 a night or $4,800 for the season. The outlay was given as follows: $1000 for scenery and costumes, $39.07 per night for current expenses, amounting for the sixteen nights to $625. This left a credit balance for the season of $1,550, from which salaries and living expenses had still to be deducted.

The season began November 19, 1761, with Rowe's " Fair Penitent " followed by Garrick's farce " Lethe." Later bills were " The Provoked Husband," " Hamlet,"[1] " Tamerlane," " Cato," " Venice Preserved " and Shakespeare's " King Henry IV." On this last occasion Mr. Douglass played Sir John Falstaff. He was the first actor to impersonate the fat knight on the American stage.

While his company had maintained its high standard of individual excellence there were constant changes in the organization. Mr. and Mrs. Harman and Mrs. Love had disappeared from the casts. Mrs. Morris we find playing Ophelia instead of Mrs. Harman, while Mr. Morris succeeds Mr. Harman as Polonius. Mrs. Douglass was still the principal attraction of the company, although by this time she had lost her youth, and in fact, four years later surrendered her best rôles to a younger actress, Miss Cheer. Lewis Hallam was now the leading actor of the American stage, playing " Hamlet " when he was only twenty-one and " Lear " at twenty-six.

Although most of the theatre advertisements of the time contained the notice: " No person admitted behind the scenes," the pernicious practice [2] of allowing male spectators to mingle with the actors and actresses—a custom dating from Shakespeare's time and which led to many abuses and immoralities—was still common, and occasioned many scandals. The

---

[1] This was given November 26th and was the second performance of "Hamlet" in America and the first performance in New York. Mr. Hallam acted the title rôle, Mr. Douglass was the King and Mr. Quelch the Ghost, while Mrs. Morris played Ophelia.

[2] What a nuisance this became is told by Tate Wilkinson in his description of Covent Garden: "It was the beaux who usually affected that part of the house. There was only one entrance on each side of the stage, which was always particularly crowded. First they sported their own figures to gratify selfconsequence and impede and interfere with the performers who had to come on and go off the stage. They loved to affront the audience, particularly the gallery part, who would answer by showering down oranges, half-eaten apples, to the great terror of the ladies in the pit, who were so closely wedged they could not move." Colley Cibber tells us how he and his fellow patentees

practice had been abolished in England, but Douglass had conceded this privilege, which he regretted later, for in a card published December 31, 1761, he made the following announcement:

> Complaints having been several times made that a number of Gentlemen crowd the Stage and very much interrupt the performance, and as it is impossible the actors, when thus obstructed, can do justice to their parts they otherwise would, it will be taken as a particular favour if no gentleman will be offended that he is absolutely refused admittance at the Stage Door, unless he has previously secured himself a place in either the Stage or Upper Boxes.

The egg throwing episode, which had occurred just previously to the publication of this advertisement, is supposed to have been caused by local resentment at the continuance of the objectionable practice. A few days after the disturbance, Mr. Douglass published in the *Mercury* the following:

> Theatre in New York, May 3, 1762.
> A Pistole Reward will be given to whoever can discover the person who was so very rude as to throw Eggs from the Gallery upon the Stage last Monday, by which the Cloaths of some Ladies and Gentlemen were spoiled, and the performance in some measure interrupted.   D. DOUGLASS.

In this instance the eggs were probably not used by way of dramatic criticism nor was the attack directed at the players at all. It is more likely that it was a homely but none the less effective protest at

---

abolished the practice at Drury Lane: "The plagues and inconveniences of which custom we found so intolerable when we afterwards had the stage in our hands that at the hazard of our lives we were forced to get rid of them and our only expedient was by refusing money from all persons without distinction at the stage door. By this means we preserved to ourselves the right and liberty of choosing our own company there, and by a strict observance of this order we brought what had been before debased into all the licences of a lobby into the decencies of a drawing room."

the behavior of the bucks of the town who, with their powdered wigs, long stiff skirted coats and waistcoats, with flaps reaching nearly to the knees, their silk stockings, short quartered shoes, and silver or paste buckles, crowded and ogled the actresses on the stage, thus interfering with the action of the play.

The season closed April 26, 1762, after which the company went to the West Indies, where they spent four years awaiting the new and more extensive theatrical campaign which the indefatigable Douglass was preparing for Philadelphia and New York.

Notwithstanding the high character of the company, the opposition to the players continued in some quarters as determined and bitter as ever. There were constant attacks in the form of anonymous communications to the newspapers. " Philodemus " charged that all ladies who attended the theatre lacked modesty. " Armanda," defending the actors, pointed out that often in plays vice is painted in the most glaring colors. " Philodemus " returned to the attack, asking which was the best teacher, the playhouse or the Bible? Douglass himself took no part in this newspaper warfare. He contented himself by having his company repeat Thomson's Epilogue defending the stage, already recited on several occasions, and in giving benefits for " such poor families as are not provided for by the public."

Religious or moral grounds were not the chief causes of the hostility to the players. There was another and still more potent reason. For some time resentment against England had been growing everywhere in the Colonies. The actors, being English, were naturally looked upon as being friendly to British aggression. The Stamp Act of 1765 immediately precipitated trouble. A mob collected in front of the Beekman Street Theatre and, after some fiery speeches, started to demolish the playhouse. The company was absent at the time, but it is probable that the actors were expected soon to return and that the structure was attacked in the hope of preventing their reappearance. That it was not totally destroyed is proved by the newspapers which announced performances there on April 10, 1765, and also on April 9 and May 5, 1766.

This anti-English feeling was directed at all the players until after the Revolution, and was no doubt the real reason that led Douglass to change the name of his organization from " Company of Comedians from London " to " The American Company," by which appellation it was afterwards known.

In spite of the difficulties that beset the players on every side, the drama steadily gained ground. The audiences had grown in size; the actors, by the excellence of their performances, had succeeded in arousing interest. Douglass was shrewd enough to see his opportunity and make the most of it. No doubt he would have found his path strewn with fewer obstacles in the more hospitable towns of the South. But there the populations were small. Profits would be so trifling as not to make it worth while. The prejudice in the North did not deter him. Douglass was the kind of man who is spurred by difficulties to greater exertions. He liked the excitement of the fray. Philadelphia, where the opposition was hottest, appealed to him particularly, and there he decided on another and more important season in 1766.

THE THEATRE IN AMERICA

While the drama in America still had its narrow minded defamers, the more liberal and intelligent part of the community enjoyed seeing good plays well acted, and did not hesitate to patronize the playhouse. The drama, he considered, was worthy of a more substantial home than the flimsy wooden buildings which until now had given it shelter. He determined, therefore, to erect in Philadelphia a theatre of a more permanent character. As a result of this decision, he built the old Southwark Theatre in South Street, above Fourth, the original walls of which are still standing, and which continued to be used for dramatic performances until the beginning of the Nineteenth Century. This was the first permanent theatre erected in America.

The upper part of the building was of wood, only the walls of the first story being of brick. It was partly destroyed by fire in 1821. Soon afterwards the walls were raised and it was known for many years as Young's Distillery, which fact prompted Dunlap, in 1832, to remark facetiously: " Once pouring out a mingled strain of good and evil, it now dispenses purely evil." It was an ugly, ill-contrived affair both outside and inside. " The brick-work," says Seilhamer, " was rude but strong, and the wooden part of the building rough and primitive. The whole was painted a glaring red. The stage was lighted by plain oil lamps, without glasses, and the view from the boxes was intercepted by large wooden pillars supporting the upper tier and the roof."

The erection of the new theatre naturally aroused a storm of protest. The Quakers looked upon it as an unlawful encroachment on their religious views and habits and presented to the Assembly a remonstrance demanding that the proposed "stage-playing" be forbidden on the ground that plays "divert the minds of unwary youths and prevent their becoming useful members of society." Governor Penn, less bigoted than the subscribers, refused to entertain the complaint and the anti-theatrical party found themselves powerless.

The season at the Southwark theatre began November 21, 1766, the players now being known as the American Company. The organization was, in fact, American in more than name. The early actors were all English, but now that could no longer be said of the company. "Most of its members," says Seilhamer, "made this country their home, and at least one of them who made his first appearance during this period became a distinguished officer in the patriot army."

An important addition to the company during this Philadelphia season was Margaret Cheer, a new leading woman and an actress of established reputation whom Douglass engaged in the West Indies to play his wife's rôles. This young actress, according to tradition, was an admirable artiste. She must also have possessed marked personal attributes to win as she did a place in the British Peerage. The *Pennsylvania Gazette* described her as one of the best of living English actresses. This, probably, was an extravagant statement, but that she was an actress of no ordinary ability may be judged by the wide range of parts with which she was identified. She made her début November 21, 1766, in "Catharine and Petruchio" ("The Taming of the Shrew"), playing Catharine to Mr. Hallam's Petruchio. Other rôles in which she was seen in Philadelphia, before making her New York debut, were Lady Anne in " Richard III," Portia in " The Merchant of Venice," Ophelia in " Hamlet," Juliet in " Romeo and Juliet," Imogene in " Cymbeline," Cordelia in " King Lear," Lady Macbeth, Desdemona in " Othello," Lady Percy in " Henry IV," Lady Constance in " King John," etc., altogether forty-six parts in less than two years—a remarkable record for any actress! In 1769 she retired from the stage, having married into the English nobility.[3]

Other newcomers in Philadelphia were Miss Wainwright and Mr. Woolls, pupils of the celebrated Doctor Arne and both of whom had good singing voices. Miss Wainwright's début was made as Polly in Gay's " Beggar's Opera."

Additions to the repertoire about this time were: " The Orphan of China," by Murphy; " The Miser," by Fielding; " Love Makes a Man," by Cibber; " Love in a Village," by Bickerstaff.

The season was also memorable for the production of " The Prince of Parthia," the first piece written by an American to be performed by professional players. The author, Thomas Godfrey, Jr.,[4] was born in Philadelphia in 1736. Early in life he was appren-

---

[3] She married in August, 1768, the Right Hon. Lord Rosehill, son and heir of the sixth Earl of Northesk in the Scotch peerage. According to Burke's "Peerage," Lord Rosehill married "Catharine Cameron" in 1768, which would indicate either that Margaret Cheer was only the stage name of the actress, or that Lord Rosehill was married twice that same year. She left the stage after her marriage, but was seen again in New York in 1773, when she played Queen Elizabeth in "Richard III" for Mrs. Douglass' benefit. Nothing more was heard of her for many years, when she reappeared on the stage as Mrs. Long.

[4] Thomas Godfrey died in North Carolina, August 3, 1763. His poems, including "The Prince of Parthia," were published in a small folio volume in 1765. The book is now very scarce.

ticed to a watchmaker, but in 1758 he joined the army, serving as a lieutenant in the expedition against Fort Duquesne. In 1759 he went to North Carolina where he wrote his tragedy. As an acting play it has no merit. There is little plot and practically no action, while the speeches in blank verse are long and dull. But the poet, who had died four years previously, had many influential friends in Philadelphia and by these Douglass was persuaded to produce the play, which he did on April 24, 1767. The announcement of the performance ran as follows:

ADVERTISEMENT.

by authority.

By the American Company.

At the new Theatre in Southwark, tomorrow, being the 24th of April, will be presented a Tragedy, written in America by the late ingenious Mr. Thomas Godfrey, of this city, called

"The Prince of Parthia,"

To which will be added

"The Contrivances."

To begin precisely at seven o'Clock.

Vivant Rex et Regina.

There is no record of the cast, but it no doubt included the principal members of the company: Mr. Hallam, Mr. Douglass, Mr. Wall, Mr. Morris, Mr. Allyn, Mr. Tomlinson, Mr. Broadbelt, Mr. Greville, Mrs. Douglass, Mrs. Morris, Miss Wainwright and Miss Cheer. The piece was not a success and there is no record of a second performance.

Another play written by an American, a comedy with the ill omened title "The Disappointment" and based on the exploits of Bluebeard the pirate, was also offered to Douglass and put in rehearsal by him.

123

It was billed for production on April 20, 1767, but was withdrawn at the eleventh hour, an announcement in the *Pennsylvania Gazette* making the following ingenuous explanation:

" The Disappointment " (that was advertised for Monday), as it contains personal reflections, is unfit for the stage.

The season ended early in July and was followed by a supplementary season, lasting from September to November, during which time Douglass was busy completing his new theatre in John Street, New York. During this supplementary season John Henry, the original Sir Peter Teazle in New York, who, both as player and manager, soon assumed a most conspicuous position on the American stage, was seen for the first time with the company.

John Henry was born in Ireland and made his début at Covent Garden in 1762. A tall and uncommonly handsome man, of commanding presence, he won much favor in leading rôles, but, instead of continuing in London, he went out to the West Indies, joining the Douglass forces in Jamaica. His American début was made in Philadelphia, October 6, 1766, as Publius Horatius in " The Roman Father." He was also seen as Othello, as Jaffier in " Venice Preserved," Charles in " The Jealous Wife," and Edmund in " Lear." " He played Othello better," Dunlap tells us, " than any man had done before him in America. His Irishmen were very fine and he had great merit in serious and pathetic fathers." His value as an actor was at once apparent and before his New York début (December 7, 1767, at the John Street Theatre as Aimwell in " Beaux' Stratagem ")

Douglass and Hallam had realized the wisdom of securing the permanent services of so popular an actor by taking him into the management.

On the same night that he made his début there appeared on the bill the name of Miss Storer. This was Ann Storer who, as Mrs. Hogg, later became a great favorite at the Park Theatre in New York. "The Storer family in Jamaica," says Seilhamer, "comprised Mrs. Storer (once a singer at Covent Garden) and her four daughters. John Henry married the eldest, but the vessel on which she made the voyage from Jamaica was burnt and she was lost at sea. Henry subsequently lived with Ann Storer as his wife, by whom he had a son. Ann afterwards married John Hogg, who was the comic old man when she was the comic old woman of the New York theatre. . . . The third sister, Fanny Storer (who afterwards became Mrs. Mechler), and Maria Storer, the youngest, was the last Mrs. Henry." [5]

[5] Henry was the matinee idol of his day and the first actor in America whose irregularities in private life gave an excuse to those ever eager to rail at the "immorality of the stage." His relations with the Storer sisters, which furnished scandalous gossip at every Colonial tea-table, "give us a glimpse," says Dunlap, "at the state of manners and morals among these teachers of virtue and morality, and such instances, even if rare, accounts for that repelling principle which keeps the cautious and the pure in private society aloof from those who delight them in public." It is often claimed that the private morals of a player have nothing to do with his or her standing as an artist. This is a delicate question open to debate. While the actor's mission is "to hold the mirror up to nature" which is not always lovely, it is also true that he is often called upon to impersonate persons of virtuous and noble character. "This," claims Colley Cibber in his "Apology," "he cannot do properly, unless his own conduct is beyond reproach." Speaking of George Powel, an actor of notoriously licentious character, Cibber says: "Wilks had the advantage of a sober character in private life, while Powel, not having the least regard to, labour'd under the unhappy disfavour, not to say contempt of, the publick to whom his licentious courses were no secret. Even when he did well that natural prejudice pursu'd him; neither the hero nor the gentleman could conceal from the conscious spectator the true George Powel. And this sort of disesteem or favour every actor will feel and more or less have his share of as he has or has not a due regard to his private life and reputation."

A man of violent temper, a victim to gout, there are many anecdotes told of Henry's eccentricities and choleric outbursts. Dunlap describes a visit he once paid the actor-manager. Ushered into his bedroom by Mrs. Henry, the dramatist found Henry extended on a bed apparently unable to rise.

" His gigantic figure appeared larger than ever, his face was flushed with fever, and the lower part covered by beard. His disease was gout, and he occasionally expressed his suffering, but spoke cheerfully, and even jocosely. The same evening he played the youthful lover in ' The Clandestine Marriage,' and his morning visitor saw him in apparent health and elegantly apparelled, while his brother manager Hallam, a harlequin in activity, represented Lord Ogilby, a character he had seen performed by King at Drury Lane, and mimicked those twitches and excruciating pains which Henry, feeling in reality, covered with the mask of apparent ease and enjoyment. Such is one picture of theatrical life, and by no means the most extraordinary."

Henry was the only actor in America at that time who kept a carriage. " It was in the form of a coach," says Dunlap, " but very small, just sufficient to carry himself and wife to the theatre. It was drawn by one horse and driven by a black boy. Aware of the jealousy towards players, and that it would be said he *kept a coach,* he had caused to be painted on the doors, in the manner of those coats of arms which the aristocracy of Europe display, two crutches in heraldic fashion, with the motto, ' *This or These.'* The ride was not a long one for the actor and actress from their house to the theatre in John Street, as he

lived in Fair Street (now Fulton), between Nassau
Street and Broadway, in the same two-story brick
house painted yellow in which Hodgkinson resided
for some years. Mrs. Henry used to go ready dressed
for the character she was to play, and shut up in the
little box-like vehicle. This residence in Fair Street
was still more convenient for Hodgkinson's theatrical business, as a gate opened (and still opens) from
the back of the house, directly opposite Theatre
Alley."

CHAPTER VI

OPENING OF THE FAMOUS JOHN STREET THEATRE

DESCRIPTION OF NEW YORK'S HISTORIC PLAYHOUSE. MARIA STORER'S DÉBUT. OPPOSITION TO PLAYACTING CONTINUES. THE VIRGINIA COMPANY OF COMEDIANS. "KING JOHN" PRODUCED IN PHILADELPHIA. FIRST AMERICAN ACTOR. MISS HALLAM'S BEAUTY INSPIRES A CELEBRATED PAINTER. NEW THEATRE IN ANNAPOLIS. NOTABLE PHILADELPHIA SEASON. DEATH OF MRS. HARMAN. NEW THEATRE IN CHARLESTON. OUTBREAK OF THE REVOLUTION AND CLOSING OF THE PLAYHOUSES.

WHEN Douglass returned to New York in December, 1767, the company had been completely reorganized both as regards actors and management. John Henry's name appeared for the first time as member of the theatrical firm, Douglass, Hallam and Henry.

The old Beekman Street Theatre having been destroyed, Douglass had built another one in John Street, half a dozen doors from Broadway. This historic playhouse remained New York's leading theatre for the next thirty years.

It was painted red like most theatres of that day and constructed entirely of wood. It stood back sixty feet from the street, and, to protect carriage folk from the weather, had a wooden awning extending from the sidewalk to the doors. There were two rows of boxes and a pit and gallery, the capacity of the house when full being about eight hundred dollars. The stage was fairly large and originally the actors' dressing rooms and greenroom were under it, but after the Revolution they were moved to a shed adjacent to the theatre.

In Royall Tyler's play "The Contrast," one of the characters, a Yankee Jonathan, who has been reared in the greatest horror of a theatre, is made to enter one unconsciously and, overcome by the illusion, he takes the whole performance for an actual occurrence. The theatre he is made to describe is the John Street Theatre. He says:

As I was looking here and there for it I saw a great crowd of folks going into a long entry that had lanterns over the door, so I asked the man if that was the place they played hocus pocus? He was a very civil kind of a man, though he did speak like the Hessians. He lifted up his eyes and said: "They play hocus pocus enough there, Gott knows, mine friend." So I went right in and they showed me a way clean up to the garret, just like a meeting house gallery. And so I saw a power of topping folks, all sitting around in little cabins just like father's corn-crib.

The season began December 7, 1767, with this bill:

By permission of His Excellency the Governor.

By the American Company.

At the Theatre in John Street, this present evening, a comedy called

"THE BEAUX' STRATAGEM."

Archer, Mr. Hallam; Aimswell, Mr. Henry; Sullen, Mr. Tomlinson; Sir C. Freeman, Mr. Malone; Foigard, Mr. Allyn; Gibbet, Mr. Woolls; Scrub, Mr. Wall; Boniface, Mr. Douglass; Dorinda, Miss Hallam; Lady Bountiful, Mrs. Harman; Cherry, Miss Wainwright; Gipsy, Mrs. Wall; Mrs. Sullen, Miss Cheer. An occasional epilogue by Mrs. Douglass.

To conclude with the dramatic satire entitled "Lethe."

On February 11, 1768, the name of Miss Maria Storer (John Henry's last wife) appeared for the first time in the bills, as the page in Otway's tragedy

9   129

"The Orphan." "She must," says Ireland, "have been a mere child at this period. She gradually developed talent both in singing and acting and after she became Mrs. Henry was an immense favorite with the public." Dunlap says that "she possessed both beauty and talent and until 1792 was the best public singer America had known. She played tragedy and comedy with spirit and propriety, although her figure was rather petite for the first or for the elegant females of Congreve and Cibber."

The season lasted until June 2, during which time were presented thirty-eight plays, tragedies and comedies—including eight by Shakespeare—and twenty-six farces, a remarkable record. The Shakespeare plays were "Richard III," "Hamlet," "Cymbeline," "Romeo and Juliet," "Taming of the Shrew," "King Lear," "Merchant of Venice," "King Henry IV," "Macbeth" and "Othello."

Artistically considered, it was one of the most brilliant seasons Douglass had yet given, and some indication of the quality of his audiences may be had from this announcement in the newspaper of the day in regard to the theatre traffic:

To prevent accidents by carriages meeting, it is requested that those coming to the House may enter John Street from *the* Broad-Way, and returning, drive from thence down John Street, into Nassau Street, or forward to that known by the name of Cart and Horse Street, as may be most convenient.

Yet in spite of the excellence of his bills and the patronage he received from the *élite,* the season had been far from satisfactory financially. Indeed, it had barely paid expenses and several times the outlook was so discouraging that disbandment seemed the only solution. The chief cause was the continued opposition to the drama which had never been so bitter as at this time. The attacks through the medium of anonymous newspaper communications were incessant. " Philander " wrote: " The erecting of a Playhouse in this city has been and still is a matter of uneasiness to a very great part of the inhabitants," and " hoped that those who were thus affected toward it would show their disapprobation by staying away." There was no truce to these assaults. The week following Philander urged the opponents of the drama to render the playhouse " a useless fabric by letting it remain a monument of the rashness and folly of those who erected it against the general opinion and sentiments of the people." A campaign of this virulence could not fail to influence public opinion. Feeling ran so high that the more timid were afraid to be seen at the theatre. It became virtually a boycott until, towards the close of the season, Douglass found himself playing to almost empty benches.

While the American Company was in New York performing at the John Street Theatre, a new troupe of players, among whom were some old members of the Douglass company, suddenly made their appearance at Norfolk and Williamsburg, Va., styling themselves the " Virginia Company of Comedians." [1] They were seen first at Norfolk, February 4, 1768, and then at Williamsburg on April 4 of the same year. The repertoire was practically the same as that of the Douglass company, although not nearly so extensive. It appears to have been a well equipped,

---

[1] John Esten Cooke, the novelist, confused this company with the Hallams when describing the players in his novel "The Virginia Comedians."

well managed organization which, had it persevered, might have become a formidable rival of the American Company. Mr. Godwin, a member of the Douglass organization in 1766, who played small parts in this company, will be heard from again.

Notwithstanding his disappointing experience at the John Street Theatre, Mr. Douglass proceeded to Philadelphia in the fall of that same year (1768) and was rewarded by better results. He opened at the Southwark Theatre October 21, with "The Spanish Friar" and the "Honest Yorkshireman," and lasted until January 6, 1769, the season being marked by the production of four plays never before acted in America. These were Shakespeare's "King John," Kelly's "False Delicacy," Hill's adaptation of Voltaire's "Zaire," and Lee's tragedy "Alexander the Great." The cast of "King John" was remarkable and is worth recording.

King John, Mr. Douglass; Falconbridge, Mr. Hallam; Hubert, Mr. Henry; Pembroke, Mr. Tomlinson; Salisbury, Mr. Parker; Robert Falconbridge, Mr. Roberts; King Philip, Mr. Byerly; Dauphin, Mr. Wall; Austria, Mr. Darby; Pandulph, Mr. Morris; Chatillon, Mr. Raworth; Melun, Mr. Woolls; Prince Arthur, Miss M. Storer; Prince Henry, Mrs. Harman; Queen Eleanor, Mrs. Douglass; Lady Constance, Miss Cheer; Lady Falconbridge, Miss Storer; Blanche of Castile, Miss Hallam.

From the little we know of the merits of the individual performers, this must have been an extraordinary cast. The modern manager, if he could duplicate it at all, would advertise it far and wide as "an all star" cast. "The production of a tragedy as elaborate as 'King John,'" says Seilhamer, "is at once a proof of the strength of the company and of the taste of the time. Many years afterwards, when it was revived by Charles Kean upon something like the splendid scale of his Shakespearean revivals in London, the undertaking was looked upon as an extraordinary theatrical event. It is not to be supposed that Mr. Douglass's production compared as regards *mise en scène* with Charles Kean's, but it is supposable that the acting of the earlier was fully equal to that of the later company."

One decided novelty introduced this season was an exhibition of fireworks given on the stage after the farce. When one considers the constant peril from fire in those flimsy early theatres, it is inconceivable how the city fathers permitted such a dangerous addition to the program. The display consisted of a large brilliantly illuminated wheel, a triumphal arch, colored fires and several fiery fountains. The experiment must have been a success for it was repeated later.

It was during this season that Mr. Goodman, an actor who shares with John E. Martin [2] the distinction of being one of the first two native born players to appear on the American stage, made his first appearance with the Douglass company. It is believed he was born in Philadelphia where he had studied law and where he made his stage début. He was an actor of more than ordinary ability, ranking second only in importance to Mr. Henry, and played Hardcastle in the original New York production of "She Stoops to Conquer." With the close of the

[2] See page 185. If Mr. Goodman was of American birth, as Seilhamer thinks he was (Brown says he was born in London), he was the first native actor to appear on our stage, Mr. Martin not making his début until 1790.

133

Charleston season of 1774, we hear no more of Mr. Goodman. " It has long been the habit," says Seilhamer, " to accord the honor of being the first actor of American birth to John Martin, but Goodman seems to be entitled to that distinction."

Immediately after closing in Philadelphia, Douglass returned to the John Street Theatre, New York, where his company remained until the following June. Then the players paid a brief visit to Albany and presented Otway's tragedy " Venice Preserved " in the hospital in that city.

Several novelties were added to the repertoire during this last New York engagement, among them being Steele's " Tender Husband," Garrick's " Guardian " and Bickerstaff's " Padlock," this last a Drury Lane success in which Mr. Hallam scored a great hit as Mungo.

Yet the season, as a whole, was no more successful than the year before. The anti-theatrical party continued their hostile manœuvres, and the audiences were so slim in consequence that Douglass was forced to resort to all kinds of expedients to sell his seats. One of these was the special engagement of an amateur actor, well known in social and military circles, to play Othello.[3] The announcement stated that the part " would be attempted by a *gentleman,* assisted by other *gentlemen* in the characters of the Duke and Senators of Venice, from a benevolent and generous design of encouraging the Theatre, and relieving the

---

[3] J. N. Ireland, in his "Records of the New York Stage," says there is good reason to suppose that the amateur Othello on this occasion was probably Major Moncrief, a British officer, who was the most distinguished amateur actor in the Colonies before and during the Revolution.

performers from some embarrassments in which they are involved."

On other occasions, the patronage of important societies, such as the Freemasons and the Friendly Brothers of St. Patrick, was solicited and accorded. In honor of the Friendly Brothers, the players gave " The Busybody " and " The Brave Irishman." For the Freemasons, the bill was " The Tender Husband," followed by a pantomime. As an example of the advertising dodges to which the theatre managers of those days were driven to attract audiences, the following novel request, contained in the newspaper announcement of the Freemason performance, is worth quoting:

> The company of *all the Brethren* in Town is earnestly requested to meet at Burns' at five o'clock on the day of Performance and walk from thence in *Procession* to the theatre, where the Pit will be reserved for their Accommodation.

That financial embarrassment was felt not only by Mr. Douglass, but also by the individual members of the company, is indicated by the unusually large number of benefits announced. The Misses Storer had one testimonial and another in conjunction with Mr. Henry. Mr. and Mrs. Tomlinson had two, Woolls had two, while Mrs. Harman tried to raise funds by giving a concert.

An important loss to the company at this time was the retirement of Miss Wainwright, an accomplished actress and singer, who had been a popular member of the company since she first joined it at the Southwark Theatre, Philadelphia, in 1766. The season was also marked by the promotion of Miss Hallam, who had done good work with the company for many

135

years, to be leading woman in the place of Miss Cheer, retired. Miss Hallam made her début as Juliet on May 8, and continued to play leading rôles. until the organization disbanded.

While Douglass virtually held a monopoly of the stage in the North, lovers of the drama in the South were not entirely deprived of the pleasures of the theatre, and players were offered every inducement to visit southern cities. This field, although not so tempting as the one already occupied by Douglass, could not be ignored. Norfolk and Williamsburg, Va., had, as we have seen, already extended a welcoming hand to the New Virginia Company in 1768. When that company disbanded at the close of the season it was immediately reorganized under the title, "New American Company." This troupe, headed by Mr. Verling as leading man, and Mrs. Parker and later Mrs. Osborne as leading woman, began a season at Annapolis, Md., February 18, 1769, and continued playing there until the middle of June. Mr. Godwin, who we have seen playing inferior parts in this company, was probably a backer of the enterprise, for he is found playing better parts than he was ever entrusted with before—second, in fact, to the lead. The repertoire was an ambitious one and practically included all the plays presented by Douglass, including seven Shakespearean tragedies. Colly Cibber's "She Wou'd and She Wou'd Not," a comedy new to the American stage, was also given during this season.

Douglass, meantime, had gone from New York to Philadelphia where he re-opened the Southwark Theatre, playing there from November 8, 1769, to the following June. This proved one of the most successful seasons the American Company had yet had. The repertoire was unusually attractive, the Philadelphians being treated to a number of plays not yet seen in America. Among them were O'Hara's mythological burlesque, "Midas," Dryden's version of "The Tempest," with elaborate *mise-en-scène,* which proved a sensational success, "The Siege of Damascus," by Hughes, Shirley's "Edward the Black Prince," Goldsmith's "Good-natured Man," Steele's "Funeral" and "Tender Husband," and Shakespeare's "Merry Wives of Windsor." During this season also important additions were made to the company—Mr. Goodman, who later became a great favorite, the second Mrs. Morris,[4] one of the most noted actresses of the early American stage, and Miss Richardson.

At the end of that year Douglass went south where the superior strength of his company soon eclipsed the histrionic efforts of would-be rivals. Annapolis, Md., and Williamsburg, Va., were the chief places visited, a season being played in each town. At Annapolis Miss Hallam made the first real success of her career as Imogen in "Cymbeline." An unsigned critique of her performance on that occasion, which appeared in the *Maryland Gazette,* merits reprinting as the only living document we have concerning the merit of a young actress whose talent and beauty inspired one of America's greatest painters,

---

[4] Mrs. Morris was the second wife of Owen Morris, the comedian, who died in Philadelphia in 1825. She played stately rôles and is described as a tall, elegant woman with a very mysterious manner. She was an actress of such reserved and retiring nature that she had a private path made from her lodgings in Maiden Lane to the theatre in John Street so she could escape the insolent stare of the beaux on Broadway. Such aloofness among player folk is rare. We know of only two similar instances on our modern stage—Mme. Eleanora Duse and Miss Maude Adams.

Charles Wilson Peale,[5] to paint her portrait. The anonymous reviewer wrote:

> I shall not at present expatiate on the merits of the whole performance, but confine myself principally to one object. The actors are indubitably entitled to a very considerable portion of praise. But, by your leave, gentlemen (to speak in the language of Hamlet), "here's metal more attractive." On finding that the part of Imogen was to be played by Miss Hallam, I instantly formed to myself, from my predilection of her, the most sanguine hope of entertainment. But how was I ravished on experiment! She exceeded my utmost idea. Such delicacy of manner! Such classical strictness of expression! The music of her tongue, the *vox liquida,* how melting! Notwithstanding the injuries it received from the horrid ruggedness of the roof and the untoward construction of the whole house, methought I heard once more the warbling of Cibber in my ear. How true and thorough her knowledge of the part she personated! Her whole form and dimensions how happily convertible and universally adapted to the variety of her part.

There is some doubt among stage historians as to the identity of this Miss Hallam. In her time, it was not customary to give the Christian name in the casts, which makes the identification all the more difficult. One can scarcely believe she was the daughter of Lewis Hallam I who made her début September 5, 1752, as Jessica in "The Merchant of Venice," for that would make her nearly forty years old before she was entrusted with leading rôles. Others believe

---

[5] Charles Wilson Peale was born at Chestertown, Md., in 1741 and died in 1827. He left America in 1770 to study art in England and did not return until 1774. He painted several portraits of George Washington from life and also portraits of Martha Washington, Benjamin Franklin and other notabilities of the Revolutionary period. Mystery attaches to his portrait of Miss Hallam. All trace of the painting has been lost. That it once existed is proved by the lines in the *Maryland Gazette* of November 7, 1771, praising the painter's skill and which are headed, "To Mr. Peale, on his Painting Miss Hallam in the character of Fedele in 'Cymbeline.'" It must have been executed before Peale's departure for England. It is not even mentioned in any list of his paintings and there is no record of it ever having been exhibited at the Peale Museum in Philadelphia.

she was the Nancy Hallam who occasionally played children's parts in Philadelphia in 1759. Seilhamer thinks she was a cousin of the Miss Hallam of 1752. He says:

That she was the niece of Mrs. Douglass and the cousin of Mr. Hallam (Lewis Hallam II.) may be accepted as established. It is not likely that a journalist as well informed as James Rivington would have made the mistake of calling Mrs. Douglass her aunt instead of her mother, especially as he mentions Mrs. Mattocks as Mr. Hallam's sister. Her list of parts shows her to have been first in everything, from *Statira* and *Juliet* to *Polly* in the " Beggars' Opera "—in tragedy, comedy and farce. In her day her admirers sang her praises with a fervor and passion that her predecessor, Miss Cheer, had never been able to command. Even allowing for poetic license and enthusiasm she must have had a fair share of personal beauty, else the Maryland poet would scarcely have dared to exclaim in his impassioned, pedantic way:—

Ye Gods! 'Tis Cytherea's face!

The poem accords Miss Hallam theatrical talents of the most versatile order, making her one of the few actresses who have had the ability to catch Shakespeare's glowing ray; investing her comedy with the power to compel laughter to hold his sides and make the pit resound with ios of enjoyment, and matching her elocution only with the notes of her singing voice when her looks inform the strings. Of Miss Hallam after her return to England there is no information. After being sung of by the poets and painted by Peale she was destined to be ignored, if not entirely forgotten, by the dramatic historians. She has always been confounded with her cousin, the Miss Hallam of 1752-4, and her merit as an actress denied, while her parts show that she occupied a more important position on the American stage than had ever been filled by her aunt, Mrs. Douglass.[6]

On the conclusion of its Annapolis season in September, 1770, the American Company is supposed to have gone to Virginia, but no record exists of performances there at that time. Some authorities in-

---

[6] History of the American Theatre, by George O. Seilhamer.

cline to the belief that Douglass paid a brief visit to Jamaica early in 1771, while Mr. Henry went to London for recruits. This theory is borne out by Douglass' later announcements.

There was a company of players in Williamsburg in 1771, but it was not the Douglass company. These strangers began their season October 23 with Cumberland's comedy " The West Indian," the first performance in America of this famous play which immediately scored as big a success in this country as it already had in England, and was acted continuously for many years. The hero is a young scapegrace fresh from the tropics " with rum and sugar enough belonging to him to make all the water in the Thames into punch," a libertine with generous instincts which in the end prevail.[7]

Later, the company presented " Lear " for the " first time in Virginia." They also gave Ben Jonson's " Every Man in His Humour," which was new to America. The season closed December 21 with a performance of " The Padlock."

The American Company returned to Annapolis in the fall of the same year (1771), and while there dedicated the new theatre [8] which Douglass had built by popular subscription. The building was of brick, with a seating capacity of six hundred and was situated on ground leased from St. Anne's Church in

---

[7] Richard Cumberland (1732–1811) has been called the "Terence of England." The son of a bishop, he wrote about thirty-five plays in addition to four operas and a farce. His favorite theme is virtue in distress or danger, but safe of its reward in the fifth act. "The West Indian," his most successful comedy, was afterwards translated into German and Goethe acted in it at the Weimar Court.

[8] This is the theatre which William Dunlap informs us was built in Annapolis in 1752—the "earliest temple reared in our country to the dramatic muse."

West Street. That it was a building of some pretensions may be inferred from this rhymed complaint from the local church people who inserted in the *Maryland Gazette:*

> *" Here in Annapolis alone*
> *God has the meanest House in town."*

The poem went on to beg for at least an equal portion in the indulgence and esteem of the people. Quite a different attitude toward the stage this, to what Douglass and his fellow players had to contend with in the less tolerant North!

Details of Douglass' efforts to secure the erection of this theatre are given in " Letters from America 1769–77," by William Eddis (London, 1792), who was surveyor of the customs at Annapolis and believed to be the anonymous admirer of Miss Hallam. Mr. Eddis writes :

Annapolis, June 18, 1771. When I bade farewell to England I little expected that my passion for the drama could have been gratified in any tolerable degree at a distance so remote from the great mart of genius, and I brought with me strong prepossessions in behalf of favorite performers whose merits were fully established by the universal sanction of intelligent judges. My pleasure and my surprise were therefore excited in proportion on finding performers in this country equal at least to those who sustain the best of the first characters in your most celebrated provincial theatres. Our Governor, from a strong conviction that the stage under proper regulations may be rendered of general utility and made subservient to the great interests of religion and virtue, patronizes the American Company, and as their present place of exhibition is on a small scale and inconveniently situated, a subscription by his example has been rapidly completed to erect a new theatre on a commodious if not elegant plan. The manager is to deliver tickets for two seasons for the amount of the respective subscriptions, and it is imagined that the money received at the doors from non-subscribers will enable him to conduct the business without difficulty.

The structure, Mr. Eddis wrote again in November of the same year, is not inelegant, but in my opinion on too narrow a scale for its length. The boxes are commodious and neatly decorated. The pit and gallery are calculated to hold a number of people without incommoding each other. The stage is well adapted for dramatic and pantomimical exhibitions, and several of the scenes reflect great credit on the painter.[9]

The new theatre was opened September 9, 1771, with "The Roman Father" and "The Mayor of Garratt" to a "numerous and brilliant audience, which expressed the greatest satisfaction, not only at the performance, but with the house, which is thought to be as elegant and commodious for its size as any theatre in America." The season closed February, 1772, when the company went to Williamsburg, Va., where they stayed till May, after which the players proceeded northward.

Philadelphia was the next stop of the Douglass company, the engagement opening at the Southwark Theatre October 28, 1772, and closing March 31, 1773, when the players proceeded to New York.

This long Philadelphia season was noteworthy, not only for the many new productions made, but for the quality and range of the entire repertoire. The pieces new to Philadelphia were Kelly's "A Word to the Wise," Cumberland's "West Indian," "The Fashionable Lover" and "Shipwreck," Bickerstaff's "Lionel and Clarissa," Foote's "Englishman in Paris," Garrick's "Cymon," Arthur Murphy's "Way to Keep Him" and "The Conquest of Canada," a war play by George Cockings, an Englishman resi-

[9] Douglass had previously announced that he had sent to London to engage some performers and daily expected their arrival together with a new set of scenes painted by Doll. This was apparently the first time that scenery was expressly painted in London for America.

dent in Boston, never before acted. The Shakespeare offerings included "Hamlet," "Cymbeline," "Romeo and Juliet," "Richard III," "Taming of the Shrew," "King Henry IV," "Othello," "Tempest," "Merchant of Venice."

"This list of productions, new and old," says Seilhamer, "must be acknowledged as extraordinary." He continues:

It included the best of the English dramatists from Shakespeare to Kelly and Cumberland. With the single exception of Shakespeare, the works of all these playwrights have been banished from the stage. Neither Cibber nor Farquhar, Congreve, nor Rowe, Lee or Whitehead, Steele or Macklin, Foote or Garrick, Murphy nor Colman, Bickerstaff nor O'Hara, Kelly or Cumberland, has been accorded a revival since early in the nineteenth century. Tragedies such as "The Mourning Bride" and "The Roman Father" have no modern representative. There is no actress on the English-speaking stage capable of playing these high comedy roles. No living manager has sufficient knowledge of stage business to produce one of these masterpieces of the last century. Were it possible to realize even in imagination the performance of Mr. Douglass' company for a season, we should learn how completely the nineteenth century has failed to realize the dramatic promise of the eighteenth.[10]

While it is indisputable that the standard of our drama has fallen lamentably below that of a century or even fifty years ago (who among our modern dramatists is capable of writing another "School for Scandal" a "Richelieu" or a "Francesca da Rimini"?), it is doubtful if any useful end would be gained by reviving to-day the plays of the Restora-

[10] Of recent years we have seen no revivals of the Restoration plays, but twenty-five years ago they were sometimes put forward as worth-while experiments. Daly revived Farquhar's "Recruiting Officer," February 8, 1885. He also did the same author's "Inconstant" and Cibber's "She wou'd and she wou'd not." Wallack used to do "The Clandestine Marriage" by Colman and Garrick, Colman's "Jealous Wife" and what Brander Matthews humorously describes as C. J. Mathews' alteration of Foote's alteration of Steele's "Liar." Congreve's comedy "The Way of the World" was also done in Philadelphia with Mrs. John Drew in the cast.

tion. These old comedies are now of more interest in the library than on the stage. Fashion has changed in plays as in everything else. What pleased our fore-fathers would probably appear trite and stale to us. Most of the wit in the old plays had local allusions which to-day we cannot understand. Moreover, the libertinism and general low moral tone of the plays of Congreve, Vanbrugh, Farquhar, Steele and their contemporaries would not be tolerated by this genera-tion. When the drama was first introduced into this country the favorites of England were, of course, the favorites of the Colonies. "The plays then popular," says Dunlap, "were full of wit but fraught with in-delicacies, not to say obscenities, their very plots so entwined with the loose manners and intrigues of the time as to be incapable of pruning so as to leave the better part separated from the filth."

For nearly twenty years now Mr. Hallam had played the leading rôles. Some of his best parts were Ranger in "The Suspicious Husband," Lord Ogleby in "The Clandestine Marriage," Archer in "Beaux' Stratagem," Alexander in "Alexander the Great," Marc Antony in "All for Love," Hamlet, Hotspur in "Henry IV," Roman Father, Tony Lumpkin in "She Stoops to Conquer," Antonio in "The Mer-chant of Venice," Richard III, Romeo, Othello, Iago, Captain Dormer in "Word to the Wise," Fal-conbridge in "King John," Norval in "Douglas," Marplot in "The Busybody," Sempronius in "Cato," Macheath in "Beggar's Opera," Hastings in "Jane Shore," etc. He was an excellent actor, although somewhat formal and stiff in style and high comedy was his forte. Two of his most successful rôles were Tony Lumpkin in "She Stoops to Conquer," which part he was the first to play in America, and Mungo in " The Padlock." As a pantomimist he was also notable, his Harlequin being a special favorite, remarkable for its activity and grace. " Previous to the Revolution," says Seilhamer, " he had practically no rival. There was no actor with which to compare him and he took care that there should be no opportunity for comparisons. For nearly a quarter of a century, the stage of the New World was his own. He was an absolute sovereign of the theatre. Not only did he have the choice of parts, but of plays. He was at once the star and the stage manager."

The New York season, the last in that city for many years, opened at the John Street Theatre, April 14, 1773, and continued until the following August. The first bill was a play new to New Yorkers—Murphy's comedy " The Way to Keep Him " and " Catharine and Petruchio," Mrs. Morris being seen as the Shrew for the first time in New York. Cumberland's " West Indian," Garrick's " Irish Widow " and O'Brien's " Cross Purposes " were given later.

Miss Cheer made her reappearance this season (June 14, 1773), taking the part of Queen Elizabeth in " Richard III " at the benefit for Mr. and Mrs. Douglass. A week later Miss Cheer herself took a benefit in conjunction with Mr. Woolls, Milton's celebrated " Masque of Comus " being the bill. .

Mrs. Harman, who had been a very prominent member of the company for twenty years, died on May 27, and the following notice in *Rivington's Gazette* is probably the first obituary of an actress ever published in an American newspaper:

On Thursday last, died, in the 43d year of her age, Mrs. Catherine Maria Harman, granddaughter of the celebrated Colley

Cibber, Esq., poet-laureate. She was a just actress, possessed much merit in low comedy, and dressed all her characters with infinite propriety, but her figure prevented her from succeeding in tragedy and genteel comedy. In private life she was sensible, humane and benevolent. Her little fortune she has left to Miss Cheer, and her obsequies were on Saturday night attended by a very genteel procession to the cemetery of the old English church.[11]

The season closed August 5 with Goldsmith's masterpiece " She Stoops to Conquer." The première of this comedy (the first time in America) had taken place two evenings before, with the following cast: Hardcastle, Mr. Goodman; Sir Charles Marlow, Mr. Morris; Young Marlow, Mr. Henry; Hastings, Mr. Byerly; Tony Lumpkin, Mr. Hallam; Landlord, Mr. Woolls; Diggory, Mr. Hughes; Mrs. Hardcastle, Mrs. Morris; Miss Hardcastle, Miss Hallam; Miss Neville, Miss Storer.

Shortly before the closing Mr. Douglass went to Charleston, S. C., to superintend the final preparations for the opening of the new theatre,[12] built by subscription, in which the American Company were to perform all that coming winter.

The new Charleston Theatre was opened December 22, 1773, with " A Word to the Wise " and " High Life Below Stairs." An article in *Rivington's Gazette* published a week after the première, gives some idea of the theatre:

---

[11] When the first Mrs. Morris was accidentally drowned crossing the Kill Von Kill in 1767 the *Gazette* merely chronicled the fact, adding that the victim was "of the playhouse." That there had been a marked change of the public attitude toward the players in the short period of six years is shown in this conspicuous and generous tribute.

[12] Dunlap, in his history, erroneously refers to this theatre as being the first playhouse built in Charleston. Seilhamer, in his later history, speaks of it as Charleston's first theatrical season, and strangely enough, makes no mention of previous theatricals in that city. As we have already seen, there was a theatre in Charleston and professionals acting there as early as 1736.

OPENING OF JOHN STREET THEATRE

The house is elegantly furnished and supposed for the size to be the most commodious on the continent. The scenes, which are new and well designed; the dresses, the music, and, what had a very pleasing effect, the disposition of the lights, all contributed to the satisfaction of the audience.

The season lasted until May 19, 1774, during which time forty-eight plays and twenty-nine farces were presented. Among the novelties were " Julius Caesar," seen for the first time in America.

These were the last appearances of the American company before the Revolution. On the close of the season, Mr. Hallam and Miss Hallam went to London to secure recruits in view of another theatrical campaign the following winter, and meantime Hallam sent out to America, to substitute himself, his cousin, Thomas Wignell, who afterwards became one of the most important figures on the American stage, especially in Philadelphia where he was the first manager of the Chestnut Street Theatre.

But before Wignell reached here, the relations between the Colonies and the mother country had grown so critical that a Congress met in Philadelphia, October 24, 1774, to take concerted action, and one of the resolutions adopted called for the immediate suspension of all public amusements. American patriots agreed to discountenance and discourage every species of extravagance and dissipation and among others named " gaming, cockfighting, exhibition of shows, plays and other expensive diversions and entertainments."

The theatres were immediately closed in consequence and the players sailed for the British West Indies.

CHAPTER VII
THE THEATRE DURING THE REVOLUTION

AMERICANS BEGIN TO WRITE PLAYS. MERCY WARREN'S POLITICAL
SATIRES. THE MILITARY THESPIANS. MAJOR ANDRÉ. FIRST
AMERICAN PERFORMANCE OF "THE RIVALS." BALTIMORE'S
FIRST THEATRE. MR. AND MRS. DENNIS RYAN. FIRST AMERICAN
PERFORMANCE OF "THE SCHOOL FOR SCANDAL." RETURN OF
THE HALLAM PLAYERS. HALLAM-HENRY PARTNERSHIP. RISE
OF THOMAS WIGNELL. THEATRICALS IN ALBANY.

IN its resolution of 1774 Congress had merely
recommended the suspension of all public amusements. Four years later, a more stringent decree was
issued prohibiting play-acting in any form. Thus, as
far as the Colonists themselves were concerned, the
drama might, at this troubled period, have been ex-
tinguished altogether, but for the fact that the
younger officers of the British army, finding the time
heavy on their hands when not fighting the Yankees,
took to theatricals as a pleasant diversion from the
rigors of war.. For eight years—from 1775, when
the military thespians first began to give performances in Boston, to 1783, the year before the declaration of peace—the American stage was in full control
of the British military who occupied all the existing
theatres and produced plays in the professional manner, for charity, amusement and profit.

This period in the history of the American stage
is of peculiar interest and significance from the fact
that it afforded native authors their first incentive and
opportunity to write for the theatre. Until now the
English dramatists had enjoyed a monopoly of our

stage. Not that it gave them any material advantage, seeing that American managers took their plays without leave and paid nothing for them, but at the same time the inexhaustible supply the London market afforded was sufficient to discourage the native writer from making any attempt in that direction.

This remained true for long after the Revolution, notwithstanding the attempts of Tyler, Dunlap and other native dramatists to entertain the public with home-made plays. As Bernard puts it, America, though politically free, was still "intellectually connected with England, bound fast to her by the ties of a common language and literature. London remained still her intellectual capital and its *imprimatur* was required upon all matters of art which had made English their vehicle."

But directly dramatic performances became popular in the Colonies, some of the minor authors were fired with ambition to write plays.

Benjamin Colman's tragedy "Gustavus Vasa" had been acted by Harvard students as early as 1690. Godfrey's "Prince of Parthia" was produced, as we have seen, in 1767, four years after that young poet's death. A piece called "The Military Glory of Great Britain" was acted by students in 1762, "The Conquest of Canada," the war play by George Cockings, was produced in 1766. These were some of the earliest attempts at native playwriting seen on the stage up to the Revolution.[1]

As the times became more critical and the feeling against England more bitter, the pamphleteers of the day were quick to recognize in the stage a

[1] See Chapter on the American Dramatist, page 48, Vol. II.

direct and effective medium of disseminating their political views and a number of pieces of a wholly controversial character were printed and acted. These plays had no merit as such. Written now to defend the British, now to advance American interests, they were little more than political pamphlets, and to-day are without the slightest value. The sole interest attaching to them is that they served as an entering wedge for the American playwright, one of the first of whom, Royall Tyler, was soon to win a substantial success with "The Contrast," the first comedy written by an American author on a purely American theme, acted by professional players.

First among American writers to use the play form as a vehicle for political satire was Mrs. Mercy Warren, wife of General Warren and a sister of James Otis. A distinct literary figure of the Revolution, an ardent champion of the Colonists' cause, in Mrs. Warren's house gathered the most celebrated men and women of the time, and John Adams, a great admirer of her writings, gave her every encouragement to devote her talents to the patriots' cause. She wrote two plays, "The Adulator," a satirical tragedy, and "The Group," the latter a piece holding up to ridicule some of the notables of the period. "The Blockheads, or the Affrighted Officers," another satirical piece attributed to her, came as a stinging retort to the unrehearsed incident at Faneuil Hall, Boston, January 8, 1776, when General Burgoyne's soldier thespians, while performing "The Blockade of Boston," a farce ridiculing the Americans, incontinently took to their heels on hearing that the patriots were attacking the British works on Bunker Hill.

Other pieces of this character, which created a sensation in their time, but which to-day lie forgotten on dusty bookshelves, are " The Battle of Bunker Hill " and " The Death of General Montgomery," tragedies in verse by Hugh Henry Brackenridge, and " A Cure for the Spleen," a Tory satire by Jonathan Mitchell Sewall, intended to gain adherents to the cause of King George.

The order of Congress to close the theatres was no sooner obeyed than the British reopened them, General Burgoyne taking the initiative at Boston in 1775.

Up to that time the sober Bostonians had been deaf to all appeals to permit dramatic performances in their city. The attempt made in 1750 to introduce theatricals had never been permitted to go any further and the drastic law forbidding play-acting of any kind passed by the General Court of Massachusetts in that year had proved an effective ban. But directly the Revolution began, local sentiment and susceptibilities were utterly disregarded by the British soldiery, and under the direction of General Burgoyne, himself an amateur actor and playwright, Faneuil Hall was turned into a theatre and performances were given regularly. It is not known what all the plays were, only four of the bills having been preserved. These give Mrs. Centlivre's comedy, " The Busybody," Rowe's " Tamerlane," Hill's tragedy, " Zara," and the farce, " The Blockade of Boston," the only piece that created any comment in the papers of the day, and the authorship of which is attributed to Burgoyne himself. In each of these plays the respective characters were acted by British officers of all ranks, the younger, smoothed-faced subalterns taking the feminine rôles.

The example set by the military in Boston was quickly followed by the garrison in New York, where the conditions in the winter of 1776—77 were so deplorable that it is not to be wondered at that the British turned to the distractions of the theatre as some relief from their sordid and distressing surroundings.

The fire which destroyed half the city the night the British troops took possession, had left a mass of unsightly ruins. All the buildings, with few exceptions, from the lower part of Broadway to Trinity Church and from thence to the Hudson were destroyed, and the West Side presented the same scene of devastation. On this black mass of ruins sprang up a number of tents and huts, temporary shelters which quickly became the resort of the scum of the city, a place of drunkenness, prostitution and crime, which went by the name of Canvas-town.

The places of amusement, Dunlap tells us, were the ball room of the City Tavern, the theatre in John Street, and the Mall, in front of the ruins of Trinity Church, which was the resort of beaux and belles during the summer evenings, walking in thoughtless gaiety or with measured steps to the music of the military bands placed by the officers amid the graves of the churchyard.

The soldier-actors began their dramatic performances at the John Street Theatre January 25, 1777, the opening bill being Fielding's burlesque, "Tom Thumb." Two weeks prior to the opening this notice to the public appeared in *Gaine's Mercury:*

DURING THE REVOLUTION

The Theatre in this city, having been some time in preparation, is intended to be opened in a few days for the charitable purpose of relieving the Widows and Orphans of Sailors and Soldiers who have fallen in support of the Constitutional Rights of Great Britain in America. It is requested that such Gentlemen of the Army and Navy whose talents and inclinations induce them to assist in so laudable an undertaking be pleased to send their names (directed to T. C.) to the Printer of this Paper before Thursday night next.

The manager of the company and principal low comedian was Dr. Beaumont, Surgeon General of the British Forces in America. Major Williams, of the artillery, played the tragic heroes, while the heroine, says Dunlap, bore his name though not received in society as the legal possessor. This was a beautiful English girl, the mistress of Major Williams, who later played such high comedy rôles as Mrs. Sullen in " Beaux' Stratagem " and Clarinda in " The Suspicious Husband " as well as any professional. There were other females associated with the company, such as had " followed the drum."

Other members of the company were Captain Oliver Delancy, who painted the scenery, Captain Seix, Captain William Loftus, Captain Edward Bradden, Lieutenant Pennefeather, Captain Phipps, Captain Stanley, who wrote the Prologue for the opening night, William Hulett, a dancer of the original Hallam company, and his son, William C. Hulett, described by Dunlap as " a remarkably beautiful youth."

The John Street playhouse was now called the Theatre Royal and the bills were usually headed " Charity." The issue of *Gaine's Mercury* following the opening contained this *critique:*

On Saturday evening last the little Theatre in John Street in this city was opened with the celebrated burlesque entertainment

153

"Tom Thumb," written by the late Mr. Fielding to ridicule the bathos of several dramatic pieces that at his time, to the disgrace of the British stage, had engrossed both the London Theatres. The characters were performed by gentlemen of the Army and Navy; the spirit with which this favourite was supported prove their taste and strong conception of the humor. Saturday's performance convinces us that a good education and knowledge of polite life is essentially necessary to form a good actor.

Other plays given included " Beaux' Stratagem," " Miss in Her Teens," " The Inconstant," " The Drummer," " Venice Preserved," " Rule a Wife and Have a Wife," the season lasting until May 29, 1777.

While the British officers were thus amusing themselves in New York, the war waged furiously all about them. Cannon thundered incessantly and the Jerseys were filled with marching men. Gradually, the Americans were forced to retire and late in that year Howe's troops took possession of Philadelphia.

Together with the other public buildings of the Quaker City, the Southwark Theatre was at first used as a hospital for the wounded, but when it was no longer needed for that purpose, Howe's " strolling company," as they styled themselves, at once began to make preparations to give dramatic performances. Their season opened January 19, 1778, and lasted until the middle of the following May, during which time they presented fourteen plays, including Home's " Douglas," Shakespeare's " Henry IV," " Wonder " and " Constant Couple."

It was at this time that the name of Major André [2]

---

[2] Major John André was born in London in 1751 and commissioned in the British army in 1771. While serving with his regiment in America he was sent to negotiate secretly with the American traitor, Benedict Arnold. Caught in disguise within the American lines he was tried by court martial and executed as a spy at Tappan, N. Y., October 2, 1780.

first became associated with these military thespians. Dunlap conveys the impression that André had assisted Captain Delancy in preparing the scenery of the John Street Theatre from the outset. But Seilhamer doubts that such was the case. He says:

André's exchange as a prisoner of war was only a matter of days when the theatre was opened on the 25th of January, 1777, and he had only obtained his captaincy on the 18th. His staff appointment came later and his Provincial rank of major later still. In Philadelphia in 1778 his position was entirely different. He was now at headquarters as Grey's aide and the favorite of his staff. He was a favorite, too, in his own immediate circle. . . . He was young, handsome, gay, accomplished. In Philadelphia society he was even more petted than other young men of higher lineage. . . . It is singular under such circumstances, if André really appeared in any of the plays presented at the Southwark Theatre that no tradition of his parts should exist, and I am inclined to believe that his connection with the amateur theatricals of the period was confined to his contributions as a scenic artist. The scenery painted by him was distinctly remembered by old Philadelphians for many years after the Revolution, and a full description of at least one set of scenes from his brush has come down to us.

This was the landscape back drop of which Durang wrote:

It presented a distant champagne country and a winding rivulet extending from the front of the picture to the extreme distance. In the foreground and centre was a gentle cascade—the water exquisitely executed—overshadowed by a group of majestic forest trees. The perspective was excellently preserved, the foliage, verdure and general coloring artistically toned and glazed. It was a drop scene, and André's name was inscribed on the back of it in large black letters. It was preserved in the theatre until 1821, when it perished with the rest of the scenery in that old temple of the drama.[3]

Early in 1778, news having been received that a

---

[3] History of the Philadelphia Stage, by Charles Durang.

French fleet would soon arrive off the coast, Sir Henry Clinton, who had succeeded Howe, received orders to evacuate Philadelphia. The English army departed in June and, by making a night retreat, was able to elude Washington and reach New York safely. Secure from attack, the Britishers once more settled down to a long period of inaction, which led to general demoralization. "Gaiety," says Seilhamer, "ruled the hour." He continues:

Extravagance was a virtue. Entertainments were frequent, and so grotesque were the fads of the time that dinners were often given with closed blinds and by candle light in the daytime. Under the conditions that then prevailed in New York it was fashionable to be loyal. Every belle had half a dozen danglers among the "Lords" and "Sir Georges" and the "dear Colonels" of the garrison. Elopements were common. Vice was supreme.[4]

Dramatic performances began again at the John Street Theatre, under the auspices of Sir Henry Clinton, six months before the evacuation of Philadelphia. The season commenced January 6, 1778, with Home's "Douglas," which *Gaine's Mercury* informs us was "much applauded by a crowded and brilliant audience." On January 15, Cumberland's "West Indian" was presented. On April 21, "The Rivals" was given, the first performance in America of Sheridan's comedy.

On June 8, Mrs. Tomlinson, a member of the American Company from 1758 to 1772 and whose professional experience must have been of great value to the military amateurs, was tendered a benefit, the bill being "She Stoops to Conquer," by "the late ingenious Dr. Goldsmith."

The season of 1779, which opened January 9, was

---

[4] History of the American Theatre, by George O. Seilhamer.

more important, for by this time Sir Henry Clinton's army had arrived from Philadelphia and the greater number of officers available permitted of a more extended repertoire. Unfortunately, the military players' theatrical library was limited. It lacked copies of many plays suitable for presentation. To overcome this difficulty, they advertised in the newspapers asking those persons who happened to own copies of the plays needed to kindly lend them. Among the plays advertised for in this manner were "The Lyar," "Tom Thumb," "Orphan of China," "Tancred and Sigismund," "High Life Below Stairs," "Hob of the Well," "What d'ye Call It," "Guard-ian," "Wonder" and "Cheats of Scapin."

Between this year and 1782, when they acted in New York for the last time, the military thespians presented a great number of the best plays of the day, including at least eight pieces that were new to this country. Although all these performances were ostensibly for charity, it is known that there was a salary list and that the officers exacted payment for their services as well as the civilian performers. As if apologizing for this business aspect to the military theatricals, an English journal of the time said that as necessaries were so dear in New York it was quite excusable, if not commendable, for officers to try and add to their incomes by exercising their talents.

It is not necessary to follow in detail the activities of these military players during the next three years, interesting as were their performances. While they were amateurs and only a passing incident in the history of the American theatre, they appear to have made their productions with almost professional care and skill. They must also be accorded credit for having maintained a high standard and kept alive the public interest in the acted drama during one of the darkest and most critical hours of the nation's life.

While Congress did everything possible to discourage the acting of plays during the Revolution, it had no power, of course, to prohibit theatrical entertainments in the individual states. Maryland, among others, disregarded its recommendations, and for some time before the end of the war, there were dramatic performances by professional players both at Baltimore and Annapolis.

Baltimore's first theatre, situated in East Baltimore Street, was erected in 1781. The managers were Mr. Wall, an actor and former member of the old American Company, and Adam Lindsay, a publican. Mr. Wall was ambitious to shine not only as a manager, but as an actor, and he eagerly assumed all the rôles with which Mr. Hallam had been identified: Richard III, Marplot, Tony Lumpkin, etc. His ambition, however, served him better than his ability, for he proved unequal to the task and later had to be content with lesser rôles.

The season began January 15, 1782, and lasted until the following June, among the plays presented being Shakespeare's " Richard III," Garrick's " Miss in Her Teens " and " Lethe," Otway's " Orphan " and " Venice Preserved," Centlivre's " Busybody " and " Wonder," Rowe's " Tamerlane," Hill's "Zara," Moore's " Gamester," Goldsmith's " She Stoops to Conquer," etc. The company, with the exception of Mr. and Mrs. Wall, were all strangers to the American stage. Among the newcomers were Mrs. Bartholomew, an ambitious and capable actress who played the rôles taken formerly by Miss Hallam, Mr. Heard, a new tragic actor who, fifteen years later, became a great favorite on the American stage, a Mr. Shakespeare, who, like his great namesake, was content to play modest rôles, and a Mrs. Robinson, a tragedienne of marked personality and ability, who, Seilhamer suggests, may possibly be identified with the " Perdita " famous in London Court scandal. She made her début on March 5, as Belvidera in " Venice Preserved," and was enthusiastically received, a writer in the *Maryland Journal* going into raptures over her acting. Throughout the season she divided the leading rôles with Mrs. Wall to whom she was far superior in tragedy. In " Lear " she played Aranthe [5] to Mrs. Bartholomew's Cordelia.

An important event of this season was the first production in America June 14, of Henry Brooke's tragedy " Gustavus Vasa, or The Deliverer of His Country," [6] a play which had been officially banned in England and chosen by Mrs. Bartholomew for her benefit. Mr. Wall played the King of Denmark and Mrs. Bartholomew was the Christina, while Mrs. Wall appeared as Augusta. In view of the political situation, the presentation of the patriotic drama at this time was particularly timely. It received a hearty

---

[5] The character of "Aranthe, lady-in-waiting to Cordelia," does not appear in "Lear" as originally written, but was an invention of Nahum Tate, one of the dramatists of the Restoration, who did not hesitate to commit the vandalism of freely adapting Shakespeare to satisfy what was considered the taste of the day.

[6] This play should not be confused with the American play of the same title, Benjamin Colman's tragedy "Gustavus Vasa," written in 1690. Henry Brooke (1703-1783) was the author of a number of plays. "Gustavus Vasa" was scheduled for production at Drury Lane in 1739, but the authorities forbade its production because of its revolutionary tendencies. It was not acted in London until 1805, when the young Roscius, Master Betty, appeared in the title rôle. It had previously been acted on the Dublin stage as "The Patriot."

ovation, and on this occasion and for several years later was inscribed to General Washington as " the deliverer of his country."

The season of 1782–83 began on September 13 with Miller's " Mahomet, the Imposter " and Cent-livre's " Ghost." Seven Shakespearean plays were given: " King Henry IV," " Romeo and Juliet," " Hamlet," " Othello," " King John," " Merchant of Venice," " Richard III." The only pieces new to Americans were Murphy's " Grecian Daughter " and Kelly's comedy " Romance of an Hour." The former piece, identified with Mrs. Siddons, was a great success and for a long time was very popular on our stage. Important acquisitions to the company were Mr. and Mrs. Dennis Ryan, players from Dublin, who at once began acting leading rôles. These artists, who, for a brief period, directed the destinies of the American stage, were seen for the first time on September 20 in Home's " Douglas." On October 18 the season was temporarily interrupted by a brief visit of the players to Annapolis. They returned to Baltimore November 15 and continued playing until February 7, after which Lindsay and Wall retired from the management in favor of Dennis Ryan.

The sudden change of management naturally leads one to infer that the two previous seasons had not been financially successful. It is probable that salaries were unpaid, for when Ryan assumed control he repudiated his predecessor's obligations, adding that old tickets would " not be received for the new performances." Possibly he was himself in difficulties, for a number of Baltimore amateurs came forward, offering to act in " The West Indian " to

" enable Mr. Ryan to accomplish the purpose of his undertaking." This was a shrewd move, for the house on the opening night was filled with Baltimoreans eager to see their local favorites. The season began February 11, 1783, and—interrupted only by a brief visit to Annapolis—lasted until June 9, the company then proceeding to New York, where there was a promise of a profitable summer season owing to the fact that, although the war was over, the British evacuation had not yet taken place, and the city was still full of idle English officers.

This summer season at the John Street Theatre began June 19 and lasted until August 16, the plays performed being the same as at Baltimore. New names in the casts were Mrs. Smith, Mrs. Garrison, Mrs. Fitzgerald and Mr. Coffy. A number of amateurs also lent their services on occasion.

The evacuation still being delayed, Mr. Ryan gave a brief supplementary season from October 11 to October 25, alternating performances with the military thespians.

The British marched out of New York, November 25, and Ryan's players departed for the South, where, in Baltimore, they began their regular winter season December 2, 1783. They continued playing there until February 14, 1784, when they went to Annapolis.

This Baltimore season was chiefly notable for the first production in America of Sheridan's comedy " The School for Scandal," which important première took place on February 3, 1784. Mr. Heard played Sir Peter Teazle, Mrs. Ryan was Lady Teazle, Mr. Ryan played Moses and Mr. Wall, Sir Benjamin

11   ·   161

Backbite. Other novelties were "The Times," by Mrs. Elizabeth Griffith, and "Fatal Curiosity," attributed to Lillo.

But in spite of good management, good acting, the best plays available, and a practical monopoly of the field, the season was not satisfactory financially. The company closed in the spring and Mr. Ryan died two years later.

The ending of the war, although a triumph for the American cause, left the country in a state bordering on anarchy. Jealousy between the individual states caused distrust and misunderstandings. Wild and extravagant notions of liberty led to serious disturbances, especially in New England. The action of law was opposed, the taxes denounced, the work of the courts obstructed, until even Washington feared that "mankind, when left to themselves, are unfit for their own government." From 1783 until 1789, when the newly drafted Constitution had been finally ratified and Washington was elected President of the New Republic, conditions were very alarming. The country seemed to be drifting towards irrevocable ruin. The rabble and the demagogues ruled. All sorts of absurd laws were passed and legitimate business enterprises hampered in every way—a general situation which bears a remarkable analogy to that facing the world to-day (1919)—six months after the Great War. Thus does History repeat itself!

The players found their path beset with new difficulties, particularly in Philadelphia, where the recommendation of Congress of 1778 had been adopted and a law passed prohibiting the theatre altogether. This law was not repealed until 1789.

DURING THE REVOLUTION

For the past eight years the old American Company had been playing in the West Indies. Mr. Douglass had retired from the organization in favor of Mr. Hallam and was now a British judge in Jamaica. The players gave regular performances in Jamaica all through the Revolution. The company at that time was as follows: Mr. Hallam played leads, Mr. Goodman, second leads, Thomas Wignell, comedy parts alternating with Mr. Morris. Mrs. Reynard and Mrs. Morris played feminine leads in tragedy and comedy, while Miss Storer and Miss Wainwright were seen in light comedy and opera.

With the advent of peace, the players once more turned their attention towards America. Mr. Henry came back in 1782 to look after the American Company's property rights in the theatres built under Douglass' direction, and in 1784 Mr. Hallam arrived in Philadelphia and presented a petition to the General Assembly praying for the repeal of the Act regarding stage plays and suggesting that the theatre be taxed. As a counter move, one hundred and ninety-eight prominent citizens presented another petition protesting against theatrical entertainment. The attempt to bring about the repeal of the Act failed, but, not discouraged, Hallam began lyceum entertainments as a sort of entering wedge, giving his " Lecture on Heads " and poetical addresses in honor of those fallen in freedom's cause. On December 7, 1784, he reopened the Southwark Theatre with the same entertainment, his company consisting of himself, Mr. and Mrs. Allen, John Durang, a dancer and the latter's sister, Caroline Durang, Mr. Allen being associated with him in the management. These lyceum performances continued at irregular intervals until the end of July, 1785, when the Hallam-Allen company went to New York, hoping to meet with more liberal treatment.

But the Manhattanites at that time were equally hostile to any revival of the drama. The *New York Packet* declared it was " too early yet for the stage." Nevertheless, Hallam opened the John Street Theatre on August 24, 1785, giving the same colorless kind of entertainment as in Philadelphia. He made no attempt to present a play until September 20, when he ventured to present Murphy's farce " The Citizen." This was the first play performed in New York after the Revolution. Meeting with no serious opposition, Hallam then gave in quick succession " Catharine and Petruchio," Maclyn's farce " Love à la Mode," Foote's " Devil on Two Sticks," " The Flitch of Bacon," " Cross Purposes," " The Mock Doctor," " The Countess of Salisbury " and " The Ghost." Plays were acted freely until November 1 when the season closed, Mr. Hallam, Mr. Lake, and Mr. and Miss Durang withdrawing from the organization. The others who remained under Mr. Allen's management acted at Albany during the winter of 1785.

John Henry, meantime, had kept the American Company intact. It included himself, Thomas Wignell, Mr. Harper, Mr. Woolls, Mr. and Mrs. Morris and Miss Storer, in addition to the new Jamaica players. Henry had intended playing in New York, but finding Hallam already in possession of that field, he was forced to alter his plans. As a way out of the difficulty he suggested a partnership, to which Hallam consented, and thus commenced a new era in the history of the American theatre, an epoch of almost complete and uninterrupted monopoly and which lasted seven years.

The first season under the Hallam-Henry management began at the John Street Theatre, New York, November 21, 1785. In addition to the two actor-managers, the company included Messrs. Wignell, Harper, Morris, Biddle, Woolls, Lake and Durang, and Mesdames Morris, Harper, Miss Tuke, Miss Durang and Miss Storer. Hallam, Henry, Wignell, Morris and Woolls were sharers in the profits of the enterprise.

Thomas Wignell, it will be remembered, was Lewis Hallam's cousin, an actor of Garrick's company who arrived in America just before the outbreak of the Revolution. His appearance with the Hallam-Henry company at this time was, therefore, his first appearance before an American audience.

This actor, who, later, became a manager on his own account and who, from the outset of his career in this country, was one of the conspicuous figures of the early American stage, was, says Dunlap, " a man below the ordinary height with a slight stoop of the shoulders. He was athletic, with handsomely formed lower extremities, the knees a little curved outwards and feet remarkably small. His large blue eyes were rich in expression and his comedy was luxuriant in humor, but always faithful to his author. He was a comic actor, not a buffoon."

Dunlap's descriptions of the other actors in the company are also of value, because he undoubtedly got them from Mr. Hallam himself. He goes on to say: " Mr. Hallam was of middle stature or above, thin, straight, and well taught as a dancer and fencer. In learning the latter accomplishment he had received a hurt in the corner of one of his eyes which gave it a slight cast, a scarcely perceptible but odd expression to it in some points of view. Generally his face was well adapted to his profession, particularly in comedy. Biddle was an actor merely decent. Harper, who was then considered handsome, was marked with small pox, had expressive eyes and fine teeth. He became a favorite in light comedy and was the original impersonator in America of Charles Surface. Later, he organized a company of his own, and was the first theatre manager to open in Boston. Mrs. Morris, the fine lady of the company, was a tall and elegant woman, and her acting was spirited. Mrs. Harper was a woman of no personal beauty, but played the old women of comedy respectably. Miss Tuke (later Mrs. Hallam) was young, comely and awkward. She afterwards became an actress of merit and improved in beauty and elegance."

The season of 1785–86, which proved an exceedingly prosperous one, opened with a performance of Moore's " Gamester " and Maclyn's " Love à la Mode." Hallam was not in the first bill, his place being taken by Mr. Henry, while Wignell played Levison in the first play and Squire Groom in " Love à la Mode." McLean's *Independent Journal,* commenting on this performance, wrote:

All the parts were acted with great ability by our old acquaintance, the long approved and very respectable American Company, who received unremitted plaudits from every part of the house, which, at a vast expense, is now repainted, beautified and illuminated in a style to vie with European splendor.

166

Subsequent bills included many of the old favorites and a few novelties. The familiar plays were: "Venice Preserved," "Jane Shore," "Douglas," "The Busybody," "Siege of Damascus," "West Indian," "Shipwreck," "Hamlet," "Merchant of Venice," "Wonder," "Richard III," "George Barnwell," "Conscious Lovers," etc. The novelties were: Thompson's tragedy "Edward and Eleanora," Mrs. Cowley's popular comedy "The Belle's Stratagem,"[7] the pantomime "Robinson Crusoe," attributed to Sheridan, "The School for Scandal," played for the first time by the American Company, and O'Keefe's comic opera "The Poor Soldier," in which last piece Wignell made such a hit as Darby that one of the newspapers hinted that the rôle of Tony Lumpkin in "She Stoops to Conquer" should be taken away from Hallam and given to Wignell.

Mr. Henry was the first Sir Peter Teazle in New York and Mr. Wignell the first Joseph Surface. This season, for the first time in America, the most popular among the plays presented had what might be called a run. "The School for Scandal" was repeated seven times, and "The Poor Soldier" eighteen times.

During this season, also, was first adopted the practice of selling reserved seats. Previously, there had been no reservation. Simple tickets of admission were sold and theatregoers sent their servants early to seize and to occupy the best seat available. But frequently it happened that the seat thus held was not occupied, and, as servants were not allowed to

[7] One of the few plays of the Eighteenth century that has come down to our time. The piece has been often revived by Augustin Daly and others.

remain once the curtain was up, the desirable seat remained empty all evening, while latecomers had to be content with less desirable ones. To remedy this Hallam and Henry devised the system of booking seats ahead and they issued this announcement to the public:

The public are respectfully informed that on account of a number of complaints relative to *unfair preference in boxes,* many of which have been lately taken without being occupied, the managers, ever ready to show their attention to the accommodation of their friends and patrons, have adopted a mode to prevent any similar infringement in future, by having tickets for the night, which will be delivered by the boxkeeper, on payment to the gentlemen taking boxes, with the number of the places particularized; a measure which they flatter themselves will meet with general approbation.

HALLAM AND HENRY.

On May 11 the company was strengthened by the arrival from England of the Kenna family, Mrs. Kenna making her début May 17 as Isabella in Southerne's tragedy of that name. Two nights later the Kennas appeared in "The Wonder" and also in "The Citizen." Mr. Kenna played young Philpot, Mr. J. Kenna, old Philpot and Mrs. Kenna, Maria. On July 14, when Shakespeare's "As You Like It" was presented for the first time in America, Mrs. Kenna was the Rosalind.

On May 29, Mr. Henry took his benefit, the bill being Bickerstaff's comic opera "The Maid of the Mill." Maria Storer sang the rôle of Patty, her first appearance since childhood, and made such a hit in the part that two hundred persons were turned away from the theatre unable to gain admittance.

Theatricals at this time were by no means confined to one locality. While the American Company, under Hallam and Henry, was acting in New York, and the Allen Company was giving excellent performances of the standard plays in Albany, an organization known as the Godwin and Kidd Company opened the theatre at Savannah, Ga. Mr. Godwin, a dancing master by profession, was a member of the American Company in 1766, and Mr. Kidd had appeared with the Ryan Company in Baltimore. The season in Savannah was brief, Addison's " Cato " and Shakespeare's " Taming of the Shrew " being presented and the company helped out by local talent. The enterprise was apparently unsuccessful, for Mr. Godwin soon advertised a school of dancing. Later, however, having found a backer, he went to Charleston, where a new theatre called Harmony Hall had been erected. Here, on September 27, he began a season which lasted until the end of March, 1787. The plays given were: " Venice Preserved," " Bold Stroke for a Wife," " Richard III," " Orphan," " Romeo and Juliet," and other favorites.

Maryland also saw something of the players. Hallam and Henry, on closing their John Street Theatre season, August 2, 1786, went to Baltimore, where a new theatre had been erected on Philpot's Hill. The season was very brief, ending September 12, Sheridan's two comedies " The School for Scandal " and " The Rivals " being features of the repertoire. Following this engagement the company went to Richmond, Va., where the new theatre had been erected by Alexander Quesnay, and opened there on October 10, 1786, with " The School for Scandal," subsequent bills being " Alexander the Great " and " The Poor Soldier." The Richmond season closed late in the fall of 1786.

CHAPTER VIII

FIRST SUCCESSFUL AMERICAN PLAY

ROYALL TYLER'S COMEDY WELL RECEIVED. THEATRICAL SUBTER-
FUGES IN PHILADELPHIA THE DOCTORS' MOB RIOT. WILLIAM
DUNLAP'S SUCCESSFUL DÉBUT AS PLAYWRIGHT. PRESIDENT
WASHINGTON AS A THEATREGOER. THE KENNA FAMILY. THE-
ATRICAL QUARRELS. WIGNELL LEAVES THE AMERICAN COM-
PANY AND PREPARES TO OPEN IN PHILADELPHIA. ARRIVAL OF
THE PLACIDES. JOHN HODGKINSON, THE " PROVINCIAL GAR-
RICK." PRIGMORE AND THE BREECHES.

THE year 1787 was a particularly interesting one
for the American Company, performances being
given in Philadelphia, notwithstanding the edict
against play acting, and also in New York, Baltimore and Annapolis.

The company began in Philadelphia with a brief
preliminary season of two weeks at the Southwark
Theatre, the object of the managers being, no doubt,
to see how far they could go. The players opened
January 15, the entertainment being announced as
" a concert of Music and Lectures, to be concluded
by the ' Pantomimical Finale ' called ' Robinson
Crusoe.' "

From Philadelphia the company proceeded to
the John Street Theatre, New York, opening there
on February 14 with Vanbrugh's " Provoked Husband " and Garrick's " Miss in Her Teens."

The principal event of the season was the successful production on April 16 of " The Contrast," a
comedy by Royall Tyler, the first play by an Ameri-

can author [1] on an American subject to be produced on the American stage. The cast was as follows: Jonathan, Mr. Wignell; Colonel Manly, Mr. Hallam; Jessamy, Mr. Biddle; Dimple, Mr. Harper; Van Rough, Mr. Morris; Servant, Mr. Lake; Charlotte, Mrs. Morris; Maria, Mrs. Harper; Letitia, Mrs. Williamson; Jenny, Miss Tuke.

Royall Tyler, the first American playwright to gain recognition, was born in Boston in 1758 and graduated from Harvard in 1776. As a student he had shown considerable literary ability in witty articles and sprightly verse. Later he fought in the Revolution, attaining the rank of major. While visiting New York he happened to see a performance of " The School for Scandal " and was immediately fired with the ambition to write a similar comedy on American manners. " The Contrast " was the result, the play taking its title from the contrast of character between the corrupt and frivolous world of fashion and the sturdier, more vigorous types of American manhood. Apart from the novelty of its theme and the direct appeal it made as a native product, the piece had no great merit and to-day it is unknown outside the library. It has practically no plot and is lacking both in situation and incident, the action consisting mainly of conversations between two persons. The success of the piece came largely from the fact that the character Jonathan introduced for the first time the stage Yankee, a low-comedy rôle in which Wignell made the hit of his career.

---

[1] Thomas Godfrey, the author of "The Prince of Parthia" produced by Douglass' company in 1767, was the first American author to have a play produced, but his blank verse tragedy was not American in theme. It failed to make any impression, and was withdrawn after the second performance.

The play was performed in New York five times in quick succession, an unusual occurrence in those days, but after its first season was never revived, although acted and favorably received in Philadelphia and Maryland. Later, a thousand copies of the play were printed by subscription, George Washington and others of the most notable people in the country sending in their names. The comedy was reprinted by the Dunlap Society in 1887, the work being embellished by a copperplate engraving by Maverick of the last scene in the last act from a drawing by Dunlap.

Another play by Major Tyler, a farce called "May Day," was presented by Mr. Wignell for his benefit, May 18, 1787, but as it never saw a second performance, it probably had little merit. Tyler subsequently became chief judge of the Supreme Court of Vermont where he died in 1826.

On the close of the New York season, June 8, the company returned to Philadelphia, where the Federal Convention was then in session, and opened at the Southwark Theatre, June 25.

Owing, however, to the Quaker City's legal restrictions against theatricals, the management had to resort to all kinds of expedients. The Southwark Theatre became the "Opera House, Southwark," and plays were called "Spectaculum Vitæ." Musical comedies and farces were announced as "operas," the assumption, of course, being that operas were not included in the prohibition. A play was never advertised as such. For instance, "Hamlet" was disguised as "a moral and Instructive Tale as exemplified in the History of the Prince of Denmark." "The

School for Scandal " became a " Comic Lecture in five parts on the Pernicious Vice of Scandal."

At the beginning of the season of 1787–1788 the American Company announced that instead of the usual three performances a week there would be only two thereafter, a change rendered necessary by the poor business done the previous year. New York at that time seemed incapable of giving support to more than two performances a week, in spite of the rapidly increasing population and the constantly growing popularity of the players. The season began December 21, 1787, with " The Mysterious Husband." This drama by Cumberland was new to America, and it failed to please. The afterpiece Dibdin's farce " The Deserter " met with more favor and remained a feature of the repertoire for a long time. Other novelties of the season were " First Floor," by James Cobb, and General Burgoyne's " The Heiress."

On April 14 Mr. Harper was billed to act Falstaff in " Henry IV " for his benefit, but unfortunately, no performance was possible owing to a serious disturbance which suddenly broke out in New York. This riot, known as "the Doctors' Mob," was caused by the most trivial incident. The windows of a hospital dissecting room had been accidentally left open and some of the cadavers lying on the slabs in a mutilated state were exposed to view. This, added to the popular accusation that graveyards were violated by doctors for dissecting purposes, so incensed the ignorant that the building was broken into and all connected with it threatened with death. Some of the more obnoxious physicians fell into the hands of the populace, but were rescued by magistrates and lodged in jail for safe keeping. The next day the riot was renewed and the mayor had to call out and arm a body of citizens to quell it, several being killed and wounded.

The season ended May 31 when the company went to Philadelphia.

The Southwark Theatre, Philadelphia, was still called an Opera House and the plays continued to be given under such thinly disguised titles as " Improper Education " (" She Stoops to Conquer "), " Filial Piety " (" Hamlet "), " Fate of Tyranny " (" Richard III "), " Crime of Filial Ingratitude " (" The Rivals "), etc.

These subterfuges, of course, only succeeded in angering more those who were opposed to the players and the absurdity of the situation was apparent to all. The progressive and cultured elements of Philadelphia society meantime were making strenuous efforts to bring about the repeal of the prohibitionary statute. A Dramatic Association, formed in January, 1789, and having among its promoters some of the most influential people in Pennsylvania, petitioned the General Assembly, taking the ground that if the theatre were not tolerated, a source of rational amusement would be destroyed and every free man incur the forfeiture of a natural right he ought to possess—the right of doing as he pleased in a matter indifferent to the welfare of the community. George Clymer, a signer of the Declaration of Independence, argued that the theatre was necessary and must come. " It is a concomitant," he said, " of an independent state. No civilized state is without it." Robert Morris, the friend of Washington, said : " The taste and manners of the people regulate the theatre and the theatre has a reciprocal effect upon the public taste and manners." In opposition were Dr. Logan, who thought "theatres only fit for monarchies," and Dr. Whitehill, who believed that "no regulation could prevent the vice and immorality of the theatre."

But once more common sense finally prevailed: The bill to repeal the Act became a law on March 2, 1789, and a week later the Southwark Theatre, this time sailing under its own colors, was opened to the public, "By Authority." During this brief Philadelphia engagement Shakespeare's "Much Ado About Nothing" was given for the first time in America, Mr. Hallam playing Benedict and Mrs. Morris, Beatrice.

On April 14 of the same year, the American Company was back at the John Street Theatre, presenting "The Beaux' Stratagem" and "The True Born Irishman."

Great excitement prevailed in the city and great preparations were being made in view of President Washington's coming inauguration. This historic event the theatre celebrated by displaying illuminated transparencies. Whether the theatre gave a performance on the evening of the inauguration is not known. According to the records the house was closed from April 18 to May 2, two days after the inauguration. But it seems highly improbable that the managers would voluntarily have neglected such a favorable occasion to refill their depleted coffers, or that the authorities would deny innocent diversion to the crowds that flocked to the city. Bills subsequent to the inauguration included " She Stoops to Conquer," " The Heiress," " George Barnwell," " Who's the Dupe? " and " The Choleric Man," both of which last plays were new.

Royall Tyler's success as a dramatist, small as it was measured by the large pecuniary reward that awaits the successful playwright to-day, was of great significance and importance to the American stage, because it helped to bring about a complete change in the attitude of our public toward the theatre. As the first attempt of an American dramatist to be subtly American, all classes of society now began to recognize in the theatre a worthy institution in which to reflect and perpetuate the national traits and genius. As such many were willing to forget their prejudice and give it their patronage. American plays quickly became the fashion, and William Dunlap began writing the sixty odd plays and adaptations which earned for him the title " Father of the American Drama."

William Dunlap, the first American man of letters who made the writing of plays a profession, was born at Perth Amboy, N. J., on February 19, 1766. The family came originally from Ireland, the grandfather, who spelled his name Dunlop, being a merchant at Londonderry. Samuel Dunlap, father of the dramatist, joined the army and came to America with General Wolfe, taking part in the campaign against the French with such distinction that he received a lieutenant's commission. When hostilities ceased, Lieutenant Dunlap married Margaret Sargeant, a native of New Jersey of English descent, and settled down in Perth Amboy as a storekeeper. The coming Revolution soon darkened the political sky.

Patriotic appeals to the Colonists to rise and throw off England's yoke were heard on every side, but all through the storm Samuel Dunlap and his wife remained stanch loyalists.

William—their only child—received a fair education and early showed great fondness for books and pictures. In 1777 the family moved to New York, then occupied by the British, and the youth found great delight in attending the performances of the military players at the John Street Theatre. It was about this time that he had the misfortune to lose one eye by an accidental blow given him in play. His father, meantime, had opened a china store and here William rendered such service as he was able. When not busy in the store he tried his hand at writing and began two plays. He also attempted to sketch crayon portraits of friends, with such success that it was at once recognized as his natural vocation. Meantime, the youth had been entirely converted to the patriot's cause, and later he was honored by an invitation to the headquarters of General Washington whose portrait he also painted.

On the close of the war, William Dunlap went to London to learn art under the great Benjamin West, although, according to his own admission, he spent more of his time seeing life and going the rounds of the theatres than in study of perspective and color. On his return to New York four years later, the glowing accounts he heard of Royall Tyler's success with " The Contrast " filled him with the determination to become a dramatist himself. He had already established himself in his father's home as a portrait painter, but his commissions were not so many as not to leave him ample leisure for activities in another direction.

His first play, a comedy called "The Modest Soldier or Love in New York," he wrote in 1787 and offered to Hallam and Henry, but the piece was declined for the reason, as Dunlap discovered later, that there was no part for Mrs. Henry. Not discouraged, Dunlap again set to work and produced another comedy, "The Father, or American Shandyism." This play was accepted and produced at the John Street Theatre September 7, 1789, with this cast:

Col. Campbell, Mr. Henry; Racket, Mr. Hallam; Tattle, Mr. Wignell; Haller, Mr. Harper; Rusport, Mr. Biddle; Campley, Mr. Woolls; Platoon, Mr. Ryan; Jacob, Mr. Luke; Mrs. Rackett, Mrs. Morris; Caroline, Mrs. Henry; Mrs. Grinade, Mrs. Harper; Susanna, Miss Tuke.

The play was favorably received. It was given four times in New York, not a bad record as runs went in those days—twice in Philadelphia and once in Baltimore. Dunlap himself considered it his best play. In his History he always refers to himself naively as the author of "The Father of an Only Child," a new title which he himself gave the play later. The *American Quarterly Review* said of the piece:

The plot is sufficiently dramatic to carry an interest throughout; the characters are well drawn, and well employed; and the dialogue possesses, what is indispensable to genuine comedy, a brief terseness, and unstudied ease, which few of the productions of the present era afford.

Following up his success, and at the request of the comedian, Mr. Wignell, Dunlap wrote an interlude called "Darby's Return" which was presented at the actor's benefit November 24, 1789. The sketch made a hit, and Dunlap's reputation as the coming dramatist was more firmly established. Other plays from his pen about this time were "The Miser's Wedding" (1793), which deservedly failed, "The Fatal Deception" (1794) and "Shelty's Travels" (1794)—both moderately successful—and "Fontainville Abbey" (1795), which also proved popular.

In 1796 Hodgkinson and Hallam made the proposition to Dunlap that he join them in the management of the John Street Theatre. He consented, only later to regret it. He found theatre management a thankless, unprofitable occupation and, after vainly struggling with the financial difficulties which finally overwhelmed him, in 1805 he declared himself bankrupt and left the stage to devote himself to literature and art.

In 1812 he wrote his "Memoirs of George Frederick Cooke." Two years later, he was appointed Assistant Paymaster-General of the New York Militia, and the following year he published his "Life of Charles Brockden Brown." In 1826 he helped found the National Academy of Design, and in 1828 he began his "History of the American Theatre" which was published in 1833. He died in 1839. The Dunlap Society of New York was organized to perpetuate his name and to publish in limited editions the best of his plays and also various treatises relating to the origin and history of the American theatre.

William Dunlap's memory is honored rather for the unique personality and amiable qualities of the man than for any real service he rendered the drama. As a playwright he cannot be considered even of the second rank. His greatest success in that field was as an adaptor of other men's ideas. He made no headway as a dramatist until he began to translate Kotzebue. As a writer, he was most prolific, but what he produced was quantity, not quality. He was versatile, and also superficial. He had many trades, but was a master of none. As a manager he was not more successful. He had high ideals—ideals which he did not hesitate to sacrifice immediately he found it profitable to do so. Yet in his business dealings he was upright, honorable and conscientious. As a painter he was only mediocre. The most successful of his larger compositions were merely copies of his teacher's, Benjamin West. His own pictures failed to make any considerable impression. His history of the American theatre, a work with a charm all its own, contains so many errors and misstatements that it can hardly be regarded seriously as history. Its chief value lies in it being a narrative, by an eye witness, of early theatrical happenings, in most of which he himself played a part. Yet for all his shortcomings, William Dunlap deserves a conspicuous niche in America's hall of fame. As one of his most recent biographers, Oral Sumner Coad, says:

William Dunlap has never ranked among our distinguished men of letters, and he will never do so. He labored as zealously as any, but no amount of application could make up for the gift that he lacked. He challenges our interest almost wholly as a pioneer. He took up his pen when the literature of the United States was still feeble and ill-supported. He threw himself especially into the neglected and unremunerative field of American drama, and though he produced nothing of lasting merit, he surpassed the work of his forerunners, he established playwriting as a respectable profession, he stimulated others to follow his example, and he exerted a distinct influence in determining the course of our drama during the last years of the Eighteenth century.[2]

John Bernard, the actor-manager, who was contemporaneous with Dunlap, and knew him well, has this to say of him:

> Induced by the success of his first play to make the drama his pursuit in preference to painting, he cemented the connection by becoming a manager and soon sank into a mere adapter, whose highest pretensions were tact and facility. He translated some twenty pieces from the German and French, and was so fortunate as to be the first to present Kotzebue to the Americans. His happiest effort was perhaps the drama of "Abaelino," from the German of Zschokke, and his very worst was undoubtedly the one he seemed to prize most, a drama on the death of Major André—a mass of fustian and platitude upon great names and themes.[3]

An interesting incident of the première of Dunlap's interlude "Darby's Return" at the John Street Theatre on September 24, was the presence of Washington, then living in New York as President of the United States.

From his youth, the theatre had been one of Washington's favorite diversions. It is not known where he first saw a dramatic performance, but it is only reasonable to suppose it was in Virginia where plays were constantly being acted during his early manhood. He could not have seen the Murray-Kean production of "Richard III" at Williamsburg on October 17, 1751, for he was then at sea on his way to the West Indies. He returned to Virginia in 1752

---

[2] William Dunlap. By Oral Sumner Coad.
[3] Early Days of the American Stage. By John Bernard.

and probably spent the summer at Mount Vernon. There is no record of his having been present in the theatre the night that the Hallams made their first bow to an American audience, but it is quite possible, even probable, that he was one of the spectators.

"With his resignation from the service and his marriage," says Paul Leicester Ford,[4] "came the leisure and opportunity to gratify his love of the drama. Furthermore, as a ' burgess ' or member of the Assembly of his colony, an annual visit to Williamsburg to attend the meetings of that body became necessary; and as this period was always the capital's season, when plays were given, if at all, he was at once able to attend to his senatorial duties and to enjoy the theatre. It is nowhere recorded that there was a company playing in Williamsburg in 1760, but Washington's ledger proves there must have been one acting during the session of the Assembly, for it records under October 8th, ' By Play Tickets at Sundry times £7.10.3.' Later entries are : ' 1761, March, Play Tickets £2.7.6; 1762, Play Tickets, £21.8.3; 1763, April 26, Play Tickets 5/; 29th, Play Tickets 10/; May 2, Play Tickets 12/6; 3rd Play Tickets 8/9; 19th Play Tickets 5/–.' "

In 1768 the Virginia Company of Players acted in Williamsburg for two months and in the daily record Washington kept of " Where and How My Time is Spent," he says he " went to Williamsburg with Col. Basset, Col. Lewis and Mr. Dick, dined with Mrs. Dawson and went to the play. Tickets cost £1.7.6."

---

[4] Washington and the Theatre. By Paul Leicester Ford.

From that time on, Washington was a constant theatregoer. " The School for Scandal " and the comic opera " The Poor Soldier " were his favorite plays. His diary is full of references to visits made to the playhouse both at New York, Williamsburg and Annapolis. In 1773, having occasion to come to New York, to enter his stepson at King's College, he " dined with James Delaney and went to the Play, the bill being ' Hamlet ' and ' Cross Purposes.' Play tickets 8/."

After he became President, Washington's visits to the theatre were always exceedingly formal and ceremonious. Over the box that he was to occupy was the United States coat of arms. At the entrances to the theatre soldiers were posted and four soldiers were generally placed in the gallery. Mr. Wignell, the manager, attired in a full dress of black, with his hair elaborately powdered in the fashion of the time, and holding two wax candles in silver candlesticks, was accustomed to receive the President at the box door and conduct him and his party to their seats.

When Dunlap's " Darby's Return " was presented at the John Street Theatre, Wignell played the rôle of the soldier who returns to Ireland and recounts his adventures in America, Washington was present. Many of the passages in the play made direct reference to the President, and, when Darby told of the adoption of the Federal Constitution and of the inauguration which was an event still fresh in every mind, the audience intently watched every change of expression in Washington's face. According to Dunlap, he

183

smiled at these lines alluding to the change in the
form of government:

> *There, too, I saw some mighty pretty shows,*
> *A revolution, without blood or blows;*
> *For, as I understood, the cunning elves,*
> *The people, all revolted from themselves.*

But he looked serious when Darby told of

> *A man who fought to free the land from wo,*
> *Like me, had left his farm a soldiering to go.*
> *But having gain'd his point, he had, like me,*
> *Return'd his own potato ground to sow.*
> *But there he could not rest. With one accord*
> *He call'd to be a kind of not a lord—*
> *I don't know what, he's not a great man sure,*
> *For poor men love him just as he were poor.*

When Kathleen asked,

> *How looked he, Darby? Was he short or tall?*

" His countenance," says Dunlap, " showed embarrassment from the expectation of one of those
eulogiums which he had been obliged to hear on
many public occasions, and which doubtless must
have been a severe trial to his feelings, but Darby's
answer that he had not seen him because he had mistaken a man 'all lace and glitter, botherum and
shine ' for him until all the show had passed, relieved
the hero from apprehension of further personality,
and he indulged in that which was with him extremely
rare, a hearty laugh."

The season, which ended December 9, was marked
by several scandalous disturbances in which Mr.
Henry, a very quarrelsome man,[5] was involved with

---

[5] Both Henry and his wife were constantly in trouble because of their
tempers. Gout was the excuse for the actor's irritable moods, while Mrs. Henry
was capricious and disobliging. She was once hissed in Philadelphia and in
danger of being driven from the stage for this reason.

his partner Hallam and others. After one personal encounter in New York, after which Henry was laid up for repairs, the actor published a card apologizing for his bruises, and asking that a committee of gentlemen make an inquiry so he might be exonerated from blame.

The following year, 1790, the American Company spent in Philadelphia. The players opened at the Southwark Theatre on January 6 with Sheridan's comedy " The Rivals."

On March 13, when Home's tragedy " Douglas " was given, a new actor made his appearance in the rôle of Young Norval. This was John Martin, one of the first native actors to appear on the American stage.

Martin was born in New York City, and educated for the bar, but, " induced by habits of idleness and the applause bestowed upon his recitations by his idle companions," he abandoned law for the stage. He was of fair complexion, middle height, light figure and played the youthful characters in tragedy and comedy respectably well. He " continued for some years a useful though not a brilliant actor, lived poor and died young," which Dunlap assures us, is the ultimate fate of all actors not endowed with exceptional gifts.

This season also brought forward another American playwright in the person of Colonel David Humphreys, aide-de-camp to General Washington, whose " Widow of Malabar," translated from the French, was little more than a *succès d'estime,* although it was the fashion of the moment to applaud everything of home manufacture, no matter how inferior in quality—a feeling which, as Dunlap observes, was soon exchanged for a most discouraging predilection for foreign plays and contempt for every native literary effort.[6]

From Philadelphia the American Company went to Baltimore for a short season, after which it returned to the Southwark Theatre where they continued acting until July of the following year. The weather was so hot in June that fire engines had to spray the walls and roof of the theatre to make performances possible.

While Hallam and his colleagues were appearing at the Southwark Theatre, another troupe suddenly appeared in Philadelphia and began a long season at what was then known as the Northern Liberties Theatre. This was the celebrated Kenna family, who had joined Hallam when they first came out from England but who since had been touring independently in the South. The company consisted of Mr. and Mrs. Kenna, Mr. and Mrs. T. Kenna, Miss Kenna, Mr. Vaughn and Mr. Allen. Apparently they were not afraid of the competition of the more famous American Company, for they settled down in Philadelphia for over a year, presenting an extensive repertoire and no doubt receiving enough patronage to make the enterprise possible.

[6] An unreasonable deep rooted prejudice against the American made play persisted in this country up to twenty-five years ago. Wallack, Daly, Palmer and Frohman favored foreign dramatists almost exclusively. It was not until the success of Bronson Howard's "Shenandoah" and William Gillette's "Held by the Enemy" proved that American dramatists could write plays with a "punch" that the tide began to turn. Nowadays the native author has it all his own way and a large fortune in royalties awaits the lucky playwright able to suit the popular taste, which today (1919) does not exact a very high standard.

The following season brought disaster to the American Company. A serious misunderstanding among the principal players caused a rupture which could not be healed, and finally led to the demoralization and disbandment of the splendid organization.

For some time ill feeling, partly fostered by jealousy, had existed between Henry and Wignell. There had also been much rivalry between Mrs. Henry and Mrs. Morris, Wignell invariably championing the latter. Wignell, too, knowing himself to be the favorite of the public, was dissatisfied with what he was getting out of the profits. Instead of receiving only a certain share, he had long expected to be taken into the management, a step to which both Hallam and Henry were opposed. Finally, unable to obtain satisfaction, Wignell withdrew from the company, taking Mr. and Mrs. Morris with him, and organized a rival company in Philadelphia.

When, therefore, the American Company returned to the John Street Theatre in October, 1791, there were serious gaps in the ranks of the players. Wignell, the favorite comedian, was no longer there. Gone, also, the stately and popular Mrs. Morris. These losses were serious, and the new names which this year appeared in the casts—Martin, the American actor, Robinson, Hammond, Vaughn, Ashton—could not make up for them. Apparently Hallam, then about to marry Miss Tuke, had made no attempt to find successors for the old favorites, and Henry was averse to bringing over a new leading woman who might prove a rival to his own wife.

A novel feature of the new season which began October 10 with a performance of " Douglas," and one that for a time helped to gloss over the serious loss the company had sustained, was the first appearance in America, February 3, 1792, of the Placide Troupe, world famous tumblers and tight rope dancers direct from Sadler's Wells Theatre, London, where they had created a sensation. The troupe comprised Alexander Placide,[7] the finest gymnast and most graceful rope dancer yet seen in America, Mme. Placide, also an admirable dancer and pantomimist, and Mr. Martine, a performer known as the " Little Devil." Their entertainment, which was part of a ballet called " The Two Philosophers," made a great hit. After appearing in New York, they went to Boston in the summer of 1792, later appearing at the Southwark Theatre, Philadelphia.

The American Company returned to Philadelphia on May 28, 1792, and gave performances until July 2, when Mr. Harper and Mr. Woolls left the organization and went to Boston. This was the last season of the players who had kept together so many years. " A new organization was formed," says Seilhamer, " but it was the American Company only in name. What had so long been known as the old American Company had ceased to exist."

The theatre in this country now entered upon a new era. It was a change for the better for it meant wholesome competition and the introduction of more practical methods, not the least important of which was a change in the relations of the individual players to their managers. The sharing system first introduced by the Hallams in 1752 was abolished. Instead

---

[7] Alexander Placide remained in America and became the manager of a theatre in Charleston, S. C. He was the father of the celebrated players, Henry and Thomas Placide and Caroline (Mrs. Blake) and Jane Placide.

of being partners in the various theatrical enterprises, the actors, with the exception of two or three of the principals, were from now on engaged on a salary basis. The sharing plan had not proved either popular or practical. It was also subversive of good discipline. When business was prosperous the players were in good humor, but directly things went amiss they were the first to become discontented and demoralized. It was better for all concerned that the financial responsibility should fall on one man.

Another change for the better was the added spur and stimulus given to production and acting by keen competition. The long monopoly of the theatrical field so long enjoyed by the American Company was broken at last. " Philadelphia and New York became from this time," says Dunlap, " territories of rival theatrical monarchs who, after mutual invasions and hostile incursions for a short time, found it necessary to divide the United States between them until other potentates raised independent standards and every city, town and village had its own ' king of shreds and patches.' "

Wignell's preparations for a new theatre in Philadelphia went rapidly forward. He found a backer and partner in the person of A. Reinagle,[a] an eminent musician, who at once began to raise the necessary funds by selling stock in the enterprise to his many friends. A site was purchased in Chestnut Street above Sixth Street and building operations commenced. While the new house was in course of construction, Wignell went to England to recruit a

[a] Father of Hugh Reinagle, the scenic painter.

company, following close in the footsteps of Henry who had already sailed on the same mission.

In September, 1792, Mr. Henry arrived in New York with his new players and at once proceeded to join Hallam, who was preparing to open the old Southwark Theatre in Philadelphia. Among the new people brought over were Mr. Hodgkinson, Mr. King, Mr. West, Mr. Prigmore, Miss Brett, afterwards Mrs. Hodgkinson, and Mrs. Pownall.[*]

The most notable among these newcomers was John Hodgkinson, known in England as the " provincial Garrick."

Hodgkinson's real name was Meadowcroft. His father was a farmer who, later in life, kept a public house in Manchester. As a boy, John sang in the choir of the Manchester churches. He was also a self-taught violinist and leader of a small band of amateur thespians who gave performances in a cellar. At the age of fifteen he ran away from home and went to Bristol where his voice procured him employment with the local theatrical troupe. His natural gifts now given free rein, his advancement was rapid, until he became the favorite actor of the provinces in comedy, opera and farce. Very ambitious, he played everything in the repertoire from courtier to clown, from king to cobbler—anything that might keep him before an audience. Like certain other players of conspicuous ability, his private life left much to be desired. " Co-ordinate with the rise of his fame and fortune," says Carpenter in *The Mirror of Taste,* " was the growth of the evils which were fated to endanger the one and make shipwreck of the other;

[*] Grandmother of Henry Placide.

his professional success and his gallantries, running parallel to each other, like the two wheels of a gig, left their marks on every road he travelled."

After eloping with the wife of his manager, Munden, he and his companion went to Bath where they lived as Mr. and Mrs. Hodgkinson. It was at Bath that Henry engaged the actor for America, and with him Miss Brett of the Bath Theatre, who later became Mrs. Hodgkinson. " Hodgkinson sought the American engagement," says Seilhamer, " before the engagement sought him. This is clearly shown by his letter to Hallam and Henry, which also betrays the motive of his application. He desired to quit England as a means of repudiating the woman who bore his name at Bath, so that another woman might bear it in America." The letter to Hallam is so characteristic of the man, that it is worth giving here:

To Messrs. Hallam and Henry, Managers of the Theatre, New York.

GENTLEMEN:

An ardent desire to visit America has forced me to an inquiry how your theatres are situated. Have you a *first line* vacant? or would you be glad to make one for a principal character in this kingdom? I have in all the first theatres out of the capital, maintained one, as I do now in Bath. Among my range of characters here are Young Mirabel, Young Quaker, Dashwood, Sir John Restless, The Liar, Othello, Iachimo, Belville (" Wives "), Clifford (" Heiress "), Mahomet, Scapin, Captain Plume, Jaques, Deaf Lover, Myrtle, Villeroy, Petruchio, Marplot, Don Carlos (B. S. Husband), Zanga, Richmond, Don John (" Chances "), Dyonisius, etc.

Now as it may seem singular that a man in possession of so great a line, and in a first theatre, who has refused, and has now offers of a considerable nature from London, should wish to emigrate, give me leave to say that no pecuniary extravagance has caused the idea, nor could that, without great imprudence, be the case, my receipts being near £400 a year from the theatre.

I know many who, were they once convinced of the firm establishment of your country, would be glad to visit it; and I can treat for you with as capital a singer as any this country has, Mrs. Billington excepted. My wish is, you would be candid with regard to every information relative to your towns, etc. What salary you can give *two* such people as I have mentioned; and should this meet your approbation do not disappoint in anything, for my part or those mentioned, should any take place, you shall be at liberty to relinquish in an instant. Our vacancy here takes place the beginning of August.

I should thank you to attend to these points. I am sure you'll pardon my being particular in them all, and in requesting an answer by the first return. Rest assured that on my part, or the person I treat for, no failure shall take place.

I am, gentlemen,   Your servant,

Bath, December 28, 1791.   JOHN HODGKINSON.

At the time of his arrival in America, Hodgkinson was twenty-six years old. " He was," says Dunlap, " five feet ten inches in height, but too fleshy to appear tall, and in a few years he became very corpulent. He was strongly and well formed in the neck, shoulders, chest and arms, but clumsily in the lower limbs, with thick ankles, and knees slightly inclined inward. His face was round, his nose broad and not prominent, his eyes gray, and of unequal sizes, but with large pupils and dark eyelashes. By some accident in early youth, one eye had been injured, and was smaller than the other, but this was not perceptible on the stage when he played in serious parts, and in the comic roles, added archness to the expression of his face. His complexion was white and almost colorless, and his hair dark brown. He had great physical strength, and a memory capable of receiving and

192

retaining the words of an author to an extent that was truly astonishing. His ignorance of all beyond theatrical limits was profound. He did not know who was the author of ' High Life Below Stairs ' at the time he played the principal character in the piece. At a time when he was the delight of the town, the companion of most of its wits, and the soul of our musical societies, he—having made out a programme for poetical recitations—was sportively asked by Judge Cozine, ' Who's this Anon you've got down on the bill among the poets? ' To the judge's astonishment, he answered in serious earnest and with an air of one showing his reading, ' Oh, he is one of our first poets, Sir.' "

John Bernard gives this further description of the actor, who until the next coming of Thomas Abthorpe Cooper, was the most important and conspicuous figure on the American stage:

Hodgkinson was a wonder. In the whole range of the living drama, there was no variety of character he could not perceive and embody, from a Richard or a Hamlet, down to a Shelty or a Sharp. To the abundant mind of Shakespeare, his own turned as a moon, that could catch and reflect a large amount of its radiance; and if, like his great precursors, it seemed to have less of the poetic element than of the riches of humour, this was more owing to association, which, in the midst of his tragic passions, would intrude other images. An exclusive tragedian will always seem greater by virtue of his specialty, by the singleness of impressions which are simply poetic—whilst Hodgkinson had one gift that enlarged his variety beyond all competition—he was also a singer, and could charm you in a burletta, after thrilling you in a play; so that through every form of drama he was qualified to pass, and it might be said he " exhausted worlds " if he could not " invent new." I doubt if such a number and such greatness of requisites were ever before united in one mortal man. Nor were his physical powers inferior to his mental; he was tall and well proportioned, though inclining to be corpulent; with a face of great mobility, that showed the minutest change of feeling; whilst his voice, full and flexible, could only be likened to an instrument that his passions played upon at pleasure.[10]

The singer described in the letter to Hallam as "second only to Mrs. Billington," and who later became Mrs. Hodgkinson, was Miss Brett, a daughter of Brett, the celebrated singer of Covent Garden and the Haymarket Theatre. "She was very fair," says Dunlap, "with blue eyes and yellow hair approaching to the flaxen. Her nose was prominent or Roman; her visage oval and rather long for her stature, which was below the middling. Her general carriage on the stage was well suited to the character she performed; and in romps, full of archness, playfulness and girlish simplicity. As a general actress, she was as valuable in female as her husband was in male characters."

Mr. King, the next player in importance to the Hodgkinsons, was an uncommonly handsome man, but not an artist of the first rank. Mrs. Wrighten, known on the American stage as Mrs. Pownall, who arrived a little later than the others, came to America with a great reputation at Drury Lane. She was one of the ablest representatives of singing chambermaids then in London.

Mr. Prigmore, the comic old man, was a vain person and had little merit as an actor, although popular with the gallery. Dunlap tells an amusing anecdote concerning him:

One of Prigmore's weaknesses was to believe every woman in love with him. A well-to-do widow, whose hobby was assisting the

---

[10] Early Days of the American Stage, by John Bernard.

indigent, came to the theatre and made inquiries about the players. Among others, she asked about Prigmore, and one of the actors, in jest, told her he had only a small salary and was pathetically shabby in appearance. Hearing this, the widow remembered she had a pair of her late husband's indispensables and she sent a note to Prigmore asking him to call. The same joker, intercepting the note, went up to the actor, exclaiming, " Prigmore, my boy, your fortune's made! Here's a rich widow in love with you!"

Prigmore hurried home to his lodgings, dreaming of golden independence, and after a sleepless night, spent an extra hour at his toilette next morning. He then proceeded to the widow's, and, on being shown into the parlor, quickly cast his eyes around, taking mental inventory of the substantial furniture, and congratulating himself on the aspect of his future home. The widow entered, and after some preliminary compliments, which only confirmed Prigmore in his fatuous belief, she went on to say she had heard that his circumstances were not exactly what he might wish, that his income was limited, etc., and that she wished to be of some assistance. Prigmore listened open-mouthed. This was surely the beginning of her proposal of marriage. At a loss for a reply, he was about to seize her hand and kiss it gallantly, when she suddenly called out to her maid:

" Rachel, bring the breeches! "

The actor, speechless, stood rooted to the spot. The widow, on receiving the trousers, folded them carefully, and, remarking they were as good as new, begged his acceptance of them.

" Was it for this you wanted me, madam? " he gasped in indignant astonishment.

" Yes, sir."

He clapped on his hat and strode furiously to the door. The widow, not understanding this sudden change in his manner, followed him with:

" Won't you take the breeches, sir? "

" Wear 'em yourself!" he flung back in angry retort, as he walked away with angry strides.

Mr. West was the dandy of the company and usually appeared on the streets in boots and leather breeches, always new, with three gold laced buttonholes on each side of the high, upright collar of his scarlet coat. Robins, an unimportant member of the organization, in addition to the gold laced collar, wore three gold bands around his hat.

All the new recruits to the American Company, Mr. Hodgkinson among them, liked to attract attention by eccentricity of dress. Long after the New Yorkers had discarded the old time wig and wore their hair short and of nature's color, Hodgkinson was seen on the streets with powdered curls on each side of his face and long braided hair twisted into a club or knot behind. Instead of boots he wore breeches, stockings and shoes. This bizarre costume, worn with a theatrical air, made him conspicuous in the crowd and gave him that grand manner which the player, with his keen instinct for publicity, has always held to be an indispensable part of his art.

CHAPTER IX

THE CHESTNUT STREET THEATRE, PHILADELPHIA

THE YELLOW FEVER SCOURGE. FIRST APPEARANCE IN AMERICA
OF MRS. MELMOTH. REAPPEARANCE OF MISS CHEER. A NOTABLE
PREMIÈRE. DUNLAP'S ACTIVITY AS A DRAMATIST. DEATH OF
JAMES FENNELL. NEW THEATRE IN BALTIMORE. DÉBUT OF
JOHN HENRY. WIGNELL'S COMPANY FOR THE CHESTNUT STREET
HOUSE. DESCRIPTION OF THE NEW THEATRE. MRS. OLDMIXON.
ANN MERRY. THOMAS ABTHORPE COOPER'S FIRST APPEARANCE
IN AMERICA. CLOSING OF THE OLD JOHN STREET THEATRE.

ANXIOUS to forestall Wignell, who was making
grand preparations to open in Philadelphia, Hallam
hurried his reorganized company to the Quaker City
and began a season at the Southwark Theatre, September 26, 1792, with Mrs. Centlivre's comedy " The
Wonder," Mr. Hodgkinson making his American
début as Don Felix. At the second performance, he
was seen as Belcour in " The West Indian." Later,
he played Petruchio to Mrs. Pownell's Catharine,
and was also seen for the first time as Othello, Richard III and Hamlet. The *Federal Gazette,* referring to him as " the American Kemble," declared his
Othello a " masterly piece of acting."

The season lasted until January 12, 1793, when
the company went to New York, opening at the John
Street Theatre January 28 in " The Dramatist," Mr.
Hodgkinson being seen for the first time before a
New York audience as Vapid. Among the novelties
given at this time were Bickerstaff's " Romp," Holcroft's " Road to Ruin " and O'Keefe's " Wild Oats,"

197

pieces which proved popular with American theatre-goers for a number of years.

Although Hallam and Henry frequently relinquished to Mr. Hodgkinson the rôles in their possession, the relations of the players were far from harmonious. /There was " a cause of discord," says Dunlap, " in the jealousy with which the old members, now considering themselves Americans, viewed the newcomers who, on their part, looked upon Americans as inferiors."/Hodgkinson, from the start, asserted his authority. Unable to tolerate a rival, either for himself or Mrs. Hodgkinson, he began to play the despot, Henry, in particular, becoming the target of his dislike. Quarrels were frequent and in measure as Hodgkinson became more popular with the public he grew in arrogance, harassing Henry at every turn and upheld by Hallam, who, quite ready to throw his old partner over if he saw any advantage to himself, sided with the new favorite, and there followed a number of intrigues which gradually undermined Henry's supremacy with the public.

A return visit to Philadelphia in July, in the hope of reaping such profit as might still be possible before Wignell's opening, was brought to a sudden end by the yellow fever epidemic of that year.

This dreadful scourge, from which the early American theatres suffered annually for a number of years, first came to this country from the West Indies in 1792. The first year of its appearance, it made comparatively few victims, but the second summer the pestilence, having gained a foothold, broke out with much greater violence and the mortality rose with frightful rapidity. All the theatres were forced to close and there was a panic among the players as well as among the rest of the population.

John Bernard, in his interesting reminiscences, speaks of the plague's effect on the theatres.

So frightful were its ravages that the first news of its approach was sufficient to empty towns of one-half of their citizens; and as it came at all periods, though chiefly in summer, it permitted no system to be planned with security. It broke up the legislatures, paralyzed trade, and, of course, put an end to all kind of amusements. The theatres, need I say, were the earliest to suffer, for, in addition to the panic which the fever created, a crowd was a medium for spreading infection; and though it is true that this scourge rarely entered New England, yet as it was here that theatricals flourished the least, the evils resulting will be readily surmised. Still, I am bound to confess, that if it shut up the theatres, it created a thirst for them, which tended greatly to balance the losses sustained. Startling as it may appear, yet the fact is unquestionable, that there never was such a disposition to enter our doors as when the fever had departed. The desire for amusement seemed to have increased by suspension. In the very first days of mourning, after thousands had been swept from the bounds of the city, let the theatre but open, and the rush to it from all quarters can be scarcely conceived. All ages and stations partook of an excitement which was usually confined to a particular class. This was scarcely to be viewed as a healthful phenomenon, and yet was as little to be traced to a want of right feeling. It was a startling reaction; in their escape from a terror which had benumbed every faculty, the mere sense of safety provoked an excess—spread an hysterical feeling that sought any amusement that would afford it a vent.[1]

The next season at the John Street Theatre saw the last of Henry's connection with the American Company. It began November 11, 1793, with a performance of "The Clandestine Marriage," for the benefit of Philadelphia's yellow fever victims, and continued until June 28, 1794.

---

[1] Early Days of the American Stage, by John Bernard.

Several interesting events marked this season. One was the first appearance in America of Mrs. Melmoth, an English actress of considerable repute who made her début November 20, 1793, as Euphrasia in Murphy's tragedy " The Grecian Daughter." She met with extraordinary success and, according to Dunlap, was " the best tragic actress the inhabitants of New York had yet seen." Tradi-tion makes her out a very handsome woman, but so corpulent that sometimes during the most tragic passages the auditors were moved to laughter instead of tears. " No actress of tragedy in New York," says Ireland, " could at this time at all compete with her, yet she was past the prime of life and her unfortunate bulk adapted her to a very limited range of parts. In Lady Macbeth and other matronly characters she displayed powers rarely equalled." She died in New York in 1823 at the age of seventy-four.

Another interesting event was the reappearance after an absence of twenty years of Miss Cheer, now known as Mrs. Long. She was seen on December 2 as Mrs. Oakley in " The Jealous Wife," but the fickle public no longer recognized in the now mature woman their old time favorite. Dunlap says, " she was received in silence by the audience and never heard of more." [2]

A notable première was the first production on March 3, 1794, of " Tammany," an opera glorifying the Indian saint, lyrics by Ann Julia Hatton and music by James Hewitt. Mrs. Hatton, a poetess of

[2] Another of Dunlap's many misstatements. Mrs. Long appeared again that same season as Almiria in "The Mourning Bride," Catharine in "Catharine and Petruchio" and Mrs. Grant in "Cross Purposes." On May 28 she took a benefit.

some standing in England and a sister of Mrs. Siddons, came to America expressly to get her opera staged, and on arriving here invoked the aid of the Tammany Society, then, as now, a powerful political organization, to secure a production. A request from such source was not to be ignored, and Hodgkinson at once began elaborate preparations to perform the piece, " which," says Seilhamer, " was the first important attempt at the composition of operatic music in America." Like most pioneer composers, Mr. Hewitt met with faint recognition so far as his original work was concerned, and he even suffered the mortification of being hissed by an angry audience on the first night of " Tammany " for not being ready with a popular air when it was called for.

Elaborate scenery was prepared for the occasion by Charles Ciceri,[3] an Italian scenic artist who had been painting scenes for the new Philadelphia theatre and had fled from that city on the outbreak of the epidemic. " Heretofore," says Dunlap, " the scenic decorations of the American theatre had been lamentably poor. Henry had not brought out with his recruits any artist to paint his scenes. Those of the old stock were originally of the lowest grade and had become black with age."

Dunlap showed at this time great activity as a dramatist. A tragedy in poetic form entitled " The Fatal Deception," based on the story of Lord

---

[3] Charles Ciceri, one of the earliest of American scenic artists, was a native of Milan who learned art in Paris. The reign of terror drove him to the West Indies and later he took refuge in America. "He was," says Dunlap, "a clever painter, and an excellent machinist, a man of exemplary habits, active mind, quick discernment, fertile in resources, and firm in purpose." He became at length an importer of French merchandise and finally retired with a handsome competence to his native Italy.

Leicester and the unfortunate Amy Robsart, was produced on April 24 without much success, but in "Shelty's Travels," a shorter piece by the same author, presented the same evening, Hodgkinson made as big a hit as had Wignell in "Darby's Return."

The breach between Hodgkinson and Henry had widened as the months went by. Determined to get rid of his rival, Hodgkinson had continued his antagonistic tactics until, finally, Henry, weary of the constant opposition, agreed to sell out his interest for $10,000 which proposition Hodgkinson eagerly accepted.

This proved the undoing of Henry. Ill, discouraged, he succumbed morally and physically and died that same year, aged forty-eight. "From the stage of life," says Dunlap, "as well as the stage of the theatre, Henry and his family were at once swept. His daughter eloped and soon after died. While on a voyage to Rhode Island on board a small coasting vessel Henry himself died and was buried without ceremony under the sand of an island in the Sound. His wife, who was with him, never recovered from the shock and died deprived of reason at Philadelphia, April 25, 1795."

Profiting by the absence of the Wignell-Reinagle Company in Baltimore, where they had gone to escape the yellow fever then raging in Philadelphia, Hallam and Hodgkinson decided on a brief season at the Southwark Theatre in the fall of 1794. It was the last ever played by the American Company in Philadelphia. When the company left on December 4 to go back to New York, the old Southwark

Theatre " closed its doors," says Seilhamer, " upon a past that covered more than twenty-eight years. For the future it was to stand, untenanted, or be given over to itinerant mountebanks or strolling companies."

Features of this short Philadelphia season were the production of " Sophia of Brabant," the first attempt at serious pantomime in America, in which Mme. Gardie,[4] a beautiful French woman and famous dancer, made her first great success, and the first performance in this country of Garrick's " Country Girl," in which Hodgkinson made a great hit as Moody, Mrs. Hodgkinson being almost equally as successful as Peggy, a rôle which Ada Rehan made familiar to theatregoers of this generation.

Returning to the John Street Theatre, the company opened there December 15, 1794, with Bickerstaff's " Love in a Village," on which occasion Mr. Hodgkinson addressed the audience for the first time in his capacity as manager. Among other reforms he promised was the abolishment of rowdyism in the

[4] This celebrated dancer had a romantic history and a very tragic end. According to Dunlap, she was the nominal wife of M. Gardie, the son of a nobleman, receiver general at La Rochelle for Louis XVI. The young man was idle and dissipated, and his father, to get him away from bad companions, sent him to St. Domingo. There the young man met the beautiful and fascinating actress to whom later he gave his name. She went back with him to France but M. Gardie's aristocratic relatives refused to receive her. One evening at the theatre, after the Revolution, the audience demanded the Marseillaise. She refused to sing it. The audience was enraged, and it became necessary for the couple to flee the country. They went first to St. Domingo, but on the insurrection of the negroes, took refuge in this country, finally settling in Philadelphia, where they lived as man and wife, he being supported chiefly by her salary as a dancer. His own source of income was copying music. When Hodgkinson in 1798 determined to leave New York for Boston, he employed Gardie to copy the orchestral music. When he went away, that source failed. The young man was hopelessly in debt and without friends. In this predicament he determined to return home, but Mme. Gardie, too proud to go where she would be unwelcome, refused to accompany him. Driven to desperation, the young man temporarily lost his reason. In the middle of the night he rose from his bed and, taking a knife, plunged it into his wife, killing her instantly. Then he turned the weapon on himself.

gallery,[5] a nuisance from which the better classes of theatregoers had had to complain for a long time.

The production of several novelties marked the season. On February 16, a new play by the industrious Dunlap entitled "Fontainville Abbey" was given its première. The piece failed to achieve any marked success, and had only a short career. The following week (February 25) Cumberland's comedy "The Jew," a piece which remained popular for forty years, had its first production, Hodgkinson being seen in the rôle of Sheva. On March 21, Prince Hoare's farce "The Spoiled Child" was presented for the first time, with Miss Harding as Little Pickle.

All this time Wignell had been straining every effort to open his splendid new theatre in Chestnut Street, Philadelphia. Thirteen months had gone by since the completion of the house. The yellow fever epidemic had been a serious cause of delay, and time had also been lost in getting the new players from England. Finally everything was ready and the new playhouse, "larger and incomparably better," says Dunlap, "than had been seen before in the New World," was opened to the public February 17, 1794, with O'Keefe's "Castle of Andalusia" and "Who's the Dupe?" by Mrs. Cowley. Seilhamer gives this interesting description of the house:

The interior of the new theatre was a perfect copy of the Theatre Royal at Bath. The façade, which was not finally finished

---

[5] The gallery element at this period was exceedingly disorderly everywhere. In Boston it was necessary for the orchestra to make a public appeal for more considerate treatment. "In Philadelphia," says Seilhamer, "even the vigilance of Mr. Reinagle could not always prevent disturbances in the gallery or protect the audience and orchestra from insult. All this was part of the rudeness of the time—a condition that has entirely passed away in our places of amusement."

until 1805, measured ninety feet in Chestnut Street, including two wings of fifteen feet each. The theatre stood back from the street, with the projections of the wings or pavilions in front of the main building extending to the line of the street. These pavilions were connected by a colonnade of ten Corinthian columns, and decorated by emblematic figures in tablets. The centre building was ornamented by two spirited and well-executed figures of Tragedy and Comedy by Rush. In the centre of the building was a great Venetian window, the niches in which the figures were placed being on each side. Over the niches in two circular tablets were emblematic insignia. In each of the wings was a green room, one being used for music rehearsals, dancing, practice, etc., and that in the west wing as a Green Room in the proper meaning of the term. The entrances to the theatre were through the projecting wings. The stairs of the galleries were under the colonnade. The left-hand door led to the pit. To the boxes the ascent was by a flight of marble stairs in front to a lobby, which communicated by corridors with all the boxes. The fronts of the boxes were handsomely gilt and decorated to correspond with the ceiling, and hung with corresponding drapery between the columns. Those in front of the stage were arranged in the form of an amphitheatre. The seats, including those of the pit and gallery, were well disposed. The extreme depth of the theatre was one hundred and thirty-four feet; that of the stage upward of seventy-one feet. Between the boxes the stage occupied a front of thirty-six feet. Over the stage, occupying a part of the entablature, was an emblematic representation of " America Encouraging the Drama," with the motto, " The Eagle Suffers Little Birds to Sing." For this was afterward substituted the words, " For useful mirth or salutary woe." It was computed that the theatre would hold about two thousand people, of which number nine hundred could be accommodated in the boxes.[6]

A company had been recruited in London of great strength, especially in the operatic department. Among the new artists were Miss George (Mrs. Oldmixon), James Fennell, Mr. Darley, John E. Harwood, Miss Broadhurst, Mr. Chalmers, Mr. and

Mrs. Charles Whitlock, Mr. and Mrs. Marshall, Mr. and Mrs. Rowson, Mr. and Mrs. Warrel, " Billy " Bates, Mr. and Mrs. Francis and Mr. Moreton.

Miss George, a Drury Lane oratorio singer, had been a great favorite with London theatregoers for a number of years. She was the daughter of a clergyman who, the story goes, was so bitterly opposed to her going on the stage that on the night of her début he stood up in the audience and hissed her. But her success was so great that at the close of her first season she was hailed as the English Allegranti. Though rather small in person she had a trim figure and a vivacious, easy and agreeable manner. " Her eyes," Seilhamer tells us, " were expressive and her features large but pleasing and excellently adapted to the stage, while the compass of her voice was astonishing and her melody had sweetness, roundness and variety of tone." All the many years she remained on the stage she retained great vivacity and force. In the later years of her life, she frequently played comedy old women. Just previous to her American engagement she married Sir John Oldmixon, a noted beau of the day. John Bernard in his " Retrospections " says he first met Sir John at Bath in 1784:

From the refinement of his dress and manners he bore the appellation of " the Bath beau," and upon all points of good breeding was looked up to as an oracle. This distinction he was not slightly proud of. Certainly the mechanism of his dress was a profound study, and his science in manœuvering a snuff box and a cane was, for many months, in my eyes an impenetrable mystery. I have been told that Sir John was the original of Mrs. Cowley's Lord Sparkle. He certainly was of mine, accident having thrown him in my way on my first visit to Bath. Whatever success I obtained in the fops and fine gentlemen (which were the characters I played mostly in

London) I acknowledge I owe it all to the strong impressions I received from Sir John Oldmixon. The next day (after playing Lord Sparkle) Sir John stopped me in the street, saying, " Bernard, I saw your Sparkle last night. They say you imitate me, but your dress is incorrect. You wear only twelve curls to a side. I never wear under sixteen." [7]

But the long sojourn in America appears to have gradually demoralized the old beau, for in a London paper of 1796 appeared the following paragraph:

Sir John Oldmixon, whose equipage was once the gaze of Bond Street, is now a gardener near Philadelphia. He drives his own cabbages to market in his own cart. His wife, formerly Miss George, sings at the theatre and returns in the conveyance which brought the vegetables to sale.

The truth of this statement is corroborated by Dunlap, who says:

Sir John did, with the earnings of his wife, purchase or hire a cottage at Germantown, and drove vegetables to market in a conveyance which would allow of his wife's going to town to attend her professional duties and return with him. Sir John only retained of the Bath beau the snuff-box, which he certainly tapped, opened and presented with the air of a finished gentleman. In 1816 Sir John was living obscurely at Sag Harbor, Long Island.

The player next in importance in the new company was the tragedian James Fennell, a man of good family who, after first studying law, began his stage career in 1787 at Edinburgh as an amateur and with such success that he was engaged for Covent Garden where he appeared as Othello. He was described after his début as having a " most elegant and striking figure, tall, finely proportioned and graceful, together with a voice of great volume." His best parts were Othello and Iago. His powers as a tragedian, how-

---

[7] Retrospections of the Stage, by John Bernard.

ever, at that time were not so far developed as to make him indispensable at Covent Garden. He became dissatisfied with the rôles given him and when approached by Wignell was quite ready to sign for America. According to Dunlap, he was remarkably handsome although rather too tall, being considerably over six feet. His complexion and hair were light, his nose round, thick and too fleshy, and his eyes a very light gray with yellowish lashes and brows. His appearance as the Moors Othello and Zanga was noble; his towering figure superb. He was the idol of the youth of Philadelphia and for a time revelled in high living and applause on and off the stage. But days of disgrace and poverty soon followed. He had a mania for making salt by artificial means and all the money he earned as an actor he sank in all kinds of dubious commercial ventures. He became involved in various money making schemes and finally was arrested for debt and sent to prison. "This unhappy man," adds Dunlap, "appeared for the last time on the stage of the Chestnut Street Theatre where he had been idolized in 1794 and exhibited the powerless remains of what God had made man, and vice had debased to a wretched driveller. He was allowed to attempt Lear in 1815, but even his memory was gone and the scene of his former triumphs witnessed his last public exhibition of pitiable imbecility. He died shortly after."

Mrs. Whitlock was a sister of the matchless Mrs. Siddons, "whom," says Ireland, "she closely resembled and in many parts imitated. Born in 1761, she was apprenticed early in life to a mantua maker. Her sister's great success induced her to attempt the stage, and, after playing several engagements in the provinces, she was engaged in 1783 for Drury Lane where she remained until she married Charles E. Whitlock, a Newcastle theatre manager who had much success playing heavy fathers. In 1791, Mrs. Whitlock became a great favorite at the London Haymarket. Three years later Wignell engaged her for Philadelphia. In 1800 she again played in London and was afterwards in Boston, whence she came to New York in 1802 as leading woman at the Park Theatre, where, though really a fine actress, she never superseded Mrs. Melmoth, Mrs. Johnson or Mrs. Merry in the favor of the public. Her person was large and heavy and both in countenance and voice she bore a marked resemblance to the house of Kemble." She visited America again in 1812 and played in Boston, a city that had always held her in the highest esteem. She died in 1835 at the age of seventy-four.

John E. Harwood was an accomplished young Englishman whose forte was high comedy. Falstaff was among his best parts. "He was the best Falstaff," says Ireland, "until the arrival of George Frederick Cooke, and when he died in 1809 he had at the time no equal in comedy on the American stage."

Other interesting people brought over by Wignell were the Rowsons. Mrs. Rowson, the daughter of William Haswell, a British naval officer, married in 1786 William Rowson, a leader of the band attached to the Royal Guards in London. She had acted in a provincial theatre and was an agreeable singer. She had also written novels, the most popular of which was " Charlotte Temple," a best seller of its day over which thousands have sighed and wept. The couple acted at the Federal Street Theatre, Boston, in 1796, and during that season Mrs. Rowson wrote a comedy called " Americans in England " which was performed for her benefit. This was her last appearance on the stage. Later she went to Medford, Mass., where she opened a school for girls.

Of the other new members of the Wignell-Reinagle company, Mr. Darley, father of John Darley, one of the most distinguished actors on the American stage, was a large, fat man and bore such a striking resemblance to Henry VIII that he was once asked to sit to an eminent artist for a portrait of bluff King Hal. He had long been a favorite singer in London, " where," says Dunlap, " he was brought into public notice by the uncommon powers and melody of his voice." Miss Broadhurst, an agreeable singer in serious opera, sang second rôles to Mrs. Oldmixon. " Billy " Bates was a low comedian, his humor being of a rather coarse order. Mr. Chalmers acted leads in genteel comedy and second rôles in tragedy. Mr. Marshall was a good actor in fops and William Francis was noted for his Harlequin and his skill in mounting pantomime.

The season which began February 17, 1794, and lasted until July 18 was the most brilliant that had yet been played in America. Performances were given every alternate night, the order of production usually being opera, tragedy and comedy, with accompanying farces, ballets and pantomimes.

All the successful pieces of the day were given, including nine Shakespeare plays—" Catharine and Petruchio," " Macbeth," " Richard III," " Hamlet,"

"Othello," "As You Like It," "Romeo and Juliet," "Merchant of Venice" and Dryden's "Tempest." The repertory was remarkably strong in operatic productions. "Even the tragedies," says Seilhamer, "were given with musical completeness before unknown in this country, the great number of singers in the company affording the managers facilities for embellishing such plays as 'Romeo and Juliet' and 'Macbeth' with genuine artists in the vocal parts."

But the practice, then commonly followed, of mingling opera with comedy and tragedy was not profitable, as Wignell soon discovered to his cost. William B. Wood, who later managed the Chestnut Street Theatre, says in this connection:

Wignell's latest conviction (and time since his death has confirmed its truth) was that no theatre can properly do justice to opera, comedy, and tragedy in our limited audiences. One theatre, he believed, should be expressly devoted to music and dancing. I am not certain, however, whether in a pecuniary point of view these departments are ever profitable to the manager under any circumstances. Our books have constantly proved that the extra expenditure for a large chorus force, additional performers, and band, added to the enormous demands of the principal singers, render a profit scarcely within probability. Such plays as "Speed the Plough," "Poor Gentleman," "John Bull," and "Foundling of the Forest," realized more real profit to our theatre than all the operas produced during twenty-five years.[8]

Mrs. Oldmixon did not arrive from England in time for the opening bill. Her first appearance with the company was made on May 14, 1794, when she was seen as Clarinda in "Robin Hood."

Mr. Darley, Mr. and Mrs. Marshall, Mrs. Warrel, and Miss Broadhurst all made their début in

[8] Personal Recollections of the Stage, by William B. Wood.

" The Castle of Andalusia " on the first night of the season, while Mr. Fennell and Mr. and Mrs. Whitlock appeared on the second night in Southerne's tragedy " Isabella." John E. Harwood made his début February 24 as Trippet in Garrick's " Lying Valet."

Only two plays of native authorship were put forward this season. These were " Slaves in Algiers," a comedy by Mrs. Rowson, and an after piece entitled " Embargo, or Everyone Has His Own Opinion," written by a Philadelphian. Neither piece was of any value except as reflecting the public excitement of the time, feeling then running high against Algiers for its piratical acts against the American flag and war threatening with England over the embargo dispute of 1794.

Now firmly established in Philadelphia, Wignell and Reinagle sought to extend their field. The first step in this direction was the building of a new theatre in Baltimore. The new house, a huge wooden barn, was erected in Holliday Street and was Baltimore's leading playhouse until 1813 when it was replaced by the second Holliday Street Theatre. The first Baltimore season was very brief, opening on September 25, 1794, and closing October 31, when the company returned to Philadelphia. Mr. Fennell withdrew from the company at the end of the Baltimore engagement, to engage in the commercial enterprises which led to his ruin. During the next two years the company divided its time between the new house in Baltimore and the Chestnut Street Theatre.

The third Philadelphia season opened December

14, 1795. The company, weakened by the absence of
Mr. Fennell and Miss Broadhurst, failed to attract
the usual amount of patronage, and Wignell sailed
for England in search of new recruits. He returned
in 1796, bringing with him some of the most distinguished players that had yet visited America—Mrs.
Merry, Thomas Abthorpe Cooper, John Bernard
and William Warren.

On December 5, 1796, Wignell, his company now
powerfully reinforced, reopened the Chestnut Street
Theatre, Philadelphia, with " Romeo and Juliet,"
Mrs. Merry making her début as Juliet.

Ann Merry, born in 1770, was the daughter of
John Brunton, manager of an English provincial
theatre. She was one of six children, three of whom
became players of some distinction. The father
taught Ann to read Shakespeare, but had no thought
of her becoming an actress. She showed, however,
such natural talent for the stage, that she was permitted to appear in the rôle of Euphrasia. " The
audience," says Dunlap, " only expected to see a girl,
a novice, perhaps a mawkin, but they saw with astonishment a graceful and accomplished actress. The
applause and commendation in and out of the theatre
were proportionate to the surprise and admiration.
The characters of Horatio in ' The Roman Father '
and Palmyra in ' Mahomet,' parts suited to her age
and figure, succeeded and increased her fame. Thus
Siddons, the greatest tragedienne we have ever seen,
had to struggle through difficulties to reach that pin-
nacle on which she towered for almost half a century unrivalled, while Ann Brunton, a child in years,
soared at once to almost an equal height." Her suc-

cess at once opened the doors to Covent Garden where her triumphs were repeated. London confirmed the opinion that she was another Siddons. Soon after her engagement at Covent Garden she attracted the admiration of Mr. Robert Merry, a fashionable poet and dramatist, and left the stage, living in retirement until 1796, when, reduced in fortune, the poet was willing that his wife should sign with Wignell for performances in America.

On the 7th, the ballet dancers, Mr. and Mrs. Byrne, were seen for the first time, and on December 9 Thomas Abthorpe Cooper made his first appearance in America in the rôle of Macbeth.

Thomas Abthorpe Cooper, one of the great actors of the Nineteenth Century, was born in 1776. His father, an Irish doctor, died when the boy was very young, and his mother's cousin, William Godwin, author of " Caleb Williams," adopted him and looked after his education. When he was sixteen, the boy decided that he was tired of books, and wanted to become an actor. Thomas Holcroft, author of " The Road to Ruin," an intimate friend of Godwin's, was asked for advice, and he obtained an opening for the youth at the Edinburgh Theatre where Mrs. Siddons was then appearing. He failed to make any impression, and, after being hissed by the audience, was discharged from the company. This experience was a lesson to the young man better to prepare himself for his chosen profession. Returning to London, he studied Hamlet and Macbeth with Holcroft, and shortly afterwards made his début at Covent Garden. Hamlet was chosen for his trial part and every account of that night's performance mentions it as one of the most successful ever remembered. Macklin, the Nestor of the stage, so pronounced it, and congratulated the triumphant youth accordingly. Macbeth followed with equal success. " Thus," says Dunlap, " before he was nineteen years of age, the despised boy had triumphed in the two most difficult characters of the drama and received the applause of those who had witnessed the veteran skill of Garrick, Henderson and Kemble."

On arriving in London, Wignell heard of Cooper's fame and at once made overtures to the young tragedian, offering him a three year engagement for America at $25 [9] a week, and benefits guaranteeing $750 more. Cooper accepted the offer and left England for his new home in America.

" With a handsome face and noble person," says Joseph N. Ireland,[10] " a fine mellow voice, unusual dignity of manner and grace of action and in his declamation most forcible and eloquent, as a tragedian he was without a rival."

Macbeth was his best rôle. Joseph T. Buckingham, writing in 1820, said of his impersonation:

He is perfectly identified with the character. The dagger scene, which he plays in a style altogether his own, is one of the sublimest efforts of histrionic genius. The terrible agonies of his mind, which proclaim their existence with " most miraculous organ," are too powerful to be long the object of attention. In the latter part of the play, after Macbeth has " supped full with horrors," the moral reflections are given with such exquisite beauty and feeling that we almost forget the crimes of the murder, and pity the wretched victim writhing with the tortures of his own conscience.

---

[9] This was considered a large salary compared with what actors were then being paid in England, many well known players not receiving more than $6 a week.

[10] Records of the New York Stage, by Joseph N. Ireland.

In personal appearance he surpassed any actor seen on the American boards up to that time. A contemporary critic says of him:

Mr. Cooper has exceeded every actor that ever trod the American boards in personal requisites. His voice, figure, action, and countenance have never been surpassed; the first in sweetness, fulness, and flexibility; the next in beauty of proportions; the third in ease, propriety, and grace; and the last in tragic expression. In these physical excellences he was more rare than in his judgment, in which, and in the niceties of reading and power of embodying the great characters of Shakespeare, he was not equal to some other actors.[11]

In 1806 he became manager of the Park Theatre, New York, and afterward had associated with him Mr. Stephen Price, with whom he continued several years till he resigned management for the more profitable career of starring. Prior to 1830 he had played in sixty-four theatres and visited every State in the Union. He had performed four thousand five hundred nights and travelled over twenty thousand miles in this country, and as most of his time was spent between New York and Philadelphia, he frequently posted in his own vehicle from one city to the other. His greatest *coup* in his managerial capacity was his bold stroke in 1810 when he induced the great English actor George Frederick Cooke to visit America.

His first wife, formerly Miss Upton, a daughter of David Johnson, of New York, died in 1808 and by his second marriage in 1812 with the brilliant belle of the city, Miss Mary Fairlie, daughter of the celebrated wit, Major James Fairlie and granddaughter of Governor Robert Yates, Mr. Cooper became allied to some of the most eminent families of

[11] Record of the Boston Stage, by William Clapp, Jr.

the state, and his society was eagerly courted by all who made pretensions to taste or fashion. "For thirty years," says Ireland, "Mr. Cooper was the paramount favorite of the public, successfully resisting the encroachments of rivalry, even Cooke's visit leaving his professional repute unaffected, but the subsequent appearance of Kean, Booth and Macready and the discovery of his many faulty readings threw him into comparative neglect and into a line of characters in which he was ultimately superseded by younger and fresher actors."

William Warren, the father of one of America's most popular comedians, and the best actor of old men that America had yet seen, made his début November 5 as Friar Lawrence in "Romeo and Juliet." Later he married Mrs. Wignell (formerly Mrs. Merry) and became manager of the Chestnut Street Theatre, Philadelphia.

John Bernard, an excellent comedian from Covent Garden, was born in 1756, the son of a British naval officer. He was articled to an attorney, but ran away and joined a theatrical troupe, receiving as his first weekly wage eight shillings and three tallow candles. Later he married an actress and with her made his appearance at Bath as Gratiano, his wife playing Portia to Henderson's Shylock. In 1787 he was engaged for Covent Garden to play fops, fine gentlemen and the higher line of comedy. His first appearance in America was at the Greenwich Street Theatre, New York, in August, 1797, as Goldfinch in "The Road to Ruin." Later he went to Philadelphia where he stayed six years, going thence to Boston in 1803. In 1806 he went into partnership with

Powers at the Federal Street Theatre, Boston, remaining there until 1810. The next seven years he travelled in the United States and Canada, his last appearance being at Boston in 1819, after which he returned to England.

With these notable additions to his forces, Mr. Wignell looked confidently forward to the most brilliant season the American stage had yet known.

Hallam and Hodgkinson, meantime, had been enjoying a year of unprecedented prosperity in New York. It was the last season (1796) but one of the old John Street Theatre, for plans had long been maturing for the erection of a new theatre (the Park) which, in size and elegance of appointments, should eclipse the pretentious playhouses recently opened in Boston.

The season opened February 9 with Vanbrugh's " Provoked Husband," Joseph Jefferson making his New York début in the rôle of Squire Richard. On February 11, Miss Broadhurst was seen for the first time in New York as Yarico, in " Inkle and Yarico," and on the same occasion Arabella Brett, who later achieved success as a singer, made her first appearance on any stage as Narcissa. On March 30, Colman's celebrated musical play " The Mountaineers " was seen for the first time in New York, Hodgkinson appearing as Octavian.

Among other novelties presented was an opera by William Dunlap called " The Archers." The piece was favorably received, but did not have many performances. Dunlap's popularity as America's leading playwright and his great influence in theatrical circles, led Hallam and Hodgkinson at this time to make him an offer to join them as partner, the inducement held out being that he would have sole control of the plays produced, including the power to bring forward his own works. Dunlap consented and soon regretted the step, for troubles began almost immediately. Hallam, it appeared, had serious grievances against Hodgkinson whom he accused of usurping power, depriving him (Hallam) of his authority, and of misrepresenting and annoying his wife. Mrs. Hallam had an unfortunate weakness which, on more than one occasion, had resulted in her coming on the stage in a state of intoxication. The audience at first laughed and then became angry at such an insult to public decorum. The scandal grew until Hodgkinson insisted on Mrs. Hallam retiring from the company. The row went on until the following season, a riot occurred in the theatre, Hodgkinson being hissed as he tried to explain, and Mrs. Hallam receiving applause when she unexpectedly came on dressed in black and posing as a martyr. Later, she was allowed to reappear at the John Street Theatre as Lady Teazle, and she took advantage of the opportunity to apologize for her former conduct by reciting a poem so unique that it is worth reprinting here:

> These flattering plaudits cannot fail to raise
> A wish to merit such transcendent praise;
> It can but be a wish, for ah!—my heart
> Knows merit could not claim a thousandth part:
> But like the lavish hand of Heaven, you
> Give largely e'en though nothing should be due.
> O'ercome with joy, my anxious throbbing heart,
> Disdaining all the little tricks of art,
> Conceals those feelings in a grateful breast
> Which may be felt, but cannot be express'd.

Time has now swept ten rolling years away,
Since flattering plaudits graced my first essay,
Young, giddy, rash, ambitious, and untaught,
You still caress'd, excusing many a fault;
With friendly hand safe led me through the way
Where lurking error watches to betray:
And shall I such advantages forego
With my consent? I frankly answer, No:
I may through inadvertency have stray'd,
But who by folly never was betray'd?
If e'er my judgment played the foolish part,
I acted not in concert with my heart.
I boldly can defy the world to say
From my first entrée to the present day,
Whate'er my errors, numerous or few,
I never wanted gratitude to you.
On your indulgence still I'll rest my cause;
Will you support me with your kind applause?
You verify the truth of Pope's fine line—
" To err is human; to forgive, divine."

While the old American Company was playing in Boston and Newport during the summer and fall of 1797, Mr. Solee of the Charleston Theatre brought his company to the John Street Theatre, intending to stay there only two or three nights, but the engagement lasted until the middle of September. The opening bill was " The Wonder " followed by " The Spoiled Child." Giles Leonard Barrett, father of George Barrett, one of America's best light comedians, made his début on this occasion in the rôle of Don Felix. On the 30th, Mrs. Whitlock made her first New York appearance in the part of Isabella in " The Fatal Marriage."

The venture was not a paying one, chiefly owing to the presence in New York at the same time of

Wignell and Reinagle's far more brilliant company from Philadelphia.

Notwithstanding the important accessions to the company, and the famous Mrs. Merry playing all her great characters, Wignell and Reinagle had found themselves facing a deficit at the end of the Philadelphia season. This had induced them to bring their forces to New York where they had leased a theatre in Greenwich Street, then known as Rickett's Circus.

The old circus had been entirely renovated and redecorated for use as a summer theatre and Wignell expected a profitable season. But here again disappointment awaited him. There were not enough theatregoers at that time to support two theatres, and each striving against the other, both fared badly.

The Greenwich Street Theatre opened August 21, 1797, with " Venice Preserved," Thomas Abthorpe Cooper making his first appearance in New York in the rôle of Pierre, with Mrs. Merry as Belvidera.

In September, Mr. Fennell also made his first New York appearance as Zanga in " The Revenge," and made such a hit, especially with Wignell, that Mr. Cooper took umbrage, and a quarrel ensued that ended with Cooper refusing to fulfill his Philadelphia contract, and making a new one with Messrs. Hodgkinson and Dunlap for the Park.

After presenting " Bunker Hill " [12] with all its smoke and noise, Wignell finally closed his temporary establishment and withdrew to his home city.

The new Park Theatre not being quite ready,

[12] Sensational Revolutionary drama, by John Burk, first produced in Boston. See page 240.

although rapidly approaching completion, the old American Company reopened the John Street Theatre on December 11, 1797, with "Young Quaker" and "The Purse." On December 13, Mr. J. Simpson, so successful an actor of Irish parts that he became known as "Irish Simpson," made his New York début. Other débuts were those of Ellen Westray and Mr. Hogg.

On January 13, 1798, the old John Street Theatre, after a glorious career of over thirty years, saw its last performance, the closing bill being "The Comet" and "Tom Thumb."

CHAPTER X

BOSTON'S FIRST THEATRE

ALTHOUGH plays had now been acted and playhouses erected all over the country for half a century and more, it was not until the year 1792 that Boston was permitted to build its first theatre.

It will be remembered that following the attempt of two English actors in 1750 to give a performance of Otway's " Orphan " in Boston—an audacious enterprise which was followed by a small riot—the Commonwealth of Massachusetts passed a very drastic law not only forbidding play-acting, but even rendering liable to a heavy fine those who, by their mere presence, gave countenance to anything of the kind. For over forty years after the passage of this law—if we except the period when the British were in control—it was easier for a camel to pass through the proverbial needle than for play actors to find shelter in the good city of Boston.

A deep seated prejudice against play acting still prevailed throughout New England. In 1790 Hallam and Henry made a formal appeal to the Massachusetts House of Representatives asking permission

223

to open a theatre, but the application was refused and the anti-theatrical forces congratulated themselves that the profane players were disposed of for good and all. But as time went on, and reports reached Boston of the success of Hallam and his fellow actors in other American cities, a certain liberal element in the town, envying the more enlightened communities where the players were under no restrictions, began to agitate for the repeal of the theatre law.

In 1792 a company of thespians, headed by Mr. Watts, an English actor, appeared at Portsmouth, N. H., and performed "The Absent Man" and "Lethe." From Portsmouth the players went to Salem, Mass., where "The Beaux' Stratagem" and "Miss in Her Teens" were given. From Salem, Watts' players went to Dorchester and a few weeks later to Boston.

But here the players found themselves blocked. The law against acting was still in force and there was no getting round it. Finally, a group of theatre lovers formed an Association, the members of which bound themselves to subscribe funds for a building which was to be a theatre in everything but name. Ground was purchased on Broad Alley, near Hawley Street, and the building called the " New Exhibition Room." This was the first theatre in Boston. " It had," says Seilhamer, " a pit, a row of boxes forming three sides of a square, and a gallery, the theatre accommodating about five hundred persons. The structure was a temporary one, but it served its purpose before it gave way to the more pretentious theatre in Federal Street two years later."

About this time there arrived from England an

actor named Charles Stuart Powell, who later became manager of the Federal Theatre. Powell had
enjoyed some reputation as a tragedian at Covent
Garden. He made no attempt to act on first reaching
America, contenting himself by giving an entertainment advertised as "The Evening Brush, for Rub-
bing Off the Rust of Care" at the Concert Hall.

On August 10, 1792, the "Exhibition Room" was
finished and formally opened under the management
of Joseph Harper, late of the American Company,
who delivered an address. Mr. Woolls, who had
joined his old associate Harper in this enterprise,
sang. The proceedings closed with tumbling and
dancing by M. and Mme. Placide. These entertainments, consisting chiefly of ballets in which the
Placides were the feature, continued for some weeks.

Gradually the company grew in size and importance. To the names of Mr. Harper, Mr. and Mrs.
Morris, Mr. Watts and Mr. Powell were added
those of Mr. and Mrs. Solomon, Messrs. Roberts,
Adams, Jones, Redfield, Tucker, Murray, Mrs. Gray,
Miss Smith and Miss Chapman. "These," says Dunlap, "were the first professional actors who performed plays in Boston."

The players were ready but the ban against acting
was still in force. It was a trying situation and finally
Mr. Harper, his patience exhausted, began giving
entertainments, cautiously at first to see how far he
would be permitted to go.

On August 27 Mr. Roberts performed on the
slack wire; on September 18 Bickerstaff's musical
entertainment "Thomas and Sally" was given; on
September 24 Mr. Solomon sang, Mr. Watts gave

Garrick's prologue, "Drunken Sailor," and the "Citizen Outwitted" was acted by Mr. Watts and Mr. and Mrs. Solomon. Two days later, September 26, 1792, all further disguise was thrown off. Home's tragedy "Douglas" and O'Keefe's "Poor Soldier" were put boldly in the bill, and the first regular dramatic season in Boston had begun.

The performances lasted from September 26 to December 5, the plays given being the best of the American Company repertoire, including three by Shakespeare. Mr. Powell was seen as Hamlet and as Richard III. The season might have continued longer but for measures taken by the authorities.

On the night of December 5, when "The School for Scandal" was being acted, a sheriff suddenly entered the theatre and, making his way on to the stage, arrested Mr. Harper, the manager.

Until now the authorities had been inclined to wink at the violation of an unpopular law, but Governor Hancock viewed the matter differently. Holding that the players' defiance was an insult to the commonwealth, he compelled official action.

A great commotion followed Harper's arrest. Cries of "Go on! Go on!" came from the pit, and many of the spectators, furious at the interruption, and eager to show their contempt for the state law, leaped on the stage and tore down the coat of arms of the State which adorned the proscenium. But, finally, wiser counsels prevailed and the theatre was closed. The following day Harper was arraigned in court, but released on a technicality.

This was the spectacular finish of Boston's first theatrical campaign.

But while Harper's boldness had been promptly challenged by the authorities and the outcome of the adventure appeared to be a distinct triumph for the " antis," it really helped the friends of the drama, for it drew the attention of the more intelligent among the community to the manifest absurdity of the law. Another determined effort in 1793 to bring about its repeal resulted in success, and a meeting was at once called to open subscriptions for building a theatre. The number of shares was limited to one hundred and twenty at $50 a share. The site selected was at the corner of Federal and Franklin Streets where a commodious brick building was speedily erected. William Clapp gives this description of the playhouse:

The theatre in those days was considered a fine specimen of architecture and creditable to the architect, Mr. Bulfinch. It was a lofty and spacious edifice substantially built of brick, with stone facias, imposts, etc. It was one hundred and forty feet long, sixty-one feet wide, and forty feet high. The entrances to the different parts of the house were distinct, and at the time the opponents of the theatre made strong use of this fact, alleging that by affording a special door to that portion of the house usually the resort of the vile of both sexes, a premium on vice was offered. In the front there was a projecting arcade, which enabled carriages to land company under cover. The interior of the building was tastefully decorated. The stage opening was thirty-one feet wide, ornamented on each side by two columns, and between them a stage door and projecting iron balcony. Over the columns a cornice and a balustrade were carried across the opening; above was painted a flow of crimson drapery and the arms of the Union and of the State of Massachusetts blended with emblems tragic and comic. A ribbon depending from the arms bore the motto, "All the world's a stage." At the end of the building a noble and elegant dancing room was constructed, fifty-eight feet long, thirty-six wide and twenty-six high, richly ornamented with Corinthian columns and pilasters.[1]

[1] A Record of the Boston Stage. By William Clapp, Jr.

There were also spacious card and tea rooms for those who were bored by the play, and kitchens with complete equipment.

Charles Stuart Powell, who had played with Harper the previous year, was appointed manager, and early in June, 1793, he sailed for England to engage a company. Among the players he secured were Mr. and Mrs. Baker, Miss Baker, Mr. and Mrs. Collins, Mr. and Mrs. Jones, Messrs. Bartlett, Kenny Nelson and Snelling Powell, a brother of Charles Powell and who afterwards became himself one of the most successful managers Boston ever had, Mrs. Abbot and Miss Elizabeth Harrison, a Shakespearean actress and protegée of Mrs. Siddons, who afterwards became Mrs. Snelling Powell.

Under the joint management of Charles Stuart Powell and Mr. Baker, the new Federal Street Theatre, known as the Boston Theatre, was opened February 3, 1794, with Brooke's drama " Gustavus Vasa," followed by O'Keefe's farce " Modern Antiques," the season lasting until the following July. The repertoire included the best of the classics and contemporary drama, five Shakespearean plays, " Hamlet," " Romeo and Juliet," " Richard III," " Twelfth Night," " The Merchant of Venice " and six new pieces which neither New York nor Philadelphia had yet seen. These were Mrs. Inchbald's " Midnight Hour," Cumberland's comedy, " The Natural Son," " Barnaby Brittle," Oulton's " All in Good Humour," O'Keefe's " Son in Law," and Mrs. Inchbald's " Animal Magnetism," a piece ridiculing hypnotism which was then first beginning to be talked about.

Now that the Bostonians had a theatre they determined that it should be conducted in such a manner as to set a model for the rest of the country. "A master of ceremonies," says Dunlap, "was appointed whose business it was to see that those who had taken seats should be accommodated according to contract, to direct the manner of taking up and putting down those who came to the door in coaches—and other matters of equal importance, besides suppressing ' all kinds of disorder and indecorum.' The trustees reserved to themselves the power of dismissing any performer from the stage or orchestra for misconduct —a power to be exercised in the form of a request to the manager."

The theatre was well patronized, entertainments being given three evenings each week, and in order to conciliate the more rigid inhabitants it was announced that on no account would the evenings fall upon those devoted to religious services. The custom was then introduced, which prevailed for many years, of allowing the audience to call upon the orchestra for such pieces of music as suited the popular taste. The practice was not a wise one for it often led to disturbances.

Owing to the rowdyism prevalent in those days in nearly all American theatres, the situation of the musicians was not an enviable one. " As early as the 20th of February," says Seilhamer, " the musicians printed a card in the newspapers begging the thoughtless or ill disposed not to throw apples, stones or other missiles into the orchestra. While the brutality toward the orchestra indicated by this appeal was not confined to Boston, but was equally characteristic of

New York and Philadelphia, the Boston gallery audience was the only one in the country at the time that assaulted the musicians merely for the sake of assaulting them. This reprehensible conduct emanated from a class that has entirely passed away—a class that Mrs. John Adams was perhaps justified in calling the ' mobility.' " [1]

After being closed for the hot months, the second season of the Boston theatre began on December 15, 1794, with Shakespeare's " As You Like It." Baker, meantime, as the result of a quarrel, had left the company together with his wife, leaving Powell in sole control. Soon after, Powell visited England again and added several new artists to his company forces. These included Messrs. Hipworth, Taylor, Villiers, Kenny, Mr. and Mrs. Hellyer (afterwards Mrs. Graupner). Both Mr. Taylor and Mr. Hipworth gained celebrity in Boston, the first for his impersonation of Octavian in the " Mountaineers," the latter in the part of Sheva.

An event of the second season was the production on March 2 of a new American comedy entitled " The Medium," the authorship of which was anonymous, but which Seilhamer thinks may be attributed to Royall Tyler. The piece was not a success and was acted only once. Two other novelties, the younger Colman's " Mountaineers " produced April 6, and Mrs. Inchbald's " Wedding Day " produced June 10, proved great successes and remained conspicuous features of the repertoire of every theatre in the country for many years.

At the end of the first two years the trustees were

---

[1] History of the American Theatre, by George O. Seilhamer.

not entirely satisfied. Powell had shown good taste and excellent judgment in the selection of plays, but owing largely to the competition of Henry and Wignell, he had not succeeded in recruiting a very brilliant company. He had also quarreled with Mr. Baker, resulting in the loss of that actor-manager, and there were other grounds of dissatisfaction. At the end of the second season, Powell found himself bankrupt and he was politely asked to retire from the management which he did rather ungraciously, only to return to Boston a year later and take his revenge for fancied injuries by opening a rival house.

The successful introduction of theatricals in Boston could not fail to whet the dramatic appetite of the rest of New England, and many communities which had been bitterly opposed to the players now began to view the matter in a more sensible light. After his arrest in Boston in 1792, Harper went with his players to Rhode Island, where at Providence[3] he succeeded in obtaining the use of the Court House for a theatre, on the condition that the proceeds of every fifth night should be paid into the city treasury. The Court House was crowded at every performance, the plays being disguised, as on previous occasions, as "moral lectures." In 1793, the prohibitionary law was repealed, and in the spring of that same year Alexander Placide, the dancer, went to Newport, and, purchasing a large brick building previously used as a market, turned it into a theatre. This house remained the Newport Theatre for half a century.

The Harper Rhode Island Company at this time

[3] History of the Providence Stage, by Charles Blake.

included the following players: Mme. Placide, Miss Smith (afterward Mrs. Harper), Mrs. Mechler (née Storer), Messrs. Watts, Adams, Kenny, Mr. and Mrs. Moore, Mr. and Mrs. Douvillier, Mr. Trouche, Mr. Spinacuta and Mr. Mallet, Mr. Minchin, Mr. Huggins, Miss Brewer, Mr. Kenna and Mr. and Mrs. Solomon, Mr. Redfield and Mr. Prigmore.

The first Newport season began July 3 with Moore's popular drama " The Gamester " and lasted until October 8. The following year the company divided its time between Newport and Providence.

In the autumn of 1794, a temporary theatre was erected in Providence in the rear of a building known as the old Coffee House, the season opening December 30 with Moore's " Foundling " and closing April 13, 1795, with " The Beggar's Opera."

Unable to do anything in Newport that summer owing to the presence of a rival company made up of the disbanded forces of the Boston Theatre, Harper withdrew to Providence to await the opening of his new theatre, in which performances were to be given by part of the old American players in conjunction with his own company. The new house opened September 3 with " A Child of Nature " and " Rosina," and closed with a benefit for Mr. and Mrs. Hallam. When this season ended, Harper went to Boston and joined the Boston Theatre Company.

The raising of the legal ban tempted many players to invade New England's virgin dramatic soil, and a band of players, most of whom were formerly with the old American Company, appeared in July, 1794, at Hartford, then a mere village. Headed by Mr.

Martin, the actors included Mrs. Martin, Mr. and Mrs. King, Mr. and Mrs. Ashton, Messrs. Ryan, Bissett and Bergman, Miss Chaucer and Mrs. Wilson. The repertoire included most of the popular plays of the day, the season lasting until the 12th of September.

Charles Stuart Powell had been succeeded in the management of the Boston Theatre by Colonel John S. Tyler "master of ceremonies." The new manager re-engaged part of the Powell company, including Mr. and Mrs. Snelling Powell, Messrs. Taylor, Villiers, Kenny, and Mr. and Mrs. Hughes. He also arranged with Hallam and Hodgkinson for a brief engagement of the Old American Company, the two contingents which had appeared at Providence and Hartford being united. Mr. and Mrs. Harper were with this united organization which was still further strengthened by the engagement of Joseph Jefferson, grandfather of America's famous Rip Van Winkle, who had been engaged in England by Powell, but arrived after that manager's retirement. Other acquisitions were Mr. and Mrs. Johnson, Mr. and Mrs. Tyler and Mrs. Brett. This company opened the Boston Theatre November 2, 1795, the season lasting until January 20, 1796, when the New York players withdrew to reopen the John Street Theatre.

Mr. Jefferson (1774–1832), the second of that well known theatrical family, did not make his first appearance before an American audience until December 16, 1795, when he was seen as La Gloire in the younger Colman's " Surrender of Calais." He was the son of Thomas Jefferson (1728–1807), an actor for many years with Garrick at Drury Lane and afterward manager of a theatre at Plymouth. Joseph Jefferson received a good education and served his theatrical apprenticeship acting small parts on his father's stage. The elder Jefferson's second marriage resulted in an estrangement between father and son, and Joseph, who had followed with the keenest interest the revolutions in America and France, determined to leave England and make a home for himself in the new world. Dunlap says that Powell invited him to go to Boston, offering him his passage money and seventeen dollars a week. Powell having failed in the meantime, Jefferson engaged with Hallam and Hodgkinson. " He was only a youth" adds Dunlap, " but even then an artist. Of a small and slight figure, well formed, with a singular physiognomy, a nose perfectly Grecian, and blue eyes full of laughter, he had the faculty of exciting mirth to as great a degree by power of feature, although handsome, as any ugly featured low comedian ever seen."

At the Boston Theatre he at once won favor in old men roles. He also made himself generally useful, playing on occasion one of the witches in " Macbeth " and even helping to paint the scenery. Whatever skill he possessed with the brush was developed to a far greater degree by his distinguished grandson Joseph Jefferson III, who, as is well known, was a painter of no mean ability.

An amusing anecdote is told of his success in old men rôles. A kind hearted lady had watched him one evening bent over and tottering about on the stage, and she determined to help remove such an old person from the boards by raising a subscription so that his last days might be spent in comparative comfort. She went to the theatre the next morning to consult with the management about her plan, being thoroughly convinced that the actor was infirm and prompted by a charitable impulse to do good. She even carried with her a list of well known names which she had procured as probable subscribers with her own at the head. But Jefferson himself, lively and full of the buoyancy of youth, happened to pass at that moment. He was stopped and introduced to his would-be benefactress, who, astounded and confused, beat a hasty retreat.

By his wife, Miss Euphemia Fortune, of New York, whom he married in 1800, Joseph Jefferson I had a large family. His daughter Elizabeth was a great favorite at the Park Theatre during the season of 1834-5. His daughter Jane and his sons John and Thomas all died in their youth. His son Joseph Jefferson II, who married Mrs. Burke the singer, became a very excellent actor in " old men " and died in Mobile in 1842, also leaving a son of the same name. This was Joseph Jefferson III, the most famous member of the family, of whom we shall have something to say later.

About the time that Boston was first being introduced to the drama—1794 to 1796—there was considerable theatrical activity in Charleston, S. C. Since the early days of the old Dock Street Theatre, two new theatres had been built in that city—the Charleston Theatre, erected by Bignall and West in 1792, and the Church Street Theatre or Harmony Hall, built for Godwin in 1786, and now opened and managed by Mr. Solee, a Frenchman. In 1794, the latter house, called temporarily the French Theatre, was occupied by the Placide troupe, the performances being confined to pantomime, dancing and tumbling. In the summer of 1795, when the Boston Theatre company disbanded, Mr. Solee engaged the players to go to Charleston where a season began on November 10 at the Church Street Theatre, now renamed the City Theatre. The season lasted until May 3, 1796, among the artists who delighted Charleston at this time being Mrs. Watts, Messrs. Hipworth, Bartlett and Heely, Mr. and Mrs. Jones, Mr. Chalmers, Mrs. and Mrs. Collins and Mrs. Pownall[4] and her two daughters.

Two distinguished English players arrived in America in 1796 under engagement for the Boston Theatre—John Brown Williamson, long a favorite at the London Haymarket, and his wife, a popular soubrette known on the stage as Miss Fontenelle. Mr. Williamson made his début January 25, 1796, as Othello, his wife appearing as " Little Pickle " in Bickerstaff's " Spoiled Child." The critics were loud in their praise of both performers, Thomas Paine,[5] America's first professional dramatic critic, declaring Mrs. Williamson's Little Pickle to be " the

---

[4] This distinguished actress died in Charleston during this engagement under tragic circumstances. Her daughter, Caroline Wrighten, eloped with Alexander Placide and later became a distinguished actress on the Southern stage and the mother of the celebrated Placide family of actors. Mrs. Pownall is said to have been so shocked at the elopement that she died of a broken heart when only in her fortieth year.

[5] Thomas Paine was a son of Robert Treat Paine, one of the signers of the Declaration of Independence. He received a classical education and won the gold medal offered for the best prologue to be recited at the opening of the Boston Theatre, February 3, 1794. Later he married Miss Baker, an actress, and started the publication of a theatrical journal which he called *The Orrery*. "He was," remarks Seilhamer, "the first American journalist to go to the devil allured by the limelight of the stage." He died in 1812.

most astonishing and brilliant display of theatrical genius ever exhibited in America."

On April 15, Miss Arnold, afterwards Mrs. Poe, mother of the unhappy American poet, Edgar Allan Poe, was seen on the stage for the first time when she sang the *Market Lass* between the second and third acts of " Mysteries of the Castle." Her first New York appearance was with Solee's company in " The Spoiled Child " at the John Street Theatre, August 18, 1797. She was a young and beautiful woman and a very pleasing comedienne and songstress, and, in 1809, became attached to the Park Theatre.

At the end of the third season, May 16, 1796, Mr. Williamson was announced as succeeding Colonel Tyler in the management of the Boston Theatre. Charles Stuart Powell, meantime, took advantage of the political excitement of the hour to get back into management. In the closing years of the Eighteenth Century, political feeling ran very high between the Federal and Jacobin parties and this public excitement naturally found its echo in the theatres. The trustees of the Federalist Boston Theatre encouraged the manager to present pieces tending to provoke the anger of their political opponents. It was customary for the actors, who were all immigrants from the English stage, to interpolate jests and witticisms at the expense of the French who were then at war with England, and these often gave offence and sometimes created serious disturbances in the house. The character of Bagatelle in " Poor Soldier," for example, became so offensive to the Jacobin party that it was cut out of the opera by Williamson's order. Taking advantage of the situation, Powell, in the spring of 1796, started the project of building a new theatre in Boston. Subscription lists were opened and quickly filled. The capital was placed at $12,000—two hundred shares of stock at $60 per share—each share of stock carrying with it free admission. Powell was given a lease for fourteen years at an annual rental of $1200. "Such was the prevailing taste for theatricals," Dunlap tells us, "that men of capital were willing to invest their money to almost any amount in the erection of theatres, and mechanics did not hesitate to take shares in payment for their labor."

Work on the new house progressed rapidly and by the end of the year the Haymarket Theatre, an immense wooden edifice near the corner of Tremont and Boylston Street, that overtopped every other building in Boston, was completed.

The new playhouse was opened December 26, 1796, with Mrs. Cowley's popular comedy "The Belle's Stratagem" and the ballet pantomime "Mirza and Lindor," performances being given every alternate night until the 14th of June following. The company included some new players imported by Powell from England, among them Mr. Williamson, a Covent Garden singer, Giles Leonard and Mrs. Barrett, parents of George H. Barrett, Mr. and Mrs. Simpson, the Misses Westray, and old members of the Boston Theatre company, Mr. and Mrs. Hughes, Mr. Taylor, Mrs. Pick and J. H. Dickson.

Mr. Dickson, who played Saville in "The Belle's Stratagem" on the opening night, later became very prominent in Boston as a successful actor, manager and merchant. He was born in London in 1774 and at the age of twenty-one came to America. He was educated for mercantile pursuits, to which training is attributed his later success as manager. In 1796 he was engaged by Charles S. Powell to play small rôles at the Haymarket. He gave at that time but little promise of the possession of histrionic talents, but he was attentive to business, and his study being remarkably rapid, he was highly valuable to the management. When the Federal Street Theatre was rebuilt in 1798, Dickson, under Hodgkinson, became attached to it in capacity of prompter and deputy manager. During the season of 1802 and 1803 he appeared as Sir Anthony Absolute and for years he was sole impersonator of this character on the Boston boards. In 1806 he became joint lessee of the Boston Theatre with Snelling Powell and John Bernard, under whose auspices the theatre did most flourishing business. As manager, he visited England during the summer vacation to engage talent and brought over some of the most popular favorites of the day. With Thomas Abthorpe Cooper he was instrumental in inducing George Frederick Cooke to visit America. After Bernard's retirement, the firm was Powell and Dickson and, after the death of Powell in 1821, he was connected with Mrs. Powell and Kilner. His last appearance on any stage was on the 14th of May, 1821. That the esteem in which he was held as a man, as well as his ability as actor and manager, did much to elevate the theatre of his day cannot be questioned. William Clapp says of him:

When Mr. Dickson first came into the management there was existing a bitter feeling against theatres and theatrical representations. The hostility was not confined to the ignorant; but many families were so deeply imbued with puritanical ideas, that they never ventured beneath the roof of a playhouse. To conciliate this class required not only good judgment, but a personal example; and in a very few years those who had been bitter opponents became warm friends, when they perceived that men of industry and character were engaged in the management. The esteem in which Mr. Dickson was held contributed materially to the establishment of the drama on a firm foundation, not only in this city, but in Providence, Newport, Portsmouth, etc.[6]

An event of the Haymarket's first season was the production of a Revolutionary drama, "The Battle of Bunker Hill," written by John Burk, the Irish editor.[7] Anti-British throughout, the piece was full of false heroics, redfire and the crudest melodramatic situations. It had no literary or dramatic merit, and yet proved such a popular success that it ran for nine consecutive nights, an extraordinary occurrence in those days. Another patriotic piece, "West Point Preserved," by William Brown, an American poet, was almost equally successful, having a run of eight nights. But in spite of his having pleased the popular taste, the end of the season did not show a profit, and Powell, discouraged, surrendered his lease, the company being disbanded. Immediately afterward, the house passed to Mr. Hodgkinson, who used it as a summer theatre until it was finally abandoned.

John Bernard, in his reminiscences, speaks of the surprise that awaited him when he first saw the Boston Theatre. He says:

Boston had another surprise for me—an additional claim to my respect and good wishes—she was possessed of two theatres, and if

[6] A Record of the Boston Stage, by William W. Clapp.
[7] John Burk edited a New York political sheet called *The Time Piece*. He also wrote a History of Virginia. In 1778 he was arrested for libel and two years later was reported to have been killed in a duel.

one be some measure of a people's refinement, there must be much force in two, even if its not geometrical. The superior was in Federal Street, being the first that was regularly opened in Boston; and the second in the Haymarket, a large wooden building at the southern end of the Mall. Both were commodious and well-arranged houses, but the former was not only of the most desirable size (built to contain about three hundred), but displayed a taste and completeness that were worthy of London. At the time of my arrival an arrangement had been completed by which they were respectively to be opened in winter and summer (the Haymarket during the latter, by a pleasant coincidence) under the direction of Hodgkinson and a Monsieur Solee, and as the latter gentleman was also the manager at Charlestown, it was further proposed that the companies of the two cities should be annually exchanged, a plan that could not have proved more agreeable to the public than to the health of the actors after a southern campaign. Upon this scheme of action the summer house had just opened, and within it I met many London acquaintances.[8]

After closing its season June 5, 1797, the Federal Street theatre began a new season December 6 of that same year, the company including Mr. and Mrs. Bates, Mr. and Mrs. Baker, Mr. and Mrs. Barrett, Mr. and Mrs. Harper, Mr. and Mrs. C. Powell and Mr. and Mrs. Snelling Powell. On January 22, 1798, Messrs. Barrett and Harper assumed the management, opening with " The Roman Father."

During the afternoon of February 2 the theatre caught fire and was burnt to the ground, the first disaster of the kind in the United States on record.[9]

[8] Early Days of the American Stage, by John Bernard.

[9] Other early American theatres destroyed by fire were Rickett's Circus, Philadelphia, burnt down in 1799; Richmond, Va., Theatre, burnt in 1811 during a performance, when seventy persons lost their lives, resulting in the enactment of a law prohibiting all amusements for four months; Chestnut Street Theatre, Philadelphia, burnt in 1820; Park Theatre, New York, burnt first in 1820 and again in 1848; Theatre at Natchez, Miss., burnt in 1822; Bowery Theatre, New York, burnt down in 1828, 1836, 1838 and again in 1845. The worst fires in American theatres on record from the viewpoint of the number of victims, were the Brooklyn Theatre fire, December 5, 1876, during a per-

16

William Clapp, Jr., gives this account of the occurrence:

On the afternoon of the 2d of February, 1798, the porter built the fires as usual, and left wood under the stove to dry, which probably ignited; for a few hours afterwards fire broke out in that portion, and the building fell a prey to the destructive flames. Nothing of consequence was saved, though in the attempt to rescue a portion of his wardrobe, Mr. Barrett was seriously injured by the falling of a door.[10]

This left Boston temporarily with only one theatre, the Haymarket, and Mr. Hodgkinson, already discouraged with the outlook in New York, began negotiations with a view to establishing himself permanently in Boston.

In July, 1798, Mr. Hodgkinson reopened the Haymarket, and on the 27th Thomas Abthorpe Cooper made his first appearance in Boston as Hamlet, Mrs. Hodgkinson playing Ophelia. The engagement, however, had occurred at an unfortunate time. Owing to the yellow fever scare, the attendance on the second night was so slim that Hodgkinson had to dismiss the audience. For the rest of that summer Bostonians had no theatrical diversions, but during the enforced vacation the Federal Street house was rebuilt and in October Mr. Hodgkinson reopened with "Wives as They Were and Maids as They Are," the company including Whitlock, Chalmers, Simpson, Williamson, Villiers, Kenny, Mrs. Hodgkinson, Mrs. King and Snelling Powell. That same month Hodgkinson reopened the Haymarket, but the

formance of "The Two Orphans," in which 295 persons perished, and the Iroquois Theatre, Chicago, fire on December 30, 1903, when 587 persons were burnt to death. Since the introduction of electricity in our theatres and the strict enforcement of the fire laws danger from fire has been reduced to a minimum.

[10] A Record of the Boston Stage. By William Clapp, Jr.

receipts were so discouraging that he decided to give up management altogether and return to the Park Theatre, New York, in the more lucrative rôle of actor.

Giles L. Barrett was the next manager of the Federal Street house, the season opening October 14, 1799, with " Laugh When You Can, Be Happy When You May." In the summer of 1800, Mr. Whitlock took a lease of the theatre, but he was no more successful than his predecessors. It was not until Snelling Powell secured control of the Federal Street Theatre in 1802 that the tide turned. He was the first successful manager of a theatre in Boston. " He adopted," says William Clapp, Jr., " a straightforward policy and honorably kept his engagements, and, by offering to the public entertainments worthy of patronage, conjured back into the boxes the long absent taste and beauty of Boston."

CHAPTER XI

THE FIRST PARK THEATRE

DESCRIPTION OF THIS CELEBRATED AMERICAN PLAYHOUSE. OPEN-
ING BILL. DUNLAP'S "ANDRÉ" PRODUCED. WILLIAM B. WOOD
MAKES HIS DÉBUT IN PHILADELPHIA. SALARIES AT THE PARK.
TRIALS OF AN IMPRESARIO. SUCCESSFUL PRODUCTION OF "THE
STRANGER." THE KOTZEBUE CRAZE. DEATH OF PRESIDENT
WASHINGTON CLOSES ALL THE THEATRES. EX-COOK BECOMES A
NEW YORK THEATRE MANAGER. BALLET DANCERS SCANDALIZE
THE QUAKER CITY. DEATH OF JOHN HODGKINSON. DUNLAP
GIVES UP A LOSING FIGHT. DÉBUT OF JOHN HOWARD PAYNE.

THE foregoing chapters have covered what may
be termed the first period in the history of the American theatre—the period of experiment. We have
seen the drama introduced in this country by strolling
players from the British West Indies and later well-
equipped companies sent out from England. We
have seen how plays were acted and theatres built
first in Virginia, then in New York, Charleston,
Philadelphia, Annapolis, Baltimore, Boston and
Newport, until gradually the drama came to be
accepted everywhere as a social institution only third
in importance to the school and the church. We
have described these timid beginnings, the extraordinary difficulties which such courageous pioneers as
Hallam and Douglass had to overcome before their
art was even permitted a hearing. We have seen
Puritanical intolerance and prejudice gradually give
place to a realization that the theatre, at its best, is
not a place of frivolous amusement, but a potent educational force in the community. This the more lib-

eral minded among our forefathers understood, the light was soon allowed to prevail, vexatious legal restrictions were removed one by one, theatregoing soon became fashionable, the playhouses prospered and multiplied.

With the opening in 1798 of the Park Theatre, the most celebrated of the early American theatres, on the boards of which trod for half a century the famous actors of the most brilliant era of our theatrical history, the experimental period ends, and the modern history of the American stage may be said to commence. The American theatre was no longer a mere outpost of the London stage. If it still looked to the land of Shakespeare for most of its plays and players, the day was fast approaching when American genius would produce a Forrest, a Cushman, a Jefferson and an Edwin Booth.

On June 24, 1797, an agreement was signed by which William Dunlap and John Hodgkinson became joint lessees of the new Park Theatre. Hallam was given one-fourth of the profits and the managers agreed to engage him and his wife as members of the company.

After numerous delays, and although still in an unfinished condition, the much heralded Park Theatre, the corner stone of which had been laid three years previous, was thrown open to the public on January 29, 1798. The bill was as follows:

NEW THEATRE
The public is respectfully informed that the New Theatre
will open this evening,
Monday, January 29, 1798,
with an Occasional Address, to be delivered by
MR. HODGKINSON,

and a prelude written by Mr. Milne, called
" All in a Bustle, or The New House."
The characters by the company.
After which will be presented Shakespeare's comedy of

" As You Like It."

Jacques	Mr. Hodgkinson	Le Beau	Mr. Hallam, Jr.
Touchstone	Mr. Hallam	Corin	Mr. Simpson
Orlando	Mr. Martin	William	Mr. Jefferson
Banished Duke	Mr. Tyler	Sylvius	Mr. Miller
Usurping Duke	Mr. Fawcett	Jacques de Bois	Mr. Seymour
Adam	Mr. Johnson	Rosalind	Mrs. Johnson
Amiens	Mr. Prigmore	Celia	Miss Broadhurst
Oliver	Mr. Hogg	Phoebe	Mrs. Collins
Charles	Mr. Lee	Audrey	Mrs. Bennett

To which will be added a musical entertainment called

" The Purse, or American Tar."

Will Steady	Mr. Hodgkinson	Page	Mast. Stockwell
Edmund	Mr. Tyler	Sally	Mrs. Hodgkinson

There was so much curiosity to see the new theatre that a mob besieged the doors. "The crush was so great," says Dunlap, "that many persons entered without paying until Mr. Cooper, seeing the confusion, took the place of one of the door keepers and helped restore order."

The nights of performance were Monday, Wednesday, Friday and Saturday, and the prices of admission: Boxes, $2; Pit, $1.50; Gallery, $1. The doors were open at five o'clock and the curtain rose at a quarter past six. According to a notice in the house bill, the custom of sending servants early to keep boxes for their masters was still in vogue. The company, at the beginning of the career of this historic house, comprised the following players:

THE FIRST PARK THEATRE

Messrs. Hallam, Hodgkinson, Tyler, Johnson, Jefferson, Martin, Simpson, Chalmers, Williamson, Fawcett, Prigmore, Hallam, Jr., Miller, Seymour, Lee, Leonard, Master Stockwell, Mesdames Johnson, Melmoth, Hodgkinson, Hallam, Brett, Simpson, Seymour, Tyler, and Collins, and Misses J. Westray, E. Westray, Broadhurst, Brett, Harding, and Hogg. Mr. Hodgkinson was stage manager; Mr. Dunlap, treasurer; Messrs. Ciceri and Audin, scene painters, and Mr. Hewitt, leader of the orchestra.

The New Theatre, as it was at first called, was situated in Park Row, about 200 feet east of Ann Street. It had a frontage of 80 feet and a depth of 165 feet. Constructed of stone, the building was three stories high, with six steps leading from the street up to the box entrance. " It was," says Ireland, " one of the most substantial buildings ever erected in New York, and though externally devoid of architectural pretension, was in its interior harmoniously proportioned and admirably well adapted for the purposes of light and sound. The plans for its construction were originally furnished by Marc Isambard Brunel, the celebrated French engineer and the builder of the Thames Tunnel (London), who, during the stormy days of the French Revolution, was an exile in America."

The centre of the façade was ornamented by a statue of Shakespeare. The lobby was spacious and carpeted and in cold weather two blazing fires were kept up at either end. There were three tiers of boxes, a gallery and a pit, the general color scheme being light pink and gold. Cushioned seats took the place of chairs in both boxes and pit. The stage was well equipped and provided with excellent scenery.

The first night's receipts at the new theatre were $1232. The next night they were only $513 and on the third night they sank as low as $265. This was not a very encouraging beginning and Mr. Hodgkinson was the first to become uneasy.

On February 5 Mrs. Melmoth made her first appearance as Queen Elizabeth in " The Earl of Essex." The following week she was seen as Margaret of Anjou in " The Earl of Warwick."

Meantime, Wignell had been vainly trying to hold Cooper to his contract. Undeterred by threats or even by actual arrest, the actor refused to go to Philadelphia, and finally it was arranged by the managers of the New York theatre that the monetary penalty exacted by Wignell should be paid, the amount to be raised by a special performance of " Hamlet," which took place February 28, Mr. Cooper appearing in the title rôle for the first time in New York. The forfeit was paid and the actor was now free to join the New York company.

Following his début as Hamlet, Cooper was next seen as King John. Later, he appeared as Romeo.

On March 30, Dunlap's tragedy " André," one of the author-manager's most ambitious efforts, was seen for the first time. Hodgkinson appeared in the title rôle, Cooper taking the part of Bland, the young American officer who intercedes with Washington for the life of the spy. The play was not a success, although Brander Matthews has written of it: " ' André ' is a better piece of work than most of the plays even of higher pretensions, which were produced in Great Britain and the United States toward the end of the last century."

On June 11 Hodgkinson appeared as Tamerlane for the benefit of Messrs. Hallam, Jr., and Martin.

He was not seen again in New York that season. Sometime before this, Hodgkinson and Dunlap had come to an understanding by which the former was to retire from the management, leaving Dunlap in sole control, and on June 29 the season closed and Hodgkinson and part of the company went to Boston, opening at the Haymarket. The Federal Street theatre was then being rebuilt, and Hodgkinson was to occupy that house during the winter and the Haymarket during the warm months.

That same summer, the Wignell and Reinagle company played engagements at Annapolis and Baltimore. At the former city, on June 26, William B. Wood, a comedian who afterwards became a conspicuous figure in the stage history of Philadelphia, made his début in the rôle of George Barnwell.

William B. Wood, whose father was a New York goldsmith, was born in Montreal in 1779. He began life as a clerk, developed extravagant habits in addition to ill health, and was imprisoned for debt. On his release, the young man saw no other career open except that of the stage, and he applied to Wignell, a friend of his father, then at Annapolis, for a position. The début as George Barnwell followed, but it was not a success, and in other tragic rôles the young man made no better impression. His health still failing, he left the stage and went to the West Indies, only to return eight months later and make a decided hit as Dick Dowlas in " The Heir at Law," a comedy part and a line of business entirely different to anything he had yet essayed. From now on, Mr. Wood devoted his attention to genteel comedy and his reputation steadily grew. Not only as an actor, but as a business man he soon commanded attention, and Wignell, recognizing his executive ability, made him treasurer of the Chestnut Street Theatre. When Wignell died in 1803 and Warren undertook the management, young Wood became assistant manager and in this capacity went to England in search of new players. This naturally brought him in contact with the most brilliant men and women of the day, and from that time on his rise in the managerial field was rapid. On his return from England he married Miss Juliana Westray, the actress, and a few years later joined Warren in the joint management of the Chestnut Street house.

Dunlap, meantime, was busy reorganizing the Park Theatre company. Mr. Cooper, Mr. Jefferson, Mrs. Melmoth and Miss Westray had remained faithful to him. To these he added Mr. and Mrs. Hallam, Mrs. Oldmixon, Mr. and Mrs. Simpson, Mr. and Mrs. G. Barrett, from the Boston Theatre, and Mr. Bates, the comedian.

It is interesting to compare the weekly salaries paid at this period with those which artists of the same rank would receive to-day. According to figures furnished by the manager himself, Mr. and Mrs. Hallam were paid $25 each; Mr. Cooper, $25; Mrs. Oldmixon, $37; Mr. Jefferson, $23; Mrs. Melmoth, $20. Corresponding salaries to-day (1919) would be: Mr. Hallam, $600; Mr. Cooper, $600; Mrs. Oldmixon, $500; Mr. Jefferson, $300; Mrs. Melmoth, $200.

That Dunlap fully realized the heavy responsibilities he had assumed in taking over the sole directorship may be inferred from his own remarks:

THE FIRST PARK THEATRE

That the reader may decide how far the person who in 1798 assumed the direction of that powerful and complicated engine, the theatre of a great metropolis, was fitted for the delicate task and great responsibility, it is necessary that a brief retrospect of his past life should be taken. The opinion of the writer is (an opinion perhaps founded upon the result of the experiment) that he was not fitted for the arduous task. Had it been his lot to direct a theatre patronized by an enlightened government, having no care but that of selecting such dramas and such performers as would best promote the great end of human happiness, he might perhaps have been entitled to the grateful remembrance of his fellow-men; but he was now, after a trial of management in conjunction with another person, forced by previous circumstances to burthen himself with a hazardous speculation, which, as far as it had been proved, was unsuccessful; and the power he once possessed of meeting temporary losses and providing the means of success had been lamentably diminished. Instead of having an unembarrassed mind, whose entire powers could be directed to that which should be the object of such an institution, he was tempted to seek resources for the supply of the treasury and the fulfillment of his moneyed engagements. Instead of studying to gain the approbation of the wise, pressing necessities turned his thoughts to the common methods of attracting the vulgar.[1]

The foregoing, no doubt, was intended as a sort of apologetic explanation of the painful necessity the manager was under, at that time, of presenting the Kotzebue plays and other melodramas calculated to attract the crowd, rather than dramatic fare of a higher quality.

"The School for Scandal" and "High Life Below Stairs" was the opening bill of the 1798–1799 season which began December 3 under the most inauspicious circumstances. The dreaded yellow fever had broken out again with unprecedented violence in the early fall, no fewer than 2086 deaths occurring

[1] History of the American Theatre, by William Dunlap.

in New York alone, out of a population of only 50,000. The epidemic terrorized the stoutest hearted. New York was a city of mourning. Most of the population had fled the pestilence, and those who remained were little disposed either to seek amusement or incur expense.

The outlook for the new management was unpromising enough when the successful production on December 10 of "The Stranger," the first Kotzebue drama to be produced in the New World, with Cooper in the title rôle, gave promise of more substantial receipts.

This success marked the beginning of the extraordinary Kotzebue craze which made the German dramas the most popular plays on our boards for a number of years. To-day such pieces as "The Stranger," "Pizarro," "The Virgin of the Sun," "Lovers' Vows," etc., are entirely forgotten, but at the beginning of the Nineteenth Century, they outrivalled the plays of any other author in their bid for popularity.

August Friedrich Ferdinand von Kotzebue, the most popular German dramatist of the Eighteenth Century, and called by some the German Shakespeare, was the author of over two hundred plays. Born in Weimar in 1761, he studied for the bar, but his natural bent was toward the theatre, and in 1783 he began writing the numerous plays that made him famous. In 1798 he accepted the office of dramatist to the court theatre of Vienna. Owing to his reactionary political writings he made many enemies, and in 1819 a student revolutionist called at his house and stabbed him to death.

His fame as a dramatist was not confined to Germany. England soon caught the Kotzebue fever and Sheridan, eager to try anything that promised to prop up the failing fortunes of Drury Lane, produced "The Stranger" in 1798. Of it the London *Times* declared: "Its beauties are not of an age but of all time." "Pizarro" was even more successful. For ten years it remained one of the most popular plays on the English boards. "The chief reasons for Kotzebue's meteoric rise," says Oral Sumner Coad, " are: First, Kotzebue was extremely skilful in producing superficial effectiveness and showy characters; while, except for Schiller, there was no other German playwright at this time capable of making a popular appeal. Second, by presenting the aristocrat as vicious, the common man as the embodiment of virtue, he caught the favor of the growing spirit of democracy which had been fostered by the French Revolution. Third, he hit the taste of the time by constant use of sentimentality." [2]

So favorable was "The Stranger's" reception here, that Dunlap determined to get better acquainted with the German language so he might be able to secure more of the same material. Kotzebue proved, indeed, the manager's salvation at this time. Other pieces, hastily adapted from the same source, likewise proved highly popular and helped ward off an impending deficit.

A picture of the audiences at the Park Theatre about this period is given by Washington Irving:

I observed that every part of the house has its different department. The good folks of the gallery have all the trouble of order-

---

[2] William Dunlap—a Study, by Oral Sumner Coad.

ing the music (their directions, however, are not more frequently followed than they deserve). The mode by which they issue their mandates is stamping, hissing, roaring, whistling, and when the musicians are refractory, groaning in cadence They also have the privilege of demanding a bow from John (by which name they designate every servant at the theatre who enters to move a table or snuff a candle), and of detecting those cunning dogs who peep from behind the curtain.

"My friend," said I (to the countryman, who complained of candle-grease falling on his coat), "we must put up with a few trifling inconveniences when in the pursuit of pleasure." "True," said he, "but I think I pay pretty dear for it—first to give six shillings at the door, and then to have my head battered with rotten apples, and my coat spoiled with candle-grease; by and by I shall have my other clothes dirtied by sitting down, as I perceive everybody mounted on the benches. I wonder if they could not see as well if they were all to stand upon the floor."

Here I could no longer defend our customs, for I could scarcely breathe while thus surrounded by a host of strapping fellows standing with their dirty boots on the seats of the benches. The little Frenchman who thus found a temporary shelter from the massive compliments of his gallery friends, was the only person benefited. At last the bell again rung, and the cry of "Down, down—hats off," was the signal for the commencement of the play.[3]

In January of the following year, Mr Cooper was seen as Macbeth, a rôle in which he had been already applauded in Philadelphia, but apparently the New Yorkers of that day had little taste for Shakespeare, for, according to Dunlap's testimony, Kotzebue's drama, "The Stranger," was "still the support of the theatre."

On February 11 a new comedy by Dunlap entitled "The Natural Daughter" was produced without much success. On February 24 Ben Jonson's comedy "Every Man in His Humour" was seen for the first

[3] Washington Irving's communications to his brother's paper, the *Morning Chronicle*, published under the pseudonym "Jonathan Oldstyle."

time in New York. On March 11 another Kotzebue play " Lovers' Vows " also proved very successful, and in April Dunlap staged the same author's " Count Benjowski," with the same gratifying results. On May 6 Schiller's " Don Carlos " was put in the bill, but it was not a success and was not repeated. On May 13 Shakespeare's " Henry VIII " was seen for the first time in America, Mr. Hallam appearing in the title rôle and Mr. Barrett as Cardinal Wolsey.

The yellow fever this year commenced in Philadelphia earlier than in New York, and Wignell, after his Baltimore season, took his company to Annapolis. Boston had luckily escaped the terrible scourge, and Mr. Hodgkinson opened at the Haymarket with a brilliant company which included himself and wife, Mr. and Mrs. Whitlock, Mr. and Mrs. S. Powell, Mrs. Brett, Miss Brett, Mr. and Mrs. Harper, Mr. Williamson, the singer, Mr. Chalmers, Mr. Simpson (Irish Simpson), Miss Solomon and others. But in spite of good performances and interesting bills, the receipts fell far below what had been expected, and at the close of the season Hodgkinson was hopelessly in debt and at variance with the proprietors of the new house in Federal Street. Under these circumstances, he decided to resign, his place at the Haymarket being taken by Mr. Barrett. Before the Park Theatre closed, Dunlap received a letter from Hodgkinson stating that, owing to financial embarrassment, he was leaving Boston and offering the services of himself and wife as actors. After some negotiation, Dunlap engaged the couple for the Park Theatre at $100 a week, Mr. Cooper, by agreement, surrendering some of the rôles which Hodgkinson wished to play.

The next season at the Park opened November 18, 1799, with " The Heir at Law," followed by " The Old Maid." On the second evening Mrs. Melmoth appeared in " The Carmelite." The receipts were only fair and the business continued unsatisfactory until December 11 when " False Shame," another. melodrama by the prolific Kotzebue, was seen for the first time. Like " The Stranger," this piece, by the same author, ran for the entire winter.

On December 14, 1799, the whole nation was stirred by the death of Washington. There being no telegraph at that time, the news was not generally known in New York until the 20th. The Park Theatre then closed its doors until the 30th when it reopened, the façade of the building meantime being draped with mourning and covered with appropriate emblems. Similar marks of respect to the memory of the Father of His Country were paid by theatres everywhere throughout the United States. In Philadelphia, on the 28th, the Chestnut Street Theatre, which was filled to overflowing, presented a solemn scene. Says a contemporary writer:

The pillars supporting the boxes were encircled with black crepe, the chandeliers decorated with the insignia of woe, and the audience, particularly the female part, appeared covered with badges of mourning. About seven o'clock the band struck up *Washington's March,* after which a dirge was played, when the curtain slowly rising, discovered a tomb in the centre of the stage, in the Grecian style of architecture. In the centre of it was a portrait of the General, encircled by a wreath of oaken leaves; under the portrait, a sword, shield, and helmet, and the colors of the United States. The top was in the form of a pyramid, in the front of which appeared the American Eagle, weeping tears of blood for the loss of her General, and holding in her beak a scroll, on which was inscribed: "A Nation's Tears." The sides of the stage were decorated with black banners, containing the names of the several States of the Union.

Meantime, Mr. Cooper had been to Philadelphia to settle matters arising out of the breach of the old contract with Wignell. On his return, considering himself injured by the bill being changed after he had been announced to appear, but really jealous of the many appearances and growing popularity of Hodgkinson in the Kotzebue plays, he served notice that the Park Theatre could no longer count on his services. The quality of the plays presented at this time was also a legitimate cause of dissatisfaction not only to Cooper, but to many of the patrons of the theatre. The more cultured theatregoers wanted Shakespeare and the classics, but the larger public found the highly flavored Kotzebue drama more to its taste, and the manager, to make both ends meet, was forced to neglect the few and cater to the many— a state of affairs which bears a striking analogy with the theatrical situation to-day (1919), showing that, in the matter of public taste, we have not made much, if any, progress in a hundred years.

Cooper's defection was a severe blow to the management, not only because of his standing as an actor, but because his presence in the company acted as a check on the encroachments of Hodgkinson, who, now that he found himself alone in the field, began to assert himself aggressively, making the most extravagant demands. On Dunlap's refusal to comply, he immediately became hostile and in consequence the relations of star and manager remained strained for some time.

With the disappearance of Cooper's name from the bills, the theatre receipts at once dropped, but fortunately Dunlap had some more of Kotzebue's plays up his managerial sleeve. One of them, "The Force of Calumny," had been produced on February 5 with great success. On March 12 "The Virgin of the Sun" was produced with great elaboration of scenery and costumes and proved a potent drawing card for the balance of the season. Sheridan's adaptation of "Pizarro," by the same author, was put on the 28th and also helped to eke out the season. This is the play of which the story is told that Sheridan wrote the last act upstairs in the prompter's room while the earlier acts of the play were being acted downstairs to an overflowing house. The anecdote, of course, was not intended to be taken seriously, but Dunlap proceeds gravely to demolish it by impugning its plausibility. It was merely intended to mock the public taste of the moment, showing how keen the public was at that time to get anything by Kotzebue, and the absurd slapdash manner in which melodrama was served "right off the fire," so to speak.

On July 19, 1800, New York saw the opening of its first summer theatre, a place called Mount Vernon Gardens, situated at the northwest corner of Broadway and Leonard Street. The proprietor-manager, a Frenchman named Joseph Corré, had formerly been a *chef* to a British army officer. On the termination of his culinary engagement, Corré had kept a tavern and public gardens where liquor was sold. The Park Theatre being closed for the summer, he thought there might be profit in a summer theatre and fitted up a small stage in the gardens and engaged a portion of the Park Theatre company as set forth in the following advertisement:

MOUNT VERNON GARDEN THEATRE. M. Joseph Corré presents his respects to the public. Ever anxious to merit their patronage and contribute to their amusement he has at a considerable expense engaged several of the principal performers belonging to the Theatre and proposes to exhibit theatrical entertainments on Mondays, Wednesdays, and Fridays, which he flatters himself will give additional satisfaction to those who have on former occasions honored him with their company.

On Wednesday evening, July 9th, 1800, will be presented a much admired farce in two acts, called " Miss in Her Teens," or the Medley of Lovers: Captain Flash, Mr. Jefferson; Cap. Loveit, Mr. Hallam, Jr.; Puff, Mr. Hogg; Jasper, Mr. Fox; Fribble, Mr. Martin; Tag (with a song), Mrs. Seymour; Miss Biddy Bellair (with a song), Miss Brett. Tickets of admission 4/ –. Performances to begin at 9 o'clock precisely.

The French ex-cook was the first of those American theatre managers who have taken to theatre management not from any love of, or in virtue of any special training for, the dramatic art, but solely and frankly for the more vulgar purpose of making money. As Dunlap himself puts it:

Mr. Corré and myself were now both theatrical managers, and Mr. Corré proved the most successful of the two. In regard to literary qualifications, Mr. Corré was probably not far behind other managers who have since ruled the fates of actors and destinies of authors.

Mr. Wignell, meantime, was having an anxious and busy time at the Chestnut Street Theatre, Philadelphia. His financial difficulties were almost overwhelming, yet he continued to give excellent performances. The company at that time was as follows: Messrs. Warren, Wood, Cooper, Bernard, Marshall,

Cain, Blisset, Darley, Sr., L'Estrange, Warrell, Francis, Wignell, Doctor, Morris, Robbins, Cromwell, Warrell, Jr., Mitchell, Hopkins, and Master Harris; Messrs. Holland, Milbourne and Robins, artists in the scene department; Mesdames Merry, Marshall, Morris, Warrell, Francis, Doctor, Gillingham, Salmon, Bernard; Misses L'Estrange, Arnold, Solomon and Broadhurst. Cooper's departure had left Wignell without a tragedian, and to make up for the weakness of his company the industrious manager presented a number of novelties in quick succession. Among them were Morton's sterling comedy " Speed the Plough," which met with great success and remained popular for years, and " Edwy and Elvira," a tragedy by Charles Jared Ingersoll, an American author. On Cooper's return in March (1800), the drama " Castle Sceptre " was put on with such success that the piece was performed five consecutive times, an unusual event at a time when it was the custom to change the bill nightly. Other bills were " King John," " Double Disguise," " False Shame," " Laugh When You Can," and Kotzebue's " Pizarro," which last piece occupied the remaining nights of the season.

The engagement of Mr. and Mrs. Byrne, the dancers, proved a disappointment to the management owing to the commotion aroused by their appearance, and this totally unexpected *contretemps* added not a little to Wignell's financial difficulties. Short skirt dancing up to that time had been entirely unknown in the Quaker City, and the scandalized Philadelphians loudly expressed their disapproval, many by staying away from the theatre; others by writing indignant letters to the newspapers. Yet, according to William B. Wood, the dresses worn on that occasion were models of modesty and decency compared with those to which our audiences are accustomed to-day. He writes:

> Mrs. Byrne appeared in a dress so long and ample that it would now appear unwieldy. Yet she was met by a demonstration of disapproval rarely witnessed in a theatre. After a withdrawal of a few nights she reappeared with the addition of a pair of panalettes, tied at the ankle. The attitude of the audience was wholly inconsistent, for imitation of male characters by women was tolerated to an extent which it would be dangerous now to follow, even in a minor theatre. Mrs. Whitlock's dress, as the peasant boy Fidele in " Cymbeline," consisted of a tight vest, and pantaloons of a sky-blue satin, fitting closely, and scarcely the apology for a very short cloak. This was the dress of one of the largest female performers ever seen on our stage, and excited no disapprobation or remark. Mrs. Marshall, too, degraded the stage on her benefit night by the performance of Marplot in a fashionable male habit of the day but little calculated for a character which was to undergo numerous shakings, beatings, tumblings, and other personal assaults.[4]

Even as late as the year 1827, the attitude of American theatre audiences toward scantily draped dancers had not undergone much, if any, change. When on February 7, 1827, Madame Francisquy Hutin, a very talented and graceful French dancer, made her first appearance in America at the Bowery Theatre, the women of the audience at once left the theatre because of her abbreviated skirts. It was the first introduction on the American stage of the modern French school of dancing and the house was crowded with spectators. Says Ireland:

> An anxious look of curiosity and expectation dwelt on every face, but when the graceful danseuse came bounding like a startled

---

[4] Personal Recollections of the Stage, by William B. Wood.

fawn upon the stage, her light and scanty drapery floating in air, and her symmetrical proportions liberally displayed by the force of a bewildering pirouette, the cheeks of the greater portion of the audience were crimsoned with shame, and every lady in the lower tier of boxes immediately left the house. But time works wondrous changes, and though for a while Turkish trousers were adopted by the lady, they were finally discarded and the common ballet dresses, indecent though they be, were gradually endured.[5]

What a difference between this uncompromising attitude and that of an audience at the Metropolitan Opera House in the year of grace 1918, when, at a matinee performance, a so-called rhythmic dancer exposed her person entirely undraped! There was a loud public outcry and the scandalized management immediately forbade further performances, but although the brazen audacity of the thing caused some of the ladies present to gasp, none of them, so far as known, left the theatre. *Autre temps, autre moeurs!*

Mr. Wignell, who had already made Philadelphia, Baltimore and Annapolis his particular territory, again branched out in 1800, extending his theatrical jurisdiction as far as the newly founded city of Washington. In the spring of that year he received a pressing invitation from a number of gentlemen in Washington to establish a theatre there, a building being offered in the centre of the new capital—a large spacious edifice, erected originally for a hotel, with two extensive wings. The playhouse, which was called the National Theatre, was opened with Otway's tragedy " Venice Preserved," Messrs. Wignell, Cooper and Mrs. Merry appearing respectively as Jaffier, Pierre and Belvidera.

[5] Records of the New York Stage, by Joseph N. Ireland.

THE FIRST PARK THEATRE

The play, William B. Wood tells us, was warmly received and applauded by " an audience more numerous, as well as splendid, that can be conceived from a population so slender and so scattered. The encouragement continued to exceed expectations, yet fell far below the manager's expenditure, as his company consisted of every one of the persons who composed the Philadelphia establishment. Mr. Wignell's main object was to obtain a footing in Washington, where he might keep together his company during the summer, in the event of a recurrence of the pestilence, which was regarded as but too probable."

The partial success of Wignell's experiment encouraged some friends of the drama, a few years afterwards, to erect a more durable theatre on Pennsylvania Avenue. This house was destroyed by fire in 1820.

The 1800 season at the Park Theatre, New York, did not open until October 20, the dread of the yellow fever epidemic making many people afraid to return to town. The first bill was Kotzebue's " Lovers' Vows " and " Fortune's Frolic."

The first important event of the season was the production on October 24 of another Kotzebue play " Fraternal Discord," in which Mr. Jefferson made a hit as an old sailor, Mr. Hodgkinson scoring equally well as a gouty sea captain. The play was a great success and held the stage for many years.

On October 31 Elizabeth Powell made her first New York appearance as Angela in the drama by M. G. Lewis entitled " The Castle Spectre." Mrs. Powell was formerly the Miss Harrison whom Charles Powell took to Boston in 1794. A

Shakespearian actress of the highest rank, "her beauty and talent," says Dunlap, " soon placed her at the head of her profession in the theatre of New England."

On February 11, 1801, Dunlap's adaptation of Zschokke's drama, " Abaelino," a piece which had been performed all over Europe under different disguises, was seen for the first time in New York, with Hodgkinson in the protean title rôle. The piece was well received and frequently performed on the American stage, yet according to Dunlap it was not a money maker. " Never," complains that manager-author, " was a play more successful or a successful play less productive to its author or translator."

In spite of every effort business continued very poor, and in self defense Dunlap found himself compelled to reduce salaries. This soon led to the retirement of Mr. and Mrs. Hodgkinson, the latter dying soon after and Hodgkinson himself falling a victim to yellow fever while playing in Washington with the Wignell company in 1805.

An interesting event of the summer of 1801 was the engagement of Mrs. Merry as a star. Mr. Merry had died in 1798 and his widow, although in ill health and uncertain about her future plans, had continued playing in Philadelphia. Dunlap was bitterly opposed to the star system which he rightly insisted was the cause of the degradation of the stage, but seeing in the popular actress a chance to improve the fortunes of the Park, he made her a liberal offer—$100 a week and a benefit—which was accepted and she made her appearance July 1, 1801, as Belvidera in " Venice Preserved," supported by Mr. Cooper and Mr. Hodgkinson.

Two years later, Mrs. Merry was married to Mr. Wignell and early in January, 1803, appeared for the first time as Mrs. Wignell in Philadelphia as Rosamund in " Abaelino." They had been married only a few weeks when Wignell died. His widow and Reinagle continued in joint management of the theatre while Mr. Wood went to England to secure new players.

The season of 1801 began November 16 with " Lovers' Vows," Mr. Cooper resuming his original rôle as Frederick. On January 8, Colman's comedy " The Poor Gentleman " was seen for the first time. This and the following season produced little else of any special interest, and the management still had great difficulty in making both ends meet.

In Philadelphia, the Chestnut Street Theatre company continued to do well under the management of Mr. Wood. In 1803 Joseph Jefferson joined the company and remained with that organization until he died in 1832.

The seventh season of the Park Theatre, New York, opened November 14, 1803. Mr. Cooper, Mr. Jefferson, Mr. and Mrs. Whitlock were no longer members of the company. On the 21st, the younger Colman's popular comedy " John Bull " was produced for the first time in America. It proved a great success and helped temporarily to tide over a critical financial situation.

A new place of amusement—a small house situated in Bedloe Street named the Grove Theatre—was opened March 9, 1804. The company included Frederick Wheatley (father of William Wheatley) and his wife, Messrs. McGinnis, Parsons, Bates,

Bland, Burrows, Burd and Mrs. Gordon, Mrs. McGinnis and Miss White. The house failed to attract much patronage and was soon closed.

This year two Shakespeare plays, that had not yet been seen in America, were produced at the Park for the first time. On May 25 " The Comedy of Errors " was given, and on May 30 " Twelfth Night " was presented, Mr. Martin being the Malvolio, Mrs. Johnson[6] the Viola and Mrs. Hallam the Olivia.

Mr. Cooper, who meantime had been playing in England, returned early this year and played starring engagements at Philadelphia, Boston and New York. While he was at the Park, the business was good, but after his departure the receipts fell to nothing. The following season, Dunlap, discouraged, crushed with debt, having lost all he had in a constantly losing game, at last gave up the fight. In January, 1805, the Park was closed, and Dunlap retired from the managerial field.

When next the Park opened its doors, it was under the direction of Messrs. Johnson and Tyler, officiating as presidents for a commonwealth of players. The arrangement was not of long duration, but it served to present at least one novelty of importance. This was the first performance in 'America, May 29, 1805, of John Tobin's amusing comedy, " The Honeymoon." This play was so successful and proved so popular with succeeding generations of American theatregoers, that some account of the author and the play itself may be given here.

---

[6] Mrs. Johnson, a famous Lady Townley, was a tall, beautiful woman whose taste in dress, Dunlap tells us, made her a model for the belles of her day. She was first seen in New York, February 10, 1796, and acclaimed the most perfect comedienne yet seen on the local boards.

THE FIRST PARK THEATRE

John Tobin was born in England in 1770 and trained for the bar. His ambition, however, was to become a great dramatist and to that end he wrote many plays which the London managers promptly rejected. Even " The Honeymoon " shared the same fate. Discouraged, he fell a victim to consumption and died in 1804. A year after his death " The Honeymoon " was produced and it scored an immediate success. It is believed that the author's life would have been saved if he had been able to witness his ultimate triumph, for it was disappointed hopes as much as anything else that killed him. The theme of " The Honeymoon " is similar to Shakespeare's " Taming of the Shrew." Duke Aranza, instead of escorting his newly wedded bride Juliana to his palace, as she expects, takes her to a cottage. He pretends that he deceived her about his title and that the hut is his only abode. At first she flies into a rage and tries to swim to her father, but after a month's discipline, begins to love the duke for himself alone and thereupon is raised to the exalted station which she had been led to expect.

On June 21 of this year, Mr. Dunlap was given a benefit, the bill being Dr. Young's tragedy " The Revenge," and Mr. Cooper appearing as Zanga. The occasion also served for the New York début of William Twaits, a low comedian of considerable ability, who, notwithstanding his youth and delicate constitution, played a conspicuous rôle in the theatrical activities of his time.

Mr. Twaits, who was one of the managers of the Richmond Theatre at the time of the fatal fire, was born in England in 1781 and first appeared on the

American stage in Philadelphia in 1803. Later he went into theatrical management. A comedian of the broadest kind, " his comic singing," says Ireland, " always convulsed the house wtih laughter." His personal appearance, alone, was enough to excite hilarity, he being described as short and thin, yet broad and muscular, his head large with carroty hair, face long and colorless, a prominent hook nose, projecting hazel eyes, large mouth and thin lips. He died of consumption in 1814.

The house now passed under the control of Messrs. Johnson and Tyler and opened November 18, 1805, with " Abaelino," with the following company: Mr. and Mrs. Barrett, Mrs. Jones, Mrs. Villiers, Mrs. Simpson, Mrs. G. Marshall, Miss Ross, Miss Graham, Messrs. Charnock, Burd, Ringwood, Utt, etc.

The great hit of this season was made by Mrs. Jones from the Haymarket Theatre, London, who appeared November 27 as Albina Mandeville in " The Will." Related to the Wallacks and called by her admirers the Mrs. Jordan of America, " Mrs. Jones," says Ireland, " was petite in person, had a pleasing and expressive face and was an exceedingly sprightly and piquant actress in light comedy and a very charming vocalist." She died in 1806, aged only twenty-four.

The following year (1806) Mr. Cooper undertook the management of the Park with Mr. Dunlap as his assistant, and supported by the following company: Messrs. Tyler, Harwood, Twaits, Hogg, Darley, Martin, Hallam, Jr., Saubere, Fennell, Shafter, and Rutherford, Mesdames Villiers, Darley, Simpson, Oldmixon and Miss Dellinger.

THE FIRST PARK THEATRE

Another summer resort, known as the Vauxhall Garden and Theatre, situated on the west side of Fourth Avenue, near Lafayette Place, was opened in New York this year. Attractively laid out in imitation of the famous Vauxhall of London, the place occupied a large plot of open ground, surrounded with trees which at night were illuminated with lamps and colored lanterns. The manager, Mr. Delacroix, engaged some of the members of the Park company (idle during the summer) and gave a varied entertainment including plays, exhibitions of animal magnetism and concerts. There were also daily balloon ascents. Mr. Poe, father of Edgar Allan Poe, made his first appearance in New York at this place July 18, 1806. His wife, who was seen with him, had previously appeared at the John Street Theatre. The year following its opening, the place was destroyed by fire, but it was soon rebuilt and it remained for some years one of the popular resorts of the town.

On January 7, 1807, Colman's drama " The Iron Chest," the central figure in which is Sir Edward Mortimer, a character made familiar by Kean, Junius Brutus Booth and other actors, was seen at the Park for the first time in New York, with Cooper in the leading rôle.

The following year Mrs. Warren (formerly Mrs. Merry and later Mrs. Wignell) died. In recording the death of this popular actress, Dunlap says:

The year 1808 was rendered remarkable in theatrical history wherever the English language is spoken by the death of Mrs. Anne Warren, in the thirty-eighth year of her age, and in the full possession of all those eminent qualifications which rendered her, as a tragedian, only second to Mrs. Siddons.

That same year Stephen Price, formerly manager of the Drury Lane Theatre, London, became associated with Cooper in the management of the Park Theatre, having purchased an interest in the house. Subsequently, he became sole lessee. " He was," says Ireland, " a man of great perseverance and energy of character, strict and severe though honorable in his dealings, and for a long period displayed good taste and judgment and literary ability in all his dramatic arrangements. A long residence abroad, during which he was for a time manager of Drury Lane, gave him great facilities for the engagement of distinguished talent, and through him many of the most eminent British actors were introduced to the American public. In fact, he had the entire monopoly of travelling stars, and only through him for several years could managers in other American cities obtain their services."

On February 24, 1809, at the Park Theatre, John Howard Payne,[7] the young American Roscius and author of the celebrated song, *Home, Sweet Home,* made his first appearance in New York as Young Norval in " Douglas." He was then only seventeen years old, having been born in New York, June 9, 1792. Almost from the cradle he developed a taste for theatricals. When thirteen he became clerk in a counting house, but finding mercantile life unsuited to his temperament, he started to publish a theatrical paper called the *Thespian Mirror.* In Boston where he was also seen as Young Norval, he was at once hailed as a histrionic wonder. Boy actors were then a novelty, and being remarkably handsome with fas-

---

[7] See chapter on "The American Dramatist," page 48, Vol. II.

cinating manners, he made an immediate hit. Later, he appeared in other American cities with equal success, after which he went to London, where at Drury Lane he was hailed as the American Roscius. In 1832 he retired from the stage to devote himself to literary pursuits. He was the author of several plays, one of which " Clari, or the Maid of Milan " contains that famous yet simple song, *Home, Sweet Home* which is still sung wherever the English tongue is spoken. In 1841 he was appointed United States Consul at Tunis and he died there in 1852.

On October 25, 1809, Edmund Simpson, a prominent New York theatre manager for thirty-eight years, made his first appearance on the American stage as Harry Dornton in " The Road to Ruin." Mr. Simpson was born in England in 1784, and made his début at Towchester in 1806 as Baron Steinfort in " The Stranger." He was especially good at dashing good fellows of comedy, scamps and spendthrifts. In 1810 he became assistant to Stephen Price in the management of the Park and later was sole manager of that house.

Early in 1810 Cooper sailed for England, and while abroad succeeded in engaging for America the most remarkable player of his time—the great George Frederick Cooke.

CHAPTER XII

COOKE AND THE ELDER WALLACK

THE STAR SYSTEM. CAREER OF ENGLAND'S FAMOUS TRAGEDIAN. ANECDOTES OF HIS ECCENTRICITIES. BURNING OF THE RICHMOND THEATRE. MARY ANN DUFF, THE AMERICAN SIDDONS. THEATRICALS IN ALBANY. BUILDING OF THE HOLLIDAY STREET THEATRE, BALTIMORE. THE MCKENZIE RIOTS. DÉBUTS OF GEORGE HOLMAN AND HIS DAUGHTER. HENRY PLACIDE AT THE PARK. JAMES WILLIAM WALLACK'S FIRST APPEARANCE IN AMERICA. DÉBUT OF EDWIN FORREST.

GEORGE FREDERICK COOKE was the first of the theatrical stars of the first magnitude to visit America. The star system—by which certain players, enjoying a large following, are engaged for limited periods on high terms and exploited in such a manner that all the other actors in the same company are overshadowed in consequence, a system still prevalent to-day and universally condemned as the real cause of the gradual decay of our stage—had already been tentatively introduced by the engagements of Mrs. Merry, Mr. Fennell and Mr. Cooper. These performers were, in turn, themselves overshadowed by the arrival of other and still more famous English players who had been tempted to cross the ocean by the lure of American dollars.

The story of how Cooke was persuaded to come to this country has been told too often to need repetition in any great detail here. There was much indignation in London when it became known that the great stage favorite had slipped away, and for years the English newspapers insisted that the tragedian had been kidnapped while drunk and brought over here by Cooper in that condition. All agreed, however, that inasmuch as going to America might be considered "punishment sufficient for any crime," both Cooper and Cooke received their just deserts.

George Frederick Cooke was born in London April 17, 1756. His father, an army officer, died when he was very young and the lad was apprenticed to a printer. He took no interest in the work and after he had seen Macklin and Garrick on the stage knew little rest until he himself became an actor. He made his début in the provinces in 1776 as Dumont in " Jane Shore." Two years later he was seen in London, but failed to attract much attention. Even at this early date in his career he had contracted those habits of dissipation and drunkenness which clung to him through life. For seventeen years he acted all over England, his latent histrionic powers slowly developing until at last they attained full maturity. In 1794, he appeared in Dublin as Othello, with such success that he was immediately secured for Covent Garden where he appeared as Richard III, his genius astonishing one of the most exacting audiences in the world. London critics declared him superior even to John Philip Kemble, who, until then, had reigned supreme on the tragic boards. His fame grew when, later on, he was seen as Shylock, and his position as the leading actor of the English speaking stage would have been unassailable but for his unfortunate weakness which made for him as many enemies as he had admirers. Often he appeared intoxicated before the footlights and was hissed. On other occasions, his condition was such that the audience laughed during the most tragic passages.

He was attacked unmercifully in the press, and this, as much as anything else, was responsible for his sudden determination to come to America and try to redeem himself in the New World. When Cooper found him in Liverpool, he was much depressed by the loss of his popularity, which he attributed to the machinations of jealous rivals rather than to his own failing, and he surprised Cooper by the readiness with which he listened to the proposals of an American engagement. Cooper offered him $125 a week for ten months to play at New York, Boston, Philadelphia and Baltimore, a benefit in each city and twenty-five cents a mile for travelling expenses, his Atlantic passage to be paid by Mr. Cooper.

He accepted the offer, and Cooper, confident that the tragedian's departure would be prevented if news of it reached London, took him to a friend's house near Liverpool. Here, in a state of inebriety, he remained over night, and in a few days he was taken to the dock. Cooper again repeated his terms—offering to release the tragedian if he repented the bargain—but Cooke was determined to go, and he was rowed on board the *Colombia* which sailed for New York October 4, 1810.

In America, the coming of the celebrated tragedian had been announced, but no one believed it possible. Many believed the visitor an impostor. It appeared as impossible that the great London actor should come to America as that St. Paul's Cathedral could be moved across the ocean.

Cooke arrived in New York November 16, 1810, and five days later made his first appearance on the American stage, at the Park Theatre, in the character of Richard III. He was then in the fifty-fifth year of his age and his powers were already in decline, but the long rest on shipboard, together with being deprived of the opportunity to indulge in his usual potations, had done much to make him fit and he gave a brilliant performance. His success was tremendous. There was the greatest curiosity to see the famous English actor. The doors of the theatre were besieged hours before the opening and the crush was so great that many spectators were swept in without paying. Dunlap gives this account of the actor's appearance on that occasion:

He entered on the right hand of the audience, and with a dignified, erect deportment, walked to the centre of the stage amidst their plaudits. His appearance was picturesque, and proudly noble. His head elevated, his step firm, his eye beaming fire. I saw no vestige of the venerable, grey-haired old gentleman I had been introduced to at the coffee-house, and the utmost effort of imagination could not have reconciled the figure I now saw, with that of imbecility and intemperance.

He returned the salutes of the audience, not as a player to the public, on whom he depended, but as a victorious prince, acknowledging the acclamations of the populace on his return from a successful campaign—as Richard, Duke of Gloster, the most valiant branch of the triumphant house of York.

The high key in which he pitched his voice, and its sharp and rather grating tones, caused a sensation of disappointment in some, and a fear in others that such tones could not be modulated to the various cadences of nature, or such a voice have compass for the varied expression of harmonious diction and distracting passion, which the characters of Shakespeare require; but disappointment and fear vanished, and conviction and admiration succeeded, and increased to the dropping of the curtain; when reiterated plaudits expressed the fulness with which expectation had been realized, and taste and feeling gratified.[1]

---

[1] Memoirs of George Frederick Cooke, by William Dunlap.

His next appearances were as Sir Pertinax in "The Man of the World," Shylock and Zanga in "The Revenge." As Sir Giles Overreach in Massinger's "A New Way to Pay Old Debts," his realistic acting struck terror to the audience. Says his biographer:

The acting of Mr. Cooke at this terrible point can never be forgotten. His attempt to draw his sword, and the sudden arrest of his arm, palsied and stiffened, and rendered powerless, as if by the stroke of Heaven's avenging thunder—the expression of his countenance at this moment, and his sinking convulsed, and then lifeless, into the arms of his servants, were so frightfully impressive and true to nature as to leave an image never to be erased. One night, in this situation, by some accident, the attendants were not ready to receive him when he fell back, expecting to be caught in their arms as usual; but instead of losing, the effect was heightened by the omission; for he fell so perfectly dead to appearance, and was carried off so much like a corpse, as only to increase the horror of the scene.

After appearing in New York, he went to Boston where the receipts, for that time, were enormous. His next engagement was in Philadelphia where he sat for his portrait as Richard III to the painter Sully. He performed sixteen nights in the Quaker City, the total receipts being $17,360. Later, he was seen in Baltimore.

Anecdotes of Cooke's eccentricities are countless. In Baltimore a gentleman in whose home he was visiting happened to remark that his family were among the first settlers in Maryland. "Have you preserved the family jewels?" inquired Cooke blandly. "What do you mean?" asked the host. "The chains and handcuffs," was the actor's reply.

On another occasion he was at a reception and tea

was passed around by a little negress. She offered some cake to Cooke. He rejected it with asperity. Fruit was offered to him, and he roughly told the girl that he was sick of seeing her face. Soon after she brought him wine. " Why, you little black angel," smiled the actor, taking the wine, " you look like the devil, but you bear a passport that would carry you unquestionably into Paradise."

When playing at Baltimore he was informed that Mr. Madison, president of the United States, had expressed his intention of coming from Washington to see him act. Instantly he flew into a rage: " If he does," he declared, " I'll be damned if I play before him. What? I! George Frederick Cooke! who have acted before the Majesty of Britain, play before your Yankee president! No!—I'll go forward to the audience, and I'll say, ' Ladies and gentlemen—the king of the Yankee Doodles has come to see me act. Me—me—George Frederick Cooke! who have stood before my royal master, George the Third, and received his imperial approbation! And shall I bring myself to play before one of his rebellious subjects, who arrogates kingly state in defiance of his master? No, it is degrading enough to play before rebels, but I will not go on for the amusement of a king of rebels, the contemptible king of the Yankee doodles!' "

William B. Wood tells of a characteristic frolic while the tragedian was playing in Philadelphia. One night there was a small dinner party at Wood's house. Cooke was there, also Stephen Price, his New York manager, William Dunlap and others. Cooke had not been drinking for some weeks. He was impeccably dressed and in the best of humor. At ten o'clock some of the guests departed, delighted with the gentlemanly propriety of the tragedian, whose reputation for totally different behavior seemed to them a cruel slander. The whole party was about to break up when the host, unfortunately, asked Price to thank a lady in New York who had sent him some old port wine.

Cooke pricked up his ears.

"Port wine—and a present from a lady!" he exclaimed. "Gallantry forbids that we separate before drinking to her health!"

A bottle was sent for and while standing, hat in hand, the lady's health was duly honored. The party began to move, but Cooke called for another glass, which the others declined. Price and Dunlap, fearing the consequences, were eager to go. Not so Cooke. He took a chair and asked the rest of the party to be seated as he intended to finish the bottle. This he achieved in a very short time, when the party made another effort to depart. Cooke allowed them to get near the door, when he first showed signs of excitement and coolly told them he liked the port so well that he begged the host to open another bottle.

Price and Dunlap returned very reluctantly, plainly seeing that to get him out of the house would prove a very difficult matter. The second bottle brought, Cooke reseated himself. No one could be prevailed upon to take any more, and by half past eleven he had emptied the second bottle and was far on the way with the third which he demanded in his most tragic and imperious tone. By this time he had become savage and rude to a disgusting degree. He abused the others for leaving a gentleman and visitor to drink alone and declared his intention to finish the bottle and all intercourse with such people at the same time.

Nothing could be done but let him take his course. When the last glass was emptied and he had pronounced a loud malediction on the host's inhospitality, he rose indignantly to leave the house; but suddenly recollecting that Mrs. Wood was an Englishwoman and, as he said, " of a superior class to those he had condescended to associate with," he declared his firm resolution not to leave the house without taking a respectful leave. In vain Mr. Wood urged that his wife had retired to rest some hours before— a statement of which Cooke declared his utter disbelief. Seating himself again, he repeated what he termed " his ultimatum." The rest of the story is better told in Mr. Wood's own words:

After a moment's hesitation, a note was dispatched upstairs to Mrs. Wood, with his singular request, and was answered with all possible haste and the utmost good humor. On her appearing as she had left the table, Cooke exultantly advanced, and changing from the loud, drunken tone in which he had indulged for the past two hours, suddenly addressed her in his most gentle and respectful manner, leading her with much ceremony to a chair and placing himself at her side. After thanking her courteously for this attention and trouble, he proceeded to chat for a full half hour on a variety of trifling subjects, when Mrs. Wood begged leave to retire, urging the necessity of her presence in the nursery, from whence the voice of a young person was very distinctly heard. With much deference he admitted the necessity of her retiring; and after various " good nights," led her to the foot of the stairs, repeating his acknowledgments. The gentlemen, who looked on in silence during this scene, now supposed that Cooke would consent to return home without offering any further annoyance. But he had yet another favor to ask, which he was sure my wife would not refuse him.

He stated the ill-treatment he had received from the host and his friends, with whom he was resolved not to leave the house unless the lady would honor him by her company in the carriage, with Price, the manager, and Dunlap. Mrs. Wood, as may well be imagined, was startled at this extravagant request, and urged the lateness of the hour (one o'clock), her necessity to attend to her infant, etc. He heard her with perfect composure, but insisted on her accompanying the party to the Mansion House, then the most select hotel in our city, in Third above Spruce Street, at which place he was stopping. Seeing no other prospect of relief, she determined to get rid of him, even at the price of so great an annoyance; and on a clear moonlight morning, at near two o'clock, the party set off in the carriage, which had been in waiting several hours. During the ride to Third Street nothing could exceed the gentleness and deference of Cooke; and when, on arriving at the Mansion House the coach stopped, and black Sam (Price's confidential servant) appeared with a light, the tragedian sprang lightly out first, and offering his hand to the lady, entreated the honor of her company, if only for five minutes, in his parlor, with that of the two gentlemen. While waiting an answer to this *reasonable* request, at a signal from Price, Sam shut the door of the coach, and the coachman drove off with all speed, leaving Cooke at the hotel door, shouting forth all manner of vengeance on the vile Yankee authors of this insult, who distinctly heard his voice until they had turned some distance into Spruce Street.[2]

On June 20, 1812, he was married to Mrs. Behn in New York. Meantime, his health was failing fast. He had continued drinking to excess and his course of living could have but one end. His last appearance on any stage was as Sir Giles Overreach at Providence, R. I. He returned to New York and on September 26, 1812, the great tragedian breathed his last, aged fifty-seven years and five months.

His remains were buried in a vault beneath St. Paul's Church, New York, where they were left un-

---

[2] Personal Recollections of the Stage, by William B. Wood.

disturbed for nine years. In 1821 Edmund Kean caused the remains to be disinterred and laid in a grave in the churchyard, over which he erected the monument that still marks the spot to-day. In 1846 the tomb had fallen into decay and Charles Kean had the monument repaired. Time and storms again damaged it, until Edward A. Sothern, on his visit to America, paid the expense of having it restored. It was repaired again by Edwin Booth in 1890. The inscriptions on the tomb read:

(South Side.)
Erected to the Memory
of
GEORGE FREDERICK COOKE
by
Edmund Kean
of the
Theatre Royal, Drury Lane,
1821.
Three kingdoms claim his birth,
Both hemispheres pronounce his worth.

(North Side.)
Repaired by Charles Kean,
1846.

(East Side.)
Repaired by
E. A. Sothern,
Theatre Royal, Haymarket,
1874.
Repaired by
Edwin Booth
in 1890.

During the last year of Cooke's life a disaster occurred that spread consternation throughout the country and for a time put an end to theatrical activities everywhere. This was the destruction by fire on December 26, 1811, of the Richmond, Va., theatre.

The bill on the fatal day comprised a new play and a pantomime for M. Placide. The second act had begun when a portion of the scenery took fire and sparks began to fall on the stage. Some of those in the audience, taking this to be part of the performance, did not move, but others, more nervous, started from their seats, although assured from the stage that there was no danger. The flames, however, spread more rapidly than the stage hands could tear the burning scenery down, and soon the fire was beyond control. There was a mad rush for the exits. Those on the ground floor succeeded in making their escape, but those in the boxes became panic stricken and the narrow stairways were soon choked with frenzied human beings. Many of the victims jumped from windows and were crushed to death. Seventy-one persons perished in the flames.

Being the first fatal catastrophe of its kind, the fire was looked upon in many quarters as Heaven's punishment for overindulgence in frivolous, vicious pleasures. The following day business was suspended in Richmond, banks and stores were closed and a law passed forbidding amusements of any kind for the term of four years.

Mr. Placide was associated with Mr. Twaits in the management of the Richmond theatre at the time of the fire. Since the death of Mr. Williamson in 1802, Placide had also secured control of the Charleston theatre, where in conjunction with Mr. Green and Mr. Twaits, he inaugurated a number of highly successful seasons. The company at the time included Mr. Robinson, Mat Sully, Mr. and Mrs. Claude, Mr. and Mrs. Young, Mr. and Mrs. Clarke, Messrs. Caulfield, Burke, Anderson, Sandford, Huntingdon, Mesdames Green, Placide, Poe. In 1803 Mr. Hodgkinson and Mr. and Mrs. Whitlock were engaged. During the winter of 1803-4 Mr. Hodgkinson played no fewer than eighty parts and all that year and next was the great attraction of the Charleston house, the company dividing its time between Charleston, Norfolk and Richmond.

The Boston Theatre, since 1806, had been under the joint management of Powell, Bernard and Dickson. In 1810 Mr. and Mrs. John R. Duff, who had been engaged in England by Mr. Dickson, arrived in America and made their first appearance at the Boston Theatre. Mr. Duff, an Irishman by birth, made his début as Gossamer in " Laugh When You Can " and proved an agreeable actor in genteel comedy rôles. For many years he was very popular in Philadelphia and subsequently became manager of the Federal Street theatre, Boston.

His wife, Mary Ann Duff, known as the " American Siddons " who made her début December 31st as Juliet, later became an immense favorite with our theatregoers. This actress, of whom a critic wrote " she was sacred in the majesty of grief; fascinating in tears," was born in London, one of the three Dyke sisters, all remarkable for their beauty and sweetness of disposition. It is said that she was asked in marriage by the poet Moore, whose poems contain several allusions to her and who eventually married her sister. She made her professional début

283

on the Dublin stage where she met Mr. Duff. Joseph N. Ireland, who wrote a " Life " of the actress, says of her:

> She was endowed by nature with every mental faculty and every physical requisite for pure tragedy; and in that distinct line, and in that line only, education and experience raised her to the highest rank ever attained on the stage in America. She possessed a person of more than medium height and of the most perfect symmetry—not so commanding, perhaps, as that of Mrs. Siddons, but far more available, in her maturer years, for the youthful heroines of the drama, and far more pleasing to the eye than Miss Cushman. Her face, called beautiful in her girlhood, throughout life was irradiated by eyes of the darkest hue and most speaking intelligence. The varying expression of her features has never been surpassed, while her voice was as soft and musical in its quiet tones as (we are told) was that of Mrs. Cibber—wild and plaintive in its ejaculations of distraction and despair, yet resonant and thrilling in its forceful utterances. . . . In February, 1821, Edmund Kean played an engagement in Boston. On his benefit night Mrs. Duff played Hermione to his Orestes. She had before played the character with applause, but, stimulated by the unwonted excellence of her support, her genius now essayed its highest flight and won the crown it had so long deserved. It was while rehearsing this part that Mr. Kean is said to have requested her to play with less force and intensity, or her acting would throw him into the background, to which she replied that, though she honored his rank and position in the profession, her duty to herself and the public would constrain her always to play to the best of her ability. Her hour of supreme triumph had at length arrived, for, at night, her performance fairly divided with Kean's the applause of the house, which unanimously pronounced her the equal of the greatest actor of the age.[3]

Mary Duff was identified chiefly with the Boston stage although for five years she was a member of Warren and Wood's Philadelphia company. Her best rôles were Hermione in " The Distressed

---

[3] Mary Ann Duff, by Joseph Norton Ireland.

Mother," Belvidera in "Venice Preserved," Isabella in "The Fatal Marriage," Jane Shore, Cordelia, Juliet, Portia, Mary Stuart and Lady Macbeth. Her stage career ended in New Orleans in 1838 when she married Mr. J. G. Sevier, a member of the New Orleans bar, and disappeared from public view.

In 1811 Mr. Bernard left Boston and went to play in Albany, where he became interested in a scheme to open a new and permanent theatre in that city. Albany was now a city of importance. It had more than doubled in size and for some years had been the State Capital.

It will be recalled that the earliest acting in Albany on record was in 1769 when the John Street company, then playing in New York City, obtained permission of the governor to give performances in Albany for one month. There was no theatre to play in, but permission was given the company to appear in the hospital, the leading players being Lewis Hallam, Miss Cheer, Mr. Woolls, and the play Otway's "Venice Preserved."

After this there were no theatrical performances in Albany for nearly twenty years. On December 9, 1785, Mr. and Mrs. Allen took their company there and gave performances in the hospital, presenting "Catharine and Petruchio" and other plays. The programme stated that the doors would be open at five o'clock and the curtain rise at six, also that stoves would be provided for the comfort of box patrons, a reminder of the rigor of the climate. The Allen organization continued acting in Albany for a year, after which the company went to Canada.

There were no more theatricals in Albany until

1803, when the Hallam company played a brief engagement at the Assembly Rooms, a dancing hall in Pearl Street, later known as the Thespian Hotel. Dramatic performances were given at this hall for several years, and in 1810, redecorated and greatly improved, the house was reopened under the management of Mr. Hayman. On April 5, 1811, " Hamlet " was given for the first time in Albany, J. Howard Payne appearing as the Melancholy Prince.

Late in December, 1810, a group of drama lovers advanced the project of building a permanent theatre in Albany, but nothing came of it until the following year when John Bernard, late of the Boston Theatre, played an engagement in the Thespian Hotel. It was thought that an actor and manager of such distinction and ripe experience would be just the director needed. Bernard accepted the invitation extended, and issued a note to the public stating his intention of opening " a new theatre in a convenient part of the city with a select company that shall perform such pieces as may tend to improve the minds, morals and manners of the rising generation." The Richmond fire dampened the public enthusiasm in the project for a time, but in 1812 the new theatre, situated on Green Street, was built, and on January 18, 1813, it was opened under Bernard's management. The first bill was " The West Indian." Leigh Waring, an English light comedian, was the star and Esther Young the leading lady. Miss Young was a great favorite with Albany audiences for many years and later played in New York as Mrs. Hughes.

In 1822 the old building on North Pearl Street, known as the Thespian Hotel, had been reopened as the New Constitution Theatre with the Talbot company. In 1824 a theatre called the New Pavilion was opened at the corner of Green and Division Streets and enjoyed much prosperity.

The following year the population of Albany had reached 16,000. The Erie Canal, already in partial operation, had nearly quadrupled the trade of the city. On all sides arose a demand for a larger theatre, and finally an imposing playhouse was erected on South Pearl Street. This house, named the Albany Theatre, was opened May 13, 1825, with "Laugh When You Can," under the management of Charles Gilfert, an experienced manager and late musical director of the Park Theatre, New York. The company included: Messrs. Barrett, Faulkner, Lindsley, Anderson, Spiller, Roper, Lamb, Singleton, Master Arthur and Mesdames Stone, Robertson, Barrett and Horton.

It was on the boards of the Albany theatre that Sol Smith, one of the most widely known American actor-managers of the early Nineteenth Century, made his first appearance on any stage as a super. Solomon Smith was born in New York in 1801, and at an early age went out West, where he became associated, both as actor and manager, with the various crude theatres then springing up all over the country. In 1827 he was in New Orleans where he first appeared as Billy Lackaday. The following year he went to Natchez, Miss., where he played nothing but old men characters, although only twenty-seven himself at the time. This earned for him the sobriquet "Old" Sol Smith which stuck to him all his life. Later, he became associated with N. M.

Ludlow and managed theatres at New Orleans, Mobile, St. Louis and other cities.

In Philadelphia there had been important changes in the theatre, both as regards the management and the company. In 1809 William Wood had bought a share of Warren's interest in the Chestnut Street house and the following season became acting manager, the company now including these players: Messrs. Warren, Jefferson, Barrett, Cone, Francis, McKenzie, Blissett, Wilmot, Hardings, Robins, Mesdames Wilmot, Wood, Jefferson, Francis, Seymour, Twaits, McKenzie and Misses White. The season, under the new management, opened in Baltimore in the autumn of 1810, with Mr. Fennell as the star. The actor had not been seen in Baltimore for fourteen years, and he played Othello, Lear, Macbeth, Zanga and Richard III to very large audiences. A star engagement of John Dwyer followed with almost equal success.

Playgoing had now become so popular in Baltimore that the existing theatre was no longer adequate, and the managers made arrangements to erect a larger and more convenient building. The new theatre, situated in Holliday Street, was completed in 1814 and opened on May 10 of that year with " The West Indian," and an address spoken by Mr. Wood.

Cooke was first seen in Philadelphia on March 25, 1811, his engagement of eighty-eight nights averaging $860 a night. That same summer occurred the McKenzie riots. A Scotch actor named McKenzie, who had won some popularity in heavy rôles, suddenly resigned from the Chestnut Street Theatre without stating his grievance, and that night, his retirement having been too recent to permit of the names being changed in the bill, his place was taken by Mr. Wood. It was noticed that the theatre appeared unusually well filled with a lot of rough looking characters and trouble was feared. The performance had no sooner begun when bedlam broke out. Wood tried to quiet the tumult, but in vain. He was greeted with cries of " Kill him! Drive him from the stage!" The riot went on and one of the actresses (Mrs. Wood), playing Juliet, was hurt by a musket ball thrown from an upper box. Finally, the rioters were dispersed, and, some months after, McKenzie, then out of employment and in distress, wrote to Mr. Wood asking to be reinstated as a member of the company, and making no allusion to the disturbance that he himself instigated.

On April 8, 1811, Thomas Hilson, an English actor who for many years was a great favorite with American theatregoers, made his first appearance at the Park Theatre, New York, as Walter in " The Children of the Wood." A versatile comedian, with ability to depict also strong, deep feeling and rough violent passion, Hilson played a wide range of parts from Falstaff to Richard III, from Sir Peter Teazle to Touchstone. One of his most successful parts, Paul Pry, he played in New York over two hundred nights. Possessing a fine baritone voice, he also won great applause in buffo characters in opera and for years was without a rival in that field.

In the fall of 1812 Joseph George Holman, a distinguished English actor, and his accomplished daughter, made their first appearance in America. Educated at Oxford, Mr. Holman belonged to one of the best families in England. He had acted at Covent Garden where, it was said, he had attracted the attention of Garrick and rivalled Kemble. " His Lord Townly," says a critic, " will long be remembered by the lovers of the drama in both hemispheres. He was distinguished as a gentleman and a scholar, and by the urbanity of his manners and the force of his talents contributed to enhance the character of his profession." He was also the author of several plays which had success on the American stage, among them " Abroad and at Home," " The Red Cross Knights," etc. He was first seen at the Park Theatre, New York, on September 28 as Hamlet, and shortly afterwards he and his daughter appeared with considerable success at the Chestnut Street Theatre, Philadelphia. Later, Mr. Holman was induced to open an opposition theatre in Walnut Street, but the venture proved a failure. His daughter, who married Charles Gilfert, manager of the Bowery Theatre, ranked as the first actress in America in high comedy for many years.

New York, meantime, had extended its theatrical activities. As the years passed and the city grew in size and importance, it was to be expected that other places of amusement would spring up and make a bid for public patronage. None of the newer stages could, of course, be regarded as serious competitors of the famous Park Theatre, now under the management of Price and Simpson, which was without a rival until nearly the middle of the Nineteenth Century, but the less important houses had a certain following, and call for mention here, if only as a matter of record.

COOKE AND THE ELDER WALLACK

In 1810 an establishment known as Scudder's Museum, an old two story building, once the New York City Almshouse, was opened as the American Museum. There were exhibits in the glass cases of stuffed animals, live serpents, tame alligators, etc., together with a gallery of paintings. There was also a small room where lectures were given. On December 27, 1841, the contents of the museum were purchased by Phineas T. Barnum, the world's greatest showman, who removed them to the building known as Barnum's Museum, which flourished so long at the corner of Broadway and Ann Street, New York.

The Broadway Circus, a building at the corner of White Street, on the east side of Broadway, was another early New York playhouse. At one end of the foyer it had a bar where thirsty patrons might purchase drinks during the intermission. In 1812, Dwyer and McKenzie took a lease of the house and called it the New Olympic. Under this name it was opened May 20, that same year, with " The Way to Get Married." The house was closed at the end of that season and reopened the following year as the " Commonwealth Theatre," under the direction of Twaits, Gilfert and Holland. Among the best known players who appeared on its boards were Cornelia Frances Burke, mother of Joseph Jefferson, Mr. Holman, John Dwyer and John Bernard.

The next New York playhouse of any note was the Anthony Street Theatre, situated on Anthony (now Worth) Street near Broadway. The house opened April 12, 1814, under the direction of Twaits and Holland, the opening bill being " The Midnight Hour." It was here that Henry Placide, then only fourteen years of age, appeared for the first time in New York. This popular comedian, who, in after years, established himself so firmly in the affections of American theatregoers, was born in 1799. A member of the celebrated Placide family of players, he was practically brought up on the stage, but he attracted little attention until 1823 when he made his New York début at the Park in the character of Zekiel Homespun. This performance at once ranked him as a comedian of marked originality and irresistible humor. "From clowns of the broadest Yorkshire dialect," says Ireland, "to the most mincing Cockney, in the garrulous Frenchman and the high-bred English gentleman, the simple rustic or the keenest London footman, in the clumsy hobbledehoy or the pathetic childishness of extreme old age, he was equally at home and equally superior."

Another favorite of that day was John Barnes, the English comedian who made his début at the Park Theatre April 22, 1816, as Sir Peter Teazle. Specially noted for his comic face and whimsical grimaces, Mr. Barnes probably caused more amusement and laughter than any comedian seen on our stage. "His mere appearance," Ireland informs us, "was the signal for a burst of merriment, and in such characters as Sir Anthony Absolute, Sir Abel Handy, etc., his equal has never been seen."

On January 16, 1818, Henry James Finn, a tragedian who later became a great favorite in Boston, made his first appearance in America at the Park in the rôle of Shylock. The son of a British naval officer, Finn was born at Cape Briton, Sidney, in 1785, and educated in American schools. Attracted to the stage at a very early age, he had managed to get employment for a time as the property man's assistant at the Park Theatre. Then he went to London where he made his début as an actor. The year following his début in New York, he was seen as Richard in Boston, which city from that time on became his permanent home. Subsequently, he became manager of the Boston Theatre in conjunction with Mr. Kilner. His end was tragic, he being a passenger on the ill-fated steamboat Lexington, which was burnt in Long Island Sound January 10, 1840.

In the fall of 1818 there appeared in this country for the first time a distinguished actor who was destined before long to become the acknowledged leader of dramatic art in America. This was Mr. Wallack, who made his début at the Park Theatre, New York, September 7, in the rôle of Macbeth.

James William Wallack, always referred to by later generations of theatregoers as the " elder Wallack," was the second of the four children of William Wallack, an actor at Astley's Amphitheatre and the first of the name of whom there is any record. His mother was an actress in Garrick's company. James was born in 1795 and made his stage début at the tender age of four in " Blue Beard " at the Surrey Theatre. Before he was fifteen he had filled a two years' engagement at Drury Lane and his precocious talent had won the friendship of Sheridan and Byron. When only eighteen, he made his first real success as Laertes to the Hamlet of Robert William Elliston, and he continued at Drury Lane, playing with Edmund Kean such rôles as Macduff, Edgar, Iago, etc. He was equally successful in Rob Roy, Rolla and Roderick Dhu, while in Petruchio, Mercutio, Benedict and similar rôles he was regarded as the only possible successor of Charles Kemble.

When he came to America some question rose as to what rôle he should make his first appearance in. Thomas Abthorpe Cooper was then the reigning favorite in Shakespearian tragedy and Macbeth was his best part. To the management it seemed dangerous to invite comparisons.

"What was Cooper seen in last?" demanded Wallack.

"Macbeth," was the reply.

"Then I'll play Macbeth!"

His success in the rôle was extraordinary, and he at once became a great favorite. James H. Hackett, who attended his opening performance, gives this description of his personal appearance on that occasion: "His figure and personal bearing were very *distingué,* his eye was sparkling, his hair dark, curly and luxuriant. His facial features finely chiselled and together with the natural conformation of his head, throat and chest, presented a remarkable specimen of manly beauty."

After playing some time in New York, Wallack went to Boston where he was seen as Hamlet, Rolla, Coriolanus, Richard, etc. The Boston critics differed respecting his talents. "He was," says William Clapp, "too melodramatic to please those who remembered Hodgkinson, Cooper and Cooke." Other critics asserted that he was wanting in simplicity, though his Hamlet was favorably received. The actor was, however, popular both on the stage and off, and was greeted everywhere by full houses.

COOKE AND THE ELDER WALLACK

Wallack acted in tragedy, comedy and melodrama, and he excelled in comedy. Among his rôles were Hamlet, Macbeth, Rolla, Octavian, Richard III, Don Felix, Shylock, Richard II, Coriolanus, Benedick, Martin Heywood, Massaroni, Don Caesar de Bazan, Doricourt, Dick Dashall, Rienzi, Master Walter, St. Pierre, Tortesa, Jaques, Rover, Sir Edward Mortimer, Delmar in "The Veteran," and Reuben Glenroy. "His distinguishing characteristic in comedy," says William Winter, "was the easy, graceful, sparkling, winning brilliancy with which he executed his artistic designs." The critic continues:

An actor shows the depth and quality of his nature in his ideals, but there he stands on the same ground with all other intellectual persons who are students of human nature and of life. It is in the methods by which he expresses and presents his ideals that he shows his distinctive power, ability, and resources in the dramatic art, and there he stands on ground that is his own. Wallack's ideals were made the theme of controversy. Hackett, for example, thought that his Hamlet "lacked a sufficiency of weight, in the philosophical portions, and also of depth and intensity of meditation in the soliloquies." But no observer could doubt or dispute the clearly defined purpose, or the pervasive animation, or the affluent, copious, picturesque grace and variety of execution with which his artistic purpose was fulfilled. His presence, whether in repose or motion, quickly absorbed a spectator's interest and held it, charmed and delighted, as long as he remained on the scene. His person was symmetrical and fine. His demeanor was marked by natural dignity and by engaging personal peculiarities. His voice was rich, sweet, and clear, his articulation distinct, and when he spoke under strong excitement,—as in some passages of Rolla,—his sonorous tones flowed over the action in a veritable torrent of musical sound. In acting, although he possessed the quality of repose, he was addicted to rapid movement. He was everywhere at once in such parts as Benedick and Don Felix, and he filled the scene with pictorial vitality and dazzled the observer by the opulence of his enjoyment. He was alive to the tips of his fingers, and he was entirely in earnest. As a comedian his style probably reflected that of Elliston,—the Magnificent,—as readers can still see him, in the pages of Charles Lamb; yet he had a way of his own, and he wrote his name, broad and deep and in letters of gold, across the dramatic period through which he lived.[4]

In 1820 Wallack returned to London and was once more seen at Drury Lane. He visited America again in 1822, in 1832, and from 1834 to 1836. In 1837 he became manager of the National Theatre, on the corner of Leonard and Church Streets, New York, which was thus the original " Wallack's," although it never bore that name. In 1839 the house was destroyed by fire, and after brief engagements at Niblo's and the Chatham Theatre, Wallack returned to England. In 1847 he again came to this country, appearing here for the first time as Don Caesar, and after another short trip to England, returned to America to make it his permanent home, and established the theatre which, as we shall see, became famous all over the country as " Wallack's."

Meantime, he had married the daughter of the celebrated Irish comedian known as " Irish Johnstone." Mrs. Wallack accompanied her husband to America at the time of his first visit in 1818, and her eldest son was born in New York City on December 31, 1819. This boy, likewise destined to become famous in the annals of our stage, was christened John Johnstone, but he was better known to the American public as Lester Wallack.

[4] From "The Wallet of Time." Copyright, 1913, by William Winter. Moffat, Yard & Company, Publishers. Reprinted by kind permission of Jefferson Winter, Esq.

COOKE AND THE ELDER WALLACK

Henry Wallack, elder brother of James W. Wallack, was also an actor and made his first appearance in America May 9, 1821, at the Anthony Street Theatre, New York, as young Norval in " Douglas." He was a very capable actor in a wide range of parts and a favorite with the theatregoing public for nearly half a century.

In the summer of 1819 a new theatre was built in Boston. It was a brick amphitheatre erected in Washington Gardens, Tremont Street. John Bernard was the manager and Mr. Betterton, Mr. Jones and Mr. and Mrs. Wheatley the principal performers. The entertainment consisted of vaudeville and songs. Later the house was used as a circus. A few years afterward it was renamed the City Theatre and a good dramatic company, including Mr. Burroughs, Mrs. Warring, Mr. and Mrs. Fisher, gave it standing as a legitimate theatre. This was the third playhouse built in the city of Boston. It was pulled down in 1829.

On April 2, 1820, the Chestnut Street Theatre, Philadelphia, was destroyed by fire. Happily, there was no loss of life, but a great quantity of valuable scenery and costumes were burned. The managers were at once offered a lease of the theatre in Walnut Street which they accepted, and on November 11 of the same year, the Walnut Street Theatre (originally constructed for a circus but now vastly improved and redecorated throughout) was opened with " The Poor Gentleman." Two weeks later there occurred on the stage of the new Walnut Street Theatre a début of special interest and significance—the first appearance of " a young gentleman of Philadelphia, Master Edwin Forrest."

Forrest, at this time, was only fourteen years of age, yet, according to William Wood, he was even then " a well grown young man with a noble figure, unusually developed for his age, his features powerfully expressive and of a determination of purpose which discouraged all further objections."

He was first seen on November 27, 1820, as young Norval in Home's tragedy " Douglas." This was Forrest's first appearance on any stage.

CHAPTER XIII

THE GOLDEN ERA OF THE AMERICAN STAGE

EDMUND KEAN'S DÉBUT CREATES A SENSATION. TRAGEDIAN ANGERS BOSTON PLAYGOERS. THE KEAN RIOTS. NEW PARK THEATRE OPENED. DESCRIPTION OF THE PLAYHOUSE. "GENTLEMAN GEORGE" BARRETT. CHARLES MATHEWS THE ELDER ARRIVES FROM ENGLAND. MRS. PIOZZI'S PROTÉGÉ. REOPENING OF THE CHESTNUT STREET THEATRE, PHILADELPHIA. DÉBUT OF F. C. WEMYSS. JUNIUS BRUTUS BOOTH COMES TO AMERICA. ANECDOTES OF THE FAMOUS ACTOR.

WHAT may properly be described as its golden era had now set in on the American stage. For the next half century a constant stream of artists of the first rank trod the boards of our theatres. It was a period of extraordinary brilliance that has never been equalled since and which probably will never be seen again. The present generation of theatregoers cannot have the faintest conception of acting such as delighted our fathers. Histrionic giants in those days trod the boards, players born and bred in the Kemble tradition, trained in all the thoroughness, style, elocutionary powers that go to make acting a great and noble art. In quick succession the American stage was enriched by the terrifying acting of Edmund Kean, the delicious drollery of Charles Mathews, the extraordinary genius of Junius Brutus Booth, the natural comedy of James H. Hackett, the intellectual art of William Charles Macready, the tempestuous splendor of Edwin Forrest, the irresistible comedy of John Brougham and W. E. Burton, the delightful

299

impersonations of Joseph Jefferson, the majesty and pathos of Charlotte Cushman, the humorous eccentricities of E. A. Sothern's Dundreary, the noble presence and beautiful voice of Edwin Booth, the scholarly and versatile art of Edward L. Davenport, the nobility and charm of John McCullough, the distinction of Lawrence Barrett, the spontaneous humor of the versatile John Gilbert, the loveliness of Mary Anderson, the mournful beauty of Adelaide Neilson, the grace of Fanny Elssler, and many other players of almost equal renown—the elder Wallack, Lester Wallack, George Holland, Mrs. John Drew, Charles and Fanny Kemble, Charles Kean and Ellen Tree, Tyrone Power, Henry Placide, James E. Murdoch, Mme. Rachel, Mrs. D. P. Bowers, Edwin Adams, Mrs. Mowatt, Mme. Ristori, William and George Vandenhoff, John E. Owens, Matilda Heron, Fanny Janauschek, W. J. Florence, Mr. and Mrs. Barney Williams, William Warren, Lotta, Laura Keene, Agnes Robertson, Dion Boucicault, William Davidge, Charles W. Couldock, John T. Raymond, Charles Fechter, Mme. Modjeska, Clara Morris— all names indelibly written on the annals of our stage.

The first appearance in America of Edmund Kean caused an immense sensation. An obscure country tragedian, he had only a few years before taken London by storm with his Shylock, and all England rang with his fame. "Just returned from seeing Kean in Richard," wrote Lord Byron in his diary. "By Jove, he has a soul! Life, nature, truth without exaggeration or diminution." Coleridge said his acting was "like reading Shakespeare by flashes of lightning."

In 1820, the year in which Kean had contracted to visit America, the historic Park Theatre, New York, was destroyed by fire, so arrangements were made for the English star to appear at the Anthony Street Theatre, where he made his first appearance November 29, 1820, as Richard III.

Edmund Kean was born in London on November 4, 1787. His reputed father, Aaron Kean, was a stage carpenter and his mother a strolling actress. According to tradition, he was four year old when he made his first appearance on the stage as Cupid in a ballet at the Opera House. He was a clever, good-looking boy with fine black eyes, but the want of proper restraint had fostered wayward tendencies. Finding school irksome, he ran away and shipped as a cabin boy at Portsmouth. Soon discovering that the seafaring life was not all that it seemed, he counterfeited lameness and deafness so well that even the naval surgeons were deceived and he procured his discharge. On his return to London, he turned again to the stage. An actress taught him the rudiments of her art and under her guidance he began a systematic study of the Shakespearian characters, displaying even at this early period the peculiar originality of his genius by interpretations entirely different from those of Kemble. In his fourteenth year he obtained an engagement to play leading characters at York, where he appeared as Hamlet, Hastings and Cato. In 1807, he played leading parts in the Belfast theatre along with Mrs. Siddons, who said that he " played very, very well," but that " there was too little of him to make a great actor," the actress referring, of course, to his small stature. In 1814, the committee of Drury

Lane, the fortunes of which were then so low that bankruptcy seemed inevitable, resolved to give him a chance among the " experiments " they were making to win a return to popularity. His début there on January 26 as Shylock roused the audience to almost uncontrollable enthusiasm, and successive appearances in Richard III, Hamlet, Othello, Macbeth and Lear only served to demonstrate to the fullest the greatness of his powers and his complete mastery of the whole range of tragic emotions. A critic wrote of him:

It was especially in the impersonation of the great creations of Shakespeare's genius that the varied beauty and grandeur of the acting of Kean were displayed in their highest form, although probably his most powerful character was Sir Giles Overreach, the effect of his first impersonation of which was such that the pit rose *en masse,* and even the actors and actresses themselves were overcome by the terrific dramatic illusion. His only personal disadvantage as an actor was his small stature. His countenance was strikingly interesting and unusually mobile. He had a matchless command of facial elocution. His fine eyes scintillated even the slightest shades of emotion and thought. His voice, though weak and harsh in the upper register, possessed in its lower range tones of penetrating and resistless power, and a thrilling sweetness like the witchery of the finest music. Above all, in the grander moments of his passion, his intellect and soul seemed to rise beyond material barriers and to glorify physical defects with their own greatness. Kean especially excelled as the exponent of passion.

In Boston the curiosity to see Kean was so great that the tickets were sold at auction, the premiums thus obtained being given by the management, Messrs. Powell and Dickson, to the various charitable institutions of the city. The actor opened February 12, 1821, in Richard. Says Clapp:

The house was crowded, and continued to be throughout his engagement; for the Kean fever broke out and raged without cessation. His acting was the all-engrossing topic of fashionable discussion, and Kean himself became the lion of the day. His engagement was for nine nights. He shared with the managers after $1000 per week, and had a clear benefit; and the engagement resulted in his adding to his treasury the neat sum of $3302.68. So great was the rush to see him that he was re-engaged for six nights at £50 per night and clear benefit, which gave him $2151.58. The first night of his re-engagement the premiums on the tickets amounted to $640, and though thousands of dollars were thus paid, the managers only reserved $500, which offset sundry extra expenses incurred to better accommodate the public.[1]

It was owing to the enthusiasm aroused by Kean's acting that the custom was first introduced in American theatres of calling out performers *dead* or *alive* after the curtain has dropped to receive a tribute of extra applause. William B. Wood, who probably saw plenty of this sort of thing while manager of the Chestnut Street Theatre, denounces the practice in no uncertain terms. He says:

The absurdity of dragging out before the curtain a deceased Hamlet, Macbeth or Richard in an exhausted state, merely to make a bow or, probably worse, to attempt an asthmatic address in defiance of all good taste and solely for the gratification of a few unthinking partisans or a few lovers of noise and tumult, is one which we date from Kean's time. It has always been a matter of wonder with me that the better part of the audience should tolerate these fooleries. Can anything be more ridiculous than that an actor, after laboring through an arduous character—a protracted combat and the whole series of simulated expiring agonies—should instantly revive and appear panting before the curtain to look and feel like a fool and to destroy the little illusion which he has been endeavoring to create.[2]

---

[1] Record of the Boston Stage, by William Clapp, Jr.
[2] Personal Recollections of the Stage, by W. B. Wood.

Concerning a minor branch of stage quackery exhibited in the passing across the footlight of flowers, wreaths, etc., the same manager has this to say:

These testimonials in most cases are prepared and paid for by the "grateful recipients." Even in the case of Fanny Ellsler (who certainly stood in no need of such aid) the basket of flowers, etc., formed an unconcealed part of the dressing apparatus for the evening. It is well known to me that in the career of other performers, these marks of a grateful and admiring public were made use of on several different nights, when the ambition of the performer outran his means, and not only so, but that the identical vases, goblets and cups have travelled with the performer from theatre to theatre and been presented and accepted at every place with new " emotions of the deepest sensibility."

Early the following May, having concluded his tour in the South, Kean wrote to the managers of the Boston Theatre, notifying them of his intention to again appear in their city. It was the dull season and the best people were out of town. Mr. Dickson tried to persuade him to defer the proposed visit until the fall. But Kean would not listen. He insisted that an actor of his renown was sure of good houses at any time of year. He went to Boston and opened as Lear to a fair house. The next night the attendance was slim, and when, on the third night, after Richard had been announced, only a few spectators appeared, Kean became angry. He declared he would not play to bare walls and, notwithstanding the managers' protests, he left the theatre. Meantime, the audience had been kept waiting and there was considerable impatience. Mr. Duff went before the curtain, explained the reason for the delay, and asked those present if they preferred to have their money returned or the play go on without Kean.

Assent was given to the programme being given as announced, a substitute was found for the star, and the play proceeded.

But the indignation against Kean for his conduct was general. In one of the Boston newspapers appeared the following:

ONE CENT REWARD!

Run away from the " Literary Emporium of the New World," [3] a stage-player calling himself Kean. He may be easily recognized by his misshapen trunk, his coxcomical, cockney manners, and his bladder actions. His face is as white as his own froth, and his eyes are as dark as indigo. All persons are cautioned against harboring the aforesaid vagrant, as the undersigned pays no more debts of his contracting after this date. As he has violated his pledged faith to me, I deem it my duty thus to put my neighbors on their guard against him.

PETER PUBLIC.

The feeling against Kean was not confined to Boston, but spread to New York, where, soon after his arrival in that city, Kean issued a letter professing to be entirely ignorant of having given any cause for offense at Boston, that he never knew the arts were encouraged in America only during certain months of the year, or that there could be any season in which Shakespeare was diminished in value, that he lived by his professional exertions and could not afford to give away his talents—a palpably insincere and impertinent apology that only added fuel to the fire. In view of the feeling aroused, further American appearances at the time were considered unwise, and on June 8 the actor sailed for England.

[3] In a speech, Kean had referred to Boston as the "Literary Emporium of the New World."

When he returned four years later, Kean assumed a less defiant attitude. He hoped that time had softened the former unfriendly feelings towards him. But in this he was mistaken. Since his previous visit he had lost prestige, both as an actor and as a man, even in England, where he had been mixed up in all kinds of unsavory scandals, notably a disgraceful liaison with Mrs. Alderman Cox, whose injured husband sought redress in the courts. His immoralities were flagrant and on several occasions London audiences had hissed him.

He made his reappearance at the Park Theatre, New York, November 14, 1825, as Richard, and disturbances began as soon as he came in view on the stage. An eye witness thus describes his reception by the audience:

The house was crowded from pit to the utmost gallery, but there were only two females in the first and two in the second tier of boxes; and these were soon compelled to beat a precipitate retreat. The curtain rose, and two of the minor characters of the play appeared and commenced reciting their parts; but the confusion was too great to allow them to be heard. Kean was loudly called for, and he speedily appeared, bowed, and prepared to address the audience. The moment he appeared, however, he was assailed by such a powerful and unexpected burst of catcalls and shower of hisses that he for a moment quailed. He attempted to obtain a hearing, but in vain. After standing upon the stage fully a quarter of an hour, he was compelled to retire. He soon, however, made a second attempt, and was again driven indignantly off. An orange struck him and fell upon the stage. He picked it up and again came forward, holding it in his hand, and attempted to obtain a hearing. But it was again in vain, and he retired. A gentleman—one of his friends—then arose and attempted to speak a word for him; but nothing could be heard but " Hear him! " " Kean forever! " " Down! " " Down! " " To Bridewell with him! " The pit was, with one exception, in Kean's favor, and very soon entirely so.

The dress boxes were almost unanimously his friends. The principal opposition came from the "slips" and second tier.

At length Manager Simpson came forward; but even he could not be heard. Notwithstanding the uproar, it was decreed in the green room that the play should go on. And on it went—"Richard III" in pantomime. Not a sound from the stage could be heard, and, "ever and anon each dreary pause between," a not very gentle salutation of an orange or a rotten apple greeted some part of Kean's body. Every time he made his appearance the cries were redoubled. "He, Kean, has insulted our country," cried one. "Bravo! that he has," cried another. "Down with the rioters!" "Send the Bostonians home!" At this moment a noise without attracted attention. An immense assemblage of the populace were at the doors and threatened to take the theatre by storm. Mr. Simpson then appeared and implored the audience to act with more decorum, and display a little more respect for themselves. After a short interval the pantomime was resumed. Kean became more agitated and angry. A bag of sand with a label struck his shoulder. His eyes flashed fire and he trembled with rage. At last in the dying scene he was saluted with a shower of rotten apples. This ended Kean's first reappearance in New York.

The next day Kean published the following communication to the public:

With oppressed feelings, heart-rending to my friends, and triumphant to my enemies, I make an appeal to that country famed for its hospitality to the stranger and mercy to the conquered. Allow me to say, whatever my offences, I disclaim all intention of offering anything in the shape of disrespect towards the inhabitants of New York. They received me from the first with an enthusiasm, grateful *in those hours* to my pride, *in the present* to my memory. I cannot recall to my mind any act or thought that did not prompt me to an unfeigned acknowledgment of their favors as a public and profound admiration for the private worth of those circles which I had the honor of moving. That I have committed an error appears too evident from the all-decisive voice of the public, but surely it is but justice to the delinquent, whatever may be his enormities, to make reparation where the offences were committed. My misunderstanding took place in Boston—to Boston I shall assuredly go to apologize for my indiscretions. I visit this country now under different feelings and auspices than on a former occasion. Then I was the ambitious man, and the proud representative of Shakespeare's heroes; the spark of ambition is extinct, and I merely ask a shelter in which to close my professional and mortal career. I give the weapon into the hands of my enemies; if they are brave they will not turn it against the defenceless.

EDMUND KEAN.

The actor then proceeded to Boston. He had been announced to appear as Richard and early in the afternoon of Wednesday, December 21, the street in front of the theatre was filled with rowdies. Clapp gives this account of what happened later:

All the tickets were sold the day previous, and on the opening of the doors in the evening every part of the house was soon crammed with males, not a female being present. The excitement inside the house was very evident, and the vociferation of those present commenced as soon as the house was packed. Outside there was a vast accumulation of people, attracted by curiosity, and evincing a disposition for a row. Mr. Finn, one of the managers, soon appeared in front of the curtain. He was received with great uproar, chiefly from the gallery and third row—the boxes being principally occupied by the stockholders of the theatre, and friends to Mr. Kean, who were in favor of Kean's performing. Finn announced Mr. Kean's intention to make an apology, but his voice was drowned in the shouts of the discontented. Mr. Kean appeared immediately afterwards upon the stage, dressed in his every-day clothes, and in a penitent and humble manner seemed to ask forgiveness of the public, and to be desirous of making atonement by an apology. But the wild commotion of the theatrical elements so completely astonished him that he said not a word. He was pale and dejected, but was assailed by cries of " Off! " "Off! " pelted with nuts, pieces of cake, a bottle of offensive drugs, and other missiles. He was encouraged with cries of " Silence! " " Hear Kean," etc. Having been fairly pelted from the stage, Mr. Kilner, dressed for King

Henry, came forward, and after consultation with those in the stage box, was heard to say, " Mr. Kean wishes to make an apology—an humble apology from his heart and soul; but he will not do it at the risk of his life." Cries of " Off! " " Off! " and " His hypocritical heart," was the response. One or two gentlemen in the boxes attempted to speak, but they were not heard, but those in the boxes giving some encouragement that the apology might be heard, Kean made his second appearance. No intermission of the uproar took place, and he retired to the green room, where, it is said, he wept like a child.

In the meantime, the mob without had become excited to frenzy, and made several assaults upon the house; and the audience within began to think not so much of Kean as of their own preservation from danger. The rabble began to assail the lamps, the windows, and the entrances to the boxes, gallery and pit. A large party succeeded in making a lodgment in the lower lobbies, after having been repulsed. The few police officers present were soon overpowered, but the gentlemen of the boxes maintained their ground manfully for some time. Mr. Kean having left the house, it was difficult to divine the objects of the assailants. The occupants of the pit made a retreat by the stage over the orchestra.

Kean escaped from the theatre before the riot reached its height, by passing through Mrs. Powell's house, in Theatre Alley, which, adjoining the theatre, had a door to communicate with it.[4]

On his return to England, Kean wisely retired from the stage. In 1833 an attempt was made to revive the old interest in him by announcing his appearance at Covent Garden together with his son Charles. They were seen in " Othello " on March 25 of that year—Mr. Kean playing the Moor and Charles Kean Iago. The house was crowded to the doors and the former favorite received a hearty greeting, but it was soon seen that the elder Kean was too feeble to play the part and immediately after repeating the line *" Othello's occupation's gone,"* he sank

[4] Record of the Boston Stage, by William Clapp, Jr.

exhausted into his son's arms. He died the following May, aged forty-six.

The new Park Theatre, New York, built on the same site as the one destroyed by fire a year previous, was opened to the public on September 1, 1821, with " Wives as They Were and Maids as They Are " followed by " Therese or the Orphan of Geneva."

The dimensions of the new house were the same as the old one—eighty feet on Park Row and one hundred and sixty-five feet in depth, running through to Theatre Alley. The theatre had seven entrances, opening into a spacious vestibule, which communicated with the corridor of the first row of boxes. " Its interior," says Ireland, " was neatly and conveniently fitted up with as much regard to elegance and taste as the limited time between its erection and opening allowed. In the auditorium, which was calculated to hold 2500 persons, there was a pit with a gradual rise in each succeeding row of seats. Surrounding this, rose three tiers of fourteen boxes, each supported by small columns of burnished gold six feet and six inches in height, and above was a commodious gallery entirely disconnected from the boxes and used principally for colored persons." Joe Cowell, the English comedian, who made his American début at this theatre on October 30 as L'Eclair in " The Foundling of the Forest " and Crack in " The Turnpike Gate," gives an interesting pen picture of the house as he found it in 1821 :

I sallied up Wall Street, and through Broadway. The pavement was horrible, and the sidewalks, partly brick and partly flagstones, of all shapes, put together as nearly as their untrimmed forms would permit. The Park, which Scovill had spoken of with enthusiasm, I found to be about the size of Portman Square, but of a shape defying any geometrical term to convey the form of it. It had been surrounded by a wooden, unpainted, rough fence, but a storm had prostrated the larger portion, together with some fine old buttonwood trees, which either nature or the good taste of the early settlers had planted there, and the little grass the cows and pigs allowed to remain was checkered o'er by the *short cuts* to the different streets in its neighborhood. The exterior of the theatre was the most prison like looking place I had ever seen appropriated to such a purpose. The theatre doors were open, and the audience already assembling. Phillips, the singer, was the "star," and the performance "Lionel and Clarrissa." The opera had not commenced, but I took a seat, with about twenty others, in the second tier. The fronts of the boxes were decorated, if it could be so called, with one continuous American design, a splendid subject, and very difficult to handle properly, but this was designed in the taste of an upholsterer, and executed without any taste at all. The seats were covered with green baize, and the back of the boxes with whitewash, and the iron columns which supported them covered with burnished gold! and looking as if they had no business there, but had made their escape from the Coburg. The audience came evidently to see the play, and be pleased, if they possibly could, with everything. The men, generally, wore their hats; at all events, they consulted only their own opinion and comfort in the matter; and the ladies, I observed, very sensibly all came in bonnets, but usually dispossessed themselves of them, and tied them in large bunches high up to the gold columns; and as there is nothing a woman can touch that she does not instinctively adorn, the varied colours of the ribands and materials of which they were made were in my opinion a vast improvement to the unfurnished appearance of the house.[5]

The company at the new theatre consisted of the following players: Messrs. Maywood, Pritchard,

[5] See "Thirty Years Among the Players," by Joe Cowell. This popular comedian was born in 1792, and, after some success on the English provincial stage, went to London, where he became a member of the company at Drury Lane. He proved a great favorite at the Park Theatre until 1823, when he was made acting manager of Price and Simpson's Equestrian company at the Broadway Circus with the travelling circuit of Boston, Philadelphia, Baltimore, Washington and Charleston. In 1826 he went to the Philadelphia theatre and later was applauded in almost every theatre in the country.

Simpson, Woodhull, Barnes, Kilner, Phillips, Reed, Bancker, Wheatley and Nexsen; Mesdames Barnes, Battersby, Barrett, Holman and Wheatley and the Misses Johnson, Jones, Bland and Brundage. The managers were Stephen Price and Edmund Simpson.

An important production of the new season was "Damon and Pythias," seen for the first time in America September 10, 1821. This new version, by John Banim, of a very old play of fraternal love, had been presented at Covent Garden earlier that same year with Macready as Damon and Charles Kemble as Pythias. In New York, Maywood acted the first rôle and Simpson the latter. Written in the classic manner and full of heroics, the piece was very popular with actors of the robust chool and a great favorite with American theatregoers up to two or three decades ago.

On March 5, 1822, George Barrett ("Gentleman George"), the celebrated light comedian, was seen at the Park for the first time in New York since reaching manhood, as Belcour in "The West Indian." Born in England in 1794, he had first appeared on the American stage at the Park in 1798, as one of the children in "The Stranger." An accomplished, intellectual man, Mr. Barrett was a great favorite with the American public for a number of years. In 1828 he was stage manager of the Bowery Theatre. Later he managed theatres in Boston and New Orleans, and in 1847 was first acting manager of the Broadway Theatre.

In the fall of 1822, Charles Mathews, Sr., the most famous comedian England ever sent here, made his first appearance in this country at Baltimore, Md., on September 2, in " The Trip to Paris." He was first seen in New York at the Park Theatre, November 7 of the same year as Goldfinch in " The Road to Ruin."

Charles Mathews, the elder, was born in London in 1776 and early developed a penchant for things theatrical. His father, a bookseller, was opposed to his becoming an actor, but finding his son obstinate he said to him: " Charles, here are twenty guineas. I do not approve of the stage, but I will not stand in the way. At any time hereafter, should you feel inclined to an honest calling, there are twenty guineas more if you send for them."

After leaving his father's house, Mathews went to Canterbury where he played Old Doiley and Lingo and thence to Dublin where he remained eighteen months playing all kinds of rôles. After three years more experience in the provinces, he went to London and made his first great hit May 16, 1803, at the Haymarket as Jabal in " The Jew." From that time on he was a great public favorite. He was, however, more successful in his entertainments than as an actor. " He possessed," says a critic, " a peculiar power of copying the minds of persons of whom he gave imitations and his greatest efforts were produced by imagining conversations between men which had never taken place but in which he depicted with a master hand their minds, characters and dispositions. This power, added to a copious store of anecdote, the quickest possible conception of the ridiculous, an unequalled talent for singing comic songs of a species which he himself originated, rendered his ' Evenings' very popular and his 'Mail Coach Adventures,' 'Trip to Paris,' 'At Home,' etc., always drew crowds."

In America his success was immediate. He was received everywhere with the greatest delight. The actor wrote home to his wife:

> They roared and screeched as if they had never heard anything comical before; and I don't think they have been glutted in that way. I discovered the never-to-be-mistaken token of pocket handkerchiefs crammed into the mouths of many of the pitt-ites. I had only to hold up my crooked finger when I wanted them to laugh, and they obeyed my call. I was most agreeably surprised, indeed, at finding them an audience of infinitely more intelligence and quickness than I had expected. Bartley had shrugged his shoulders at the idea of their taking the jokes. One of the London papers said I should be lost here; . . . but the neatest and best points were never better appreciated, even in London; and I am quite certain, from the effects, that the French language is generally much more understood here than in England.

On his return to England he brought out his " Trip to America " which caused considerable criticism, it being alleged that in it he burlesqued the Americans who had received him so cordially. He made a formal denial, but the controversy continued, and on his return to New York in 1834, a hostile group of theatregoers announced their intention of preventing his reappearance. Placards were posted inviting patriotic Americans to attend and trouble was anticipated. When the curtain went up at the Park Theatre October 13, 1834, the house was crowded from pit to dome. A tremendous shout greeted Mathews when he appeared and the applause kept up in spite of all the efforts of the unfriendly element to down it. Finally, silence being obtained, Mathews addressed the audience, thanking them for their generous reception and asking bluntly: was it possible, if he were guilty, that he would have come here to face them. *"No, I'm not acting now!"* he cried with great feeling. This had an electric effect, and a burst of applause effectually discouraged all further idea of an unfriendly demonstration.

During his lifetime, Mathews enjoyed the friendship of many famous men, among them being Sir Walter Scott and Byron. He was also one of the few actors received as a guest by King George IV. Kean alone excepted, he made more money than any performer of his day. A writer in the *London Times* said of him:

As a companion he was delightful, as a friend sincere, as a husband and father exemplary, and, as an actor, he had no competitor, and will, we fear, never have a successor. . . . He was on the stage what Hogarth was on the canvas—a moral satirist; he did not imitate, he conceived and created characters, each one of which was recognized as a specimen of a class. Nothing could exceed the correctness of his ear; he spoke all the dialects of Ireland, Scotland and Wales with a fidelity perfectly miraculous. He could discriminate between the pronunciation of the different writings of Yorkshire, and speak French with the Parisian accent—the *patois* of the South or the guttural tone of the Flemish. His powers in this way had no limit. His knowledge of human character was no less remarkable. Though his performances professed to be representations of manners and peculiarities, they really abounded in the fine analysations of character. Mathews did not occupy the highest place in the drama, but he was indisputably, and by the united suffrage of France, England and America, the first in his peculiar walk. . . . For seventeen years he, by his single exertions, delighted all England—" alone he did it! "

He died at Plymouth, England, June 28, 1835, and a handsome monument erected in the church bears the following inscription by Horace Smith:

All England mourned when her comedian died,
A public loss that ne'er might be supplied;
For who could hope such various gifts to find,
All rare and excellent in one combined?
The private virtues that adorned his breast,
Crowds of admiring friends with tears confessed.
Only to thee, O God! the grief was known
Of those who reared this monumental stone!
The son and widow, who, with bosoms torn,
The best of fathers and of husbands mourn.
Of all this public, social, private wo
*Here lies the cause—*CHARLES MATHEWS *sleeps below.*

The year following the first appearance here of Mathews, there came to America another English actor of note—William Augustus Conway, a tragedian whose end was tragic, but whose popularity with our audiences at one time threatened the supremacy of Cooper.

William Conway was born in London in 1789 and educated in the West Indies. He made his professional début in the English provinces as Zanga in "The Revenge" and was first seen in London at Covent Garden October 4, 1813, as Alexander the Great. He was received with favor and this good impression was increased when he appeared later in such rôles as Othello, Romeo, Henry V, Macbeth, Rolla, George Barnwell, etc. After some time spent in starring, he was engaged in 1821 as leading actor at the Haymarket. A very good looking man, over six feet tall, he had been two years previously the object of the infatuation of the celebrated Mrs. Piozzi[*] then an old lady of nearly eighty. The actor was only thirty, but that fact did not discourage Mrs. Piozzi who, it is said, went so far as to propose marriage. Her love letters to the actor, found among Conway's effects after his death, were published later in London. While playing at the Haymarket, Conway became the target of the journalistic attacks of Theodore Hook, who described him as a " fantastical person of the name of Rudd who is thrust night after night into principal parts and suffered to annoy the auditors by the deplorable coxcomity of his manner of action." Mrs. Rudd was housekeeper to Lord George Seymour, who was popularly believed to be Conway's father. This cruel allusion to his illegitimate birth so affected Conway that he decided to leave London and come to America, where he made his début at the Park Theatre January 12, 1824, as Hamlet, with such success that Thomas Cooper, then the popular idol, made him an offer to appear with him. The invitation was accepted and for many nights the Park was packed to the doors with people eager to see the two stars together.

Suddenly, in the midst of his success, Conway left New York and went to Newport, where he shut himself out from the world and devoted himself to books.

[*] Mrs. Piozzi, a celebrated literary character of 18th century London, was the daughter of John Salisbury of Bodville, Carnarvonshire. She received a better education than most girls of her time, being well versed in the dead and living languages, and was married in 1763 to Henry Thrale, a brewer. A clever, witty woman, Mrs. Thrale attracted around her some of the most distinguished men of letters of her day. Dr. Johnson, among others, was an intimate of the household and travelled with her and her husband on the continent. On Mr. Thrale's death, she married an Italian musician named Piozzi. He died in 1809. She had considerable literary ability and her "Anecdotes of Dr. Johnson" and "Letters To and From Dr. Johnson" are considered inferior in interest only to Boswell's biography. She died at Clifton, May 2, 1821.

He is believed to have broken down mentally, for, two years later, he took passage to Savannah and as the vessel was approaching Charleston, he seized an opportunity when his fellow passengers were at dinner to throw himself into the sea.

A fresh stimulus was given to theatricals in Philadelphia in 1822 by the reopening of the Chestnut Street Theatre. Notwithstanding all the expense that Messrs. Warren and Wood incurred to redecorate the Walnut Street house and make it safe, that theatre was never popular, and after a few unsuccessful seasons, there was an insistent demand for the rebuilding of the older house. Subscription lists were opened, building operations started and on December 2, 1822, the second Chestnut Street Theatre was opened with " The School for Scandal " acted with this cast: Sir Peter Teazle, Mr. Warren; Sir Oliver, Mr. Francis; Charles Surface, Mr. Wood; Joseph Surface, Mr. H. Wallack; Sir Benjamin Backbite, Mr. Johnson; Crabtree, Mr. Jefferson; Rowly, Mr. Hathwell; Moses, Mr. Burke; Careless, Mr. Darley; Trip, Mr. J. Jefferson; Snake, Mr. Greene; Lady Teazle, Mrs. Wood; Lady Sneerwell, Mrs. Lafalle; Mrs. Candour, Mrs. Francis; Maria, Mrs. H. Wallack.

An incident of the reopening and one which might have had serious results shows how easily the susceptibilities of theatre patrons are ruffled. For the convenience of the public, manager Wood had provided several separate entrances to the theatre—one from Chestnut Street for the orchestra seats, one from Sixth Street for the pit, and one from Carpenter Street for the gallery, the object being to avoid the confusion often arising from all classes of seats using the same main entrance. The pit patrons at once took offense, claiming that such an arrangement made invidious class distinctions and was out of place in a democracy. Inflammatory handbills were circulated and serious trouble might have followed, but for the conciliatory attitude of the management, which at once provided a pit entrance from Chestnut Street. The Walnut Street house, meantime, had been sub-leased to Joe Cowell's New York company.

On December 11, at the Chestnut Street house, Francis Courtney Wemyss, an agreeable English drawing-room comedian, made his first appearance in America as Vapid in "The Dramatist." This actor, who later became an important figure in American theatricals, was born in London in 1797, and began his stage career as an amateur. In 1821 he made his début at the London Adelphi as Sponge in "Where Shall I Dine?" Engaged for America by the agent of the Philadelphia theatre, he arrived in this country late in the fall of 1822. After acting for a few years he was made stage manager of the Chestnut Street Theatre and in 1829 he became sole lessee of that house. Then he went West and became manager of the new Pittsburgh Theatre. In 1848 he was lessee of the Arch Street Theatre, Philadelphia. Apart from his stage activities, he contributed to literature " A Chronology of the American Stage," and some interesting theatrical reminiscences under the title " Twenty Six Years of the Life of an Actor and Manager."

A month after Kean had sailed for England, following his first appearance in America, there arrived in Virginia from London another tragedian who so strongly resembled Kean, both in personal appearance and in his fiery style of acting, that English critics—including the famous Hazlitt—had accused him of copying the established favorite, a charge that had been followed by serious riots at Covent Garden. This was Junius Brutus Booth, the father of the most popular player with the theatregoing public America has ever known—Edwin Booth.

Junius Brutus Booth was born in London in 1796. The family, whose name is believed to have been originally Bethe, was, like the Keans, of Jewish descent. His father, Richard Booth, an attorney with revolutionary tendencies, married a Miss Game, who was lineally descended from the celebrated John Wilkes. The elder Booth, a warm admirer of the writings of Junius, named his son after the famous incognito, adding to it the second name of Brutus. The boy received a good education with a view to his adopting the law as a profession, but long before he grew to manhood, Junius Brutus had decided to become an actor. After dabbling for some time in amateur theatricals, he made his professional début in 1813 with a strolling company as Campillo in " The Honeymoon." With this organization he travelled on the Continent, visiting Ostend, Amsterdam, Antwerp, Brussels and Ghent. In Brussels he took a wife, but the marriage was not a happy one and divorce soon followed. Later, he was back in London where in 1817 he was given his first opportunity to appear at Covent Garden in the rôle of Richard III. A few days after the performance Hazlitt wrote in the *Examiner* as follows:

A gentleman of the name of Booth, who, we understand, has been acting with considerable applause at the Worthing and Brighton, came out in " Richard, Duke of Gloster," at this theatre on Wednesday. We do not know well what to think of his powers till we see him in some part in which he is more himself. His face is adapted to tragic characters, and his voice wants neither strength nor musical expression. But almost the whole of his performance was an exact copy or parody of Mr. Kean's manner of doing the same part. It was a complete, but, at the same time, a successful, piece of plagiarism. We do not think this kind of second-hand reputation can last upon the London boards for more than a character or two. . . . We do not blame Mr. Booth for borrowing Mr. Kean's coat and feathers to appear in upon a first and trying occasion, but if he wishes to gain a permanent reputation, he must come forward in his own person.

Kean was the first to take alarm. Shrewdly, he at once made overtures to Booth, urging him to leave Covent Garden and go to Drury Lane to play Iago to his (Kean's) Othello, his idea being that if he could keep Booth playing subordinate rôles there would be less danger of losing his supremacy. Booth's sudden departure incensed the patrons of Covent Garden and angry mutterings were heard. Meantime, Booth had realized the real object of Kean's apparent friendliness and returned in contrite spirit to Covent Garden. Then the storm broke. The audience, to punish him, would not let him play. Missiles were thrown and for several days pandemonium reigned. Finally, Booth made an apology and the excitement subsided.

John Howard Payne, who was one of those fortunate enough to see Booth play Iago to Kean's Othello, has left this description of the unique contest:

The house was packed from pit to gallery; it was a great performance and a grand sight. The new little man behaved himself like a great hero. Kean seemed to feel the force of the newcomer and performed up to the full height of his wonderful powers. In the jealous scene, their acting appeared like a set trial of skill, and the applause that followed the end of each of their speeches swept over the house like a tornado. The effect was almost bewildering. At the end of the play both of the actors appeared to be exhausted from the extraordinary effort they had made.

Early in 1821 Booth sailed for America with Mary Anne Holmes, an actress and one of the most beautiful women of her day, as his wife, and he made his first appearance on the American stage at Richmond, Va., as Richard, July 13, 1821.

Booth did not consider himself an imitator of Kean. They were both men of the most intense and impassioned nature and easily excited to the action of the play. James E. Murdoch, who acted with Booth in this country, says that the tragedian, while playing in Virginia, used to act Richard one night in his own style and the next in that of Mr. Kean, each of the performances being marked with individual traits of extraordinary genius. Murdoch adds: " The perfect mastery with which he treated the personal manner of Kean's acting while he exhibited his own in distinctive contrast, settled the question (on this side of the water at least) concerning Booth's imitation, while it established him as the peer of Edmund Kean."

The realism Booth put into his acting was one remarkable feature of his performances. When there was any fighting to be done, he was so much in earnest that even his fellow players were afraid of him. Murdoch tells an amusing story of the night he played the young secretary to Booth's Sir Edward

Mortimer in " The Iron Chest." The play has to do with a mystery connected with an iron chest which Sir Edward is known to visit often and always alone, returning from such visits with evident marks of the deepest agitation. One day the young secretary finds the key in the lock of the mysterious chest. Curiosity gets the better of him. He kneels and opens the lid. Murdoch tells the rest:

> The heavy hand fell on my shoulder. I turned and there with the pistol held to my head stood Booth glaring like an infuriated demon. Then, for the first time, I comprehended the reality of acting. The fury of that passion-flamed face and the magnetism of the rigid clutch upon my arm paralyzed my muscles, while the scintillating gleam of the terrible eyes, like the green and red flashes of an enraged serpent, fascinated and fixed me spellbound to the spot. A sudden revulsion of feeling caused me to spring from my knees, but, bewildered with fright and a choking sensation of undefined dread, I fell heavily to the stage, tripping Mr. Booth, who still clutched my shoulder.[7]

A man of conflicting moods, few of his friends professed to understand him. Yet he was given credit for great tenderness and many lovable qualities. Murdoch adds: " There was something peculiar about him that acted like a charm and commanded the respect and won the esteem of all whose advances he encouraged. A morbid tendency of feeling which gave rise to wild and defiant moods led him at times to things at variance with the conventionalities of society and entirely opposed to his well known gentlemanly character and these eccentricities caused coldness and reserve both with himself and his friends."

All his critics, however, are not so gentle. Joseph N. Ireland says:

---

[7] The Stage. By J. E. Murdoch.

Charity would draw a veil over his frailties, but truth obliges us to say of this man with the signet of a god on his brow, that by his own act he was often sunk below the level of the brute. In his moments of inebriation he knew not friend or foe. He forgot his engagements with his managers, his duty to the public, his respect for himself. His drunken brawls were a terror to his friends, yet up to his latest day when he appeared but as a battered and broken column, if the public felt assured that he was himself they thronged to greet him. To the last he retained their affection, if not their respect.[8]

William Winter says of him:

. . . he was heedless and imperfect as an artist, but electrical and fascinating as a man. He would, for example, when acting Macbeth, deliberately go to the wing and obtain a broadsword, from the hand of the prompter, with which to fight the final battle, and would do that in full view of the audience—just as Ristori, when acting Lady Macbeth, would carry Macbeth's letter to the side and throw it away. He did not care, when acting Richard the Third, whether he wore an old dressing gown or a royal robe, and he heeded little where other persons entered or stood, so that they appeared somewhere. ·His acting entirely lacked the finish which was so eminently characteristic of that of his great contemporary Macready and of that still greater artist, the late Henry Irving. But authentic testimony signifies that the soul that he poured into it was awful and terrible: the face, the hands, the posture, the movement,—all was incarnate eloquence; and when the lightning of the blue-gray eyes flashed, and the magnificent voice gave out its deep thunder-roll, or pealed forth its sonorous trumpet-notes, the hearts of his hearers were swept away as on the wings of a tempest.[9]

Anecdotes of his eccentricities are endless. Once, says Phelps, while playing Richard at the Park Theatre "this lunatic of an actor, sword in hand, chased the Richmond of the evening out of the back

---

[8] Records of the New York Stage, by Joseph N. Ireland.
[9] From "The Wallet of Time." Copyright, 1913, by William Winter. Moffat, Yard & Company, Publishers. ¦Reprinted by permission of Jefferson Winter, Esq.

door of the theatre into the street. Another time, while playing Othello, he bore down so heavily with the pillow on the actress playing Desdemona that she was in danger of her life and was only rescued from suffocation by the other actors who rushed upon the stage to save her." Phelps continues:

These fits are said to have come upon him irrespective of whether he had been drinking at the time or not. It was the result of some such freak that in Charleston after playing Othello one night he went to the hotel where he roomed with Tom Flynn, and assuming that he was Iago, began rehearsing the famous scene beginning " Villain, be sure thou prove," etc., with such vehemence that Flynn in self-defence grasped the fire poker and struck Booth over the nose, breaking it and marring his noble countenance forever.[10]

On October 5, 1821, Mr. Booth made his first appearance in New York at the Park Theatre as Richard III. Later he was seen as Brutus, Lear, Othello and Hamlet. Afterwards he acted in Baltimore, Boston, Philadelphia and other cities.

On January 11, 1822, Booth made his first appearance before a New Orleans audience, opening as Richard III. Several writers—the usually careful Ireland among others—have stated that during this engagement, Booth acted the rôle of Orestes in Racine's tragedy " Andromache " in the original French, supported by a company of French actors. That an English speaking player could attempt any such difficult feat, no matter how well he might be acquainted with the language, was, on the face of it, extremely doubtful. The only excuse for taking up space to contradict so obviously inaccurate an assertion is to show how loosely history is sometimes

---

[10] Players of a Century. By H. P. Phelps.

written. The real facts are given by N. M. Ludlow, the pioneer theatre manager in New Orleans, who happened to be himself a member of the cast on that particular occasion. He says:

In the second week of Booth's engagement, a deputation of French gentlemen called on Mr. Caldwell, the manager, to be introduced to Mr. Booth, with the view of ascertaining if he could not perform some tragedy of which they had more knowledge than those he had thus far presented to them, which, up to that time, had been only " Richard III," the " Iron Chest," and " A New Way to Pay Old Debts "—six nights in all, our performances being only four times per week. In the two latter plays he had created an immense sensation, and the French population were all agog to witness a performance of the great man in some play they were more familiar with, that they might see him to the best advantage. Mr. Booth told this deputation of gentlemen that he had once performed Orestes, in an English translation of Racine's " Andromache," and that, with a few days for him to recover the words of this character, it would afford him pleasure to perform it before an audience of French ladies and gentlemen. The party confessed themselves under great obligations to him for his courtesy, and a night was set apart for the purpose in the following week. This tragedy, called in the English translation " The Distressed Mother," was rendered into English by a Mr. Ambrose Phillips, of England, and was often acted during the last half of the previous century, but since has gradually vanished from the stage. Five of the principal characters of the play were cast as follows: Pyrrhus (son of Achilles), Mr. Hughes; Orestes (son of Agamemnon), Mr. J. B. Booth; Pylades (friend of Orestes), Mr. Ludlow; Andromache (Hector's widow), Mrs. Hughes; Hermione (daughter of Menelaus), Miss Seymour. When the night arrived for this tragedy to be performed, the theatre was crowded to an excess, and at least half the audience were French ladies and gentlemen, who understood but very little of the English language, but they could comprehend the tragedy so far as they were familiar with Racine's " Andromache." Mr. Booth received immense applause during the performance of the play, but the closing scene was the crowning of a brilliant triumph. The gentlemen, and even the ladies, rose from their seats and applauded, the former calling out, " Brava! Brava!" " Talma, Talma!" long after the curtain had descended.[11]

That same year (1822) Booth purchased " The Farm," an estate in Harford County, near Baltimore, and here he settled down with his family. In 1825 he went to England, appearing in London as Brutus, but soon returned to America, visiting California with great success. His last appearance on the stage was on the boards of the St. Charles Theatre, New Orleans, November 19, 1852, as Mortimer in " The Iron Chest." He died November 30 of the same year.

[11] Dramatic Life as I Found It, by N. M. Ludlow.

CHAPTER XIV

THE DRAMA IN THE WEST

EARLY BARNSTORMERS. DIFFICULTIES OF TRAVEL. NAVIGATING
THE OHIO AND MISSISSIPPI. DANGER FROM WILD BEASTS. FIRST
THEATRICAL PERFORMANCE IN PITTSBURGH. THE VIRGINS OF
THE SUN. FIRST THEATRES IN LOUISVILLE, CINCINNATI AND
ST. LOUIS. JAMES H. CALDWELL BUILDS THE ST. CHARLES THE-
ATRE, NEW ORLEANS. THEATRICALS AMONG THE MORMONS.
THE SALT LAKE THEATRE. THE RIVER SHOW-BOATS. EARLY
THEATRES IN CHICAGO AND SAN FRANCISCO.

ALTHOUGH the constantly growing interest in theatricals had by this time resulted in the building of
a chain of fine playhouses all along the Atlantic seaboard, the Nineteenth Century was already well
advanced before the sock and buskin was seen west
of the Alleghenies. In 1800 the great valley east of
the Rockies was still a vast wilderness, the primeval
silence of its mighty rivers and virgin forests broken
only by the howling of wolves and the yell of the
marauding redskin. Cincinnati, with a population
of about 1000, was the only western town of any size.
St. Louis was little more than a hamlet. A group of
frame cabins, clustered within the stockade shelter of
Fort Dearborn, occupied the site of the future city of
Chicago. It was not until the introduction of steam
navigation on the Ohio and Mississippi in 1816 that
there was any rapid growth in the settlement of the
middle West. Before that time, what little trade
existed was carried on between the widely scattered
settlements and towns by means of crudely con-

structed flat bottom boats—the famous keel boat of the Ohio and the " broadhorns " of Kentucky.

The pampered stage favorite of to-day who gazes idly out of the window, as his private car speeds smoothly across the continent, and even his less fortunate brother mummer whom bad business has reduced to the sorry expedient of " footing it " home on the railroad ties, can have little idea of the hardships and perils the pioneer actors of the West had to face when they set out a hundred years ago to carry the message of Thespis through the American backwoods.

The recorded history of the drama in the West begins in Albany, N. Y., in the year 1814. John Bernard was then manager of the Albany theatre. One day a man named Usher presented himself at the theatre, stating that he was an " actor and recently arrived from the state of Kentucky." As Kentucky in those days was literally the " far, far West," the stranger attracted more than the usual amount of attention. He wished to play an engagement of a few nights, and Mr. Bernard, who had seen him act in Boston a few years previously, engaged him. During the brief time he was with the company, Usher told Samuel Drake, then Bernard's stage manager, that his main object in coming East was to try and engage a company for Kentucky, where he said he had three theatres—one at Lexington, one at Frankfort and a third at Louisville. The adventure at once appealed to Drake, who agreed to get together a small company with which he would start for Kentucky the following spring.

But it was easier said than done. It proved no

light task to find actors and actresses courageous enough to undertake such a long hazardous journey into the unknown. The difficulties of travel were enormous and sufficient to deter the stoutest hearted. There were no roads, no stage coaches, no steamers. The only methods of travel were on horseback or by wagon and then by tow or drift boat down the great rivers.

Experienced actors, holding well-paid, comfortable positions in the already established theatres in the East, refused to listen to what they considered a crazy scheme and for some time Drake was nonplussed. Members of his own family—all actors—were willing to go, but he needed others. Finally, he approached a young actor named Noah Miller Ludlow, who had recently joined the company to play small parts, and made him an offer. Full of pluck and enthusiasm, eager for the adventure, Ludlow promptly accepted and later himself became a leader among those early barnstormers—Usher, Turner, Drake, Caldwell, Sol Smith, Isherwood, Collins and Jones, Chapman—who introduced the acted drama through the great West. After thirty-eight years of management, Ludlow wrote a book of his adventures during that early period of development and to its interesting pages the present writer is indebted for many of the otherwise inaccessible details given in this chapter.

Having assembled his players, Drake now began to make preparations for departure. His little band of mummers consisted of Samuel Drake, Sr., Samuel Drake, Jr., Alexander Drake, James Drake, N. M. Ludlow, Mrs. Lewis, Miss Denny, Miss Martha

Drake, Miss Julia Drake (afterwards the mother of Julia Dean), Mr. Lewis, stage carpenter, and Joe Tracy, man of all work. Others were to join the company at Pittsburgh.

As Drake did not wish to reach Kentucky until late in the fall, he decided to prolong his journey by performing at towns on his way to the land of promise. His course was to travel northwest in the state of New York, until he should reach Canandaigua, then to deflect to the southwest, strike the head waters of the Allegheny River, descend by boat to Pittsburgh, and perform there until the assembling of the State Legislature of Kentucky, early in December. Some time about the latter part of July, 1815, the party started from Canandaigua for the head waters of the Allegheny River. Ludlow writes:

Our means of transportation were a road-wagon, drawn by two horses, owned by Mr. Drake, and a light spring wagon owned by Mr. Lewis, drawn by one horse, and used for the convenience and comfort of his wife and occasionally one other of the ladies; the other portions of the company, after leaving town, were expected to walk the greater part of the way. The manager, being the oldest person, and rather obese, it was unanimously decided, should occupy a seat in the large wagon by the side of the driver, Joe Tracy. Sam Drake, Alexander, his brother (familiarly " Aleck "), and I started on foot before sunrise, for Sam said, " I'll not march through Coventry with them; that's flat!" and so we started on ahead, the cavalcade following about sunrise; and in this way we started for Olean, a settlement on the Allegheny River, Cataraugus County, New York, about one hundred and fifty miles southwest of Canandaigua, and through what was then almost a wilderness.[1]

In Olean, " a wild looking place," the players disposed of their wagons and horses and purchased a

[1] Dramatic Life as I Found It, N. M. Ludlow.

flat bottomed boat known in those days as an " Ark "
or " Broadhorn."

It was about twenty-five feet long by fifteen wide, boarded up
at the sides, and covered with an elliptical roof about high enough
to allow a man of medium stature to stand erect beneath the
centre. It was quadrangular, and intended to be a kind of floating
house, of small dimensions. In one end of this boat were two rooms,
partitioned off as bedrooms, one for Mr. Lewis and wife, the other
for the three single young ladies, the Misses Drake and Miss Denny.
The men, especially the young ones, were expected to " rough it,"
and rough it we did.

One evening shortly after they started out, the
younger men in the party took a skiff and rowed
ashore to reconnoitre. They soon had to beat a rapid
retreat for they suddenly came upon wolves. They
saw the beasts's eyes flashing in the dark undergrowth,
and the howling wolves were heard all that night.
The next morning the voyage was resumed. The
weather was very warm and there was no protection
from the hot sun except under the low roof.

The ladies complained very much of the heat; they could not
remain under the low roof of the boat and came to the bow, where
they could catch some portion of a breeze then blowing up stream.
There was a space of about seven feet that had not been enclosed;
but even here, screened as they were with umbrellas from the sun,
there was much complaint. At the suggestion of the manager, one
of our scenes was got out and unrolled, which being stretched over
the top of the boat, presented a painted canvas surface of twelve
by fifteen feet. This top was not far removed from a level, the
centre being raised only enough to throw off water in the event of
rain. Seated on this elevation, and screened from the sun, they
obtained more air, and consequently more comfort. Thus situated,
we floated down at a very slow rate; some reading, some sewing,
some sleeping, and all without anything to excite us or disturb the
quiet of the wilderness around until about four o'clock in the
afternoon.

They travelled only in the daytime, the men being organized into two watches, one to go on at seven in the morning about the time of starting, the other in the afternoon, Mr. Drake acting as chief navigator.

Gradually the country grew less wild and uncultivated. They were again getting into civilized regions. They met more frequently well cleared farms and better built houses. At nine o'clock one night, to their great delight, the glimmerings of a city broke upon their view. They had reached Pittsburgh, a city of no small consequence even at that early day. The theatre which Luke Usher had built and which Drake found on his arrival, was only a poor frame affair. The first brick theatre built in the Iron City was not opened until September 2, 1832, when Francis Courtney Wemyss, the well-known English actor, became manager of the theatre there and presented " The Busybody." Until that year the drama had no permanent home in Pittsburgh, which has remained an important theatrical centre ever since. The old Opera House, under the direction of Ellsler and Gotthold, played all the great stars and had a fine stock company in the seventies, while the more modern houses—the Alvin, the Duquesne, Pitt and Nixon—rank with the best in the country.

The first thing the actors from Albany did on landing was to inspect the playhouse. Ludlow writes:

Such a theatre! It was the poorest apology for one I had then ever seen; I have, I confess, seen worse since. It was situated on the eastern outskirts of the city, and fronted, I think, on Fifth Street, not far from Wood Street. It had been built, I think, by some amateur in theatricals. It contained a pit and one tier of boxes, as they were called. The form was after the old style—two parallel elongations, with an elliptical curve at the entrance. The decorations, if such they might be termed, were of the plainest kind, and every portion bore the Pittsburg stamp upon it—coal smut.

Pittsburgh's first theatrical season began the middle of August, 1815, with a performance of Tobin's popular comedy "The Honeymoon." The cast included: Mr. Williams, S. Drake, Mr. Ludlow, Mr. Drake, Sr., A. Drake, Mrs. Williams, Miss Denny, Mrs. Riddle and Mrs. Lewis. Previous to this time there had been occasional performances by amateurs and strolling "show folk," but this was the first dramatic performance given by a regularly organized professional company and marked the beginning of Pittsburgh's dramatic history. The third night's performance consisted of Sheridan's romantic play "Pizarro, or the Virgins of the Sun." Mr. Drake was opposed to attempting it, owing to the many difficulties. One of these was a lack of virgins. The company was very limited in regard to females, and the town folk would have as soon consented to walk deliberately into the infernal regions as offer their services as "supers." Yet what was the use of·a Temple of the Sun without Virgins of the Sun as worshippers? However, preparations for the production went on, and the play was finally produced on a Saturday night. The first act went off with considerable *éclat* and when the Temple of the Sun was presented to the dazzled eyes of the audience the applause was immense. The band commenced a slow, solemn piece of music to which the Virgins of the Sun were to enter on the stage in silent reverence to begin their worship of the sun. Says Ludlow:

They made their appearance, first entrance, right and left hand, one from each side; met in front at the centre of the stage; then side by side passed up, bowed a reverent salutation to the god of day, and then took their positions to the right and left sides and commenced the beautiful chant of " Oh, Power Supreme! " The first pair of virgins, provided by Mr. Williams, were the Elvira of the night, Mrs. Lewis, and Cora, Miss Denny, with long white robes and veils to disguise them. The next pair of virgins were two daughters of Mr. Drake, Miss Julia, then about fourteen years of age, and her sister Martha about thirty. The third pair of virgins were an old Irishwoman who cleaned the dressing-rooms, and the " property-man," a Pennsylvania Dutchman, whose business it was to provide all small articles of furniture required for the stage. As the old song goes, " Sure such a pair was never seen." A description of these virgins is worthy of record, in order that the present generation of playgoers may know to what shifts the pioneers of the Western drama had to resort in order to succeed with their business. Their costumes consisted of long white cotton gowns reaching to the ankles, and closed in front; around the waist a red sash; suspended from the neck, on the breast, a large golden sun; over the head and ears, and reaching to the shoulders, a white cloth or bandeau; over this a short white gauze veil reaching below the chin, in order, in this case, to conceal the features. The property official was a short, stout man, with a low forehead, a pug nose, and in no small degree corpulent. The old house-cleaner was not able to make as prominent an appearance, in the same way, as did her companion, yet when she walked up the stage there was a stern reality exhibited by her, that made her quite as conspicuous in the public eye as her companion in piety. While this ceremony of entering and doing reverence to the sun was proceeding, there was a silence such as should always exist during any devotional service, Christian or Pagan; but when the last-mentioned pair of virgins entered, bowed, and were walking up the stage, there was heard to arise from the centre of the pit a long and pious groan, and a voice, partially subdued, but loud enough to be heard in the prevailing silence, exclaimed, " Oh, such virgins! " The effect was not unlike that of dropping a lighted match into a canister of gunpowder—the explosion was tremendous. The pit shouted and the house roared with laughter, in which the actors were compelled to join.

The season ended early in November with a benefit for Mr. Drake, Sr. The next stand was Frankfort, Ky., a journey of four hundred miles. There was no way of going except by water, so, another "Broadhorn" having been secured, they started November 15, 1815, down the Ohio River. They reached Limestone, or Maysville as it was afterwards known, a week later, where they had to abandon the boat and make the rest of the journey by wagon. Two conveyances were purchased, one for the baggage and one for the ladies.

At Frankfort they were joined by other actors, John Vaughan, leading man, Henry Vaughan, Frank Blissett, who played low comedy, Tom Jefferson, oldest son of Joseph Jefferson the first, and James Douglass, a son of David Douglass, the early American theatre manager. The first Frankfort theatrical season opened early in December, 1815, with Colman's play "The Mountaineers," followed by "The Poor Soldier," Mr. Blissett playing Bagatelle in the farce. The season ended early in March, 1816, after which the players started for Louisville. Says Ludlow:

The only theatre in Louisville at that time stood on Jefferson Street, where it was in 1832. It was afterwards burned down. It belonged, I believe, to a gentleman of the name of Tyler. This season of ours in Louisville I understood to be the first that had been made by any regular company of comedians. It lasted about ten or eleven weeks, and was undoubtedly profitable to the management, for the house was well filled every night. The season closed with benefits to the company, all of them being well attended, and this in a town of not more than three thousand inhabitants at that time; but the people were prosperous, gay, and fond of theatrical amusements.

The next stand was Lexington where a brewery had been converted into a theatre.

The second story of this building, a long and narrow one, had been fitted for dramatic performances by an amateur society. It was probably seventy to eighty feet in length by about twenty-five to thirty feet in width. If I remember rightly, the seats were constructed upon the amphitheatre plan—gradually rising from the floor, one above the other, to the back, these back seats being reached by a sloping platform at one side. They were simply covered with canvas and painted, without being stuffed, or having any backs to them, and the surroundings were of the most simple, unpretending character.

After considerable sweeping, cleaning and painting, the Lexington theatre was opened by Drake and his company for the first regular season ever played there, June 15, 1816, with Colman's comedy " Speed the Plough."

The following year Mr. Ludlow married and left the company to join others of the Drake organization who had decided to form a dramatic company on the " commonwealth " system. The plan was to play their way through Kentucky to Nashville, Tenn. They reached Nashville in time to open there July 10, 1817, with the " Soldier's Daughter." The cast included: Aaron J. Phillips, Mr. Ludlow, Mr. Vaughan, H. Vaughan, Mr. Bainbridge, Mrs. Vaughan, Miss Wallace (Mrs. Ludlow). The season lasted only three weeks, when Ludlow and Phillips started on horseback for Cincinnati to seek recruits for the company.

Cincinnati at that time had grown into a bustling young town of 8,500 inhabitants. It did not become a city until 1819, but thanks to the newly introduced steam navigation, it was making rapid strides in population and prosperity. A small dramatic company was already performing there under the management of William Turner, but business was far from good and the organization was on the eve of disbandment when Ludlow arrived.

The first theatre in Cincinnati had opened in 1801. It was a frame building and stood on Front Street. In 1815 Mr. Turner went to Cincinnati with a few actors and occupied a temporary theatre erected by some amateurs. His first company consisted of: Mr. Joshua Collins, Thomas Caulfield, Thomas Morgan, Thomas Jefferson, William Anderson, Robert Laidly, A. Cargill, Lucas Beale, Mrs. Turner, Mrs. Barrett (mother of George Barrett) and Mrs. Milner. The second theatre built in Cincinnati was the Columbia Street Theatre, built by Collins and Jones in 1820. Then came the Globe and Caldwell's New Cincinnati, opened 1832. These were followed by the National, where, under the management of John Bates, a fine stock company was maintained and all the important stars appeared; Wood's Theatre, Barney McCauley's, Robinson's Opera House, all favorite stages for visiting stars, and Pike's Opera House, fifty years ago one of the most widely known and most imposing theatres in the West. Destroyed by fire, its site is now occupied by a business block. The Grand Opera House, very popular in the seventies, is still Cincinnati's leading theatre.

Ludlow returned to Nashville with the recruits from Turner's company, and, after a successful season, conceived the idea of taking the English speaking drama to New Orleans, already a city of considerable importance. Although there had been a French theatre in New Orleans since 1809, no company speaking the English language had ever performed there, and it was believed that an American company would do well, as the resident American population was large.

But there were difficulties in the way. Ludlow's players were far from sharing their leader's enthusiasm for the scheme. New Orleans in those days (1817) had not a very savory reputation. Yellow fever was rampant, and there was bitter feeling among the French and Spaniards towards anyone speaking the English language, owing to the hostility of the natives towards the Louisiana Purchase. It was no uncommon occurrence for Americans to be robbed or even assassinated in the streets of the city. Mr. Phillips refused flatly to go and left the company when he found his objections overruled. But Messrs. Vaughan and Morgan were willing to share profits or losses with Ludlow and the rest of the company were to have their usual salary.

There were no steamboats then on the Cumberland, but two or three plied on the Mississippi and the plan was to go by " keel boat " as far as Natchez and there take the steamer. The little band of players left Nashville October 20, 1817, and about a month later reached Natchez. A stop here had not been contemplated, but on the earnest solicitation of a committee of influential citizens, Ludlow consented to give a performance of " The Honeymoon " in the " little theatre on the bluff." This first performance, by any professional dramatic company, was given at Natchez, November 15, 1817. A few days later the players arrived at the levee at New Orleans City.

Having obtained permission to open from the mayor, whose representative suggested the propriety of sending his honor the compliment of a box to be set apart and reserved for himself and party whenever they wished to visit the theatre, Ludlow opened on December 24, 1817, with Tobin's ever popular comedy "The Honeymoon," followed by a farce "The Hotel, or a Servant with Two Masters." This was the first dramatic performance given by professional actors in the city of New Orleans. The cast included the following players: John Vaughan, Mr. Ludlow, Mr. Plummer, Mr. Lucas, Mr. Morgan, Henry Vaughan, Mr. Bainbridge, Mr. Jones, Mrs. J. Vaughan, Mrs. Jones, Mrs. Ludlow and Mrs. Morgan.

The theatre, situated in St. Phillippi Street, was called the St. Philip. The auditorium consisted of two tiers of boxes and a parquet and seated about seven hundred persons, the prices of admission being one dollar to all parts of the house. The theatre on the opening night "was crowded from bottom to top, half the audience being French and many of them not understanding one word in a hundred that was spoken. Nevertheless, the performance went off with great applause."

A year after the arrival of the Ludlow company, the new French theatre, called The Orleans, was completed and opened in the fall of 1818 under the management of John Davis, a Frenchman with an English name, who had imported a company of French artistes from Paris. Two years later, James H. Caldwell, another famous pioneer manager in the West, arrived in New Orleans from Virginia and opened at the St. Philip Theatre January 7, 1820, presenting " The Honeymoon " following the farce " Three and Deuce."

Mr. Caldwell, who was a conspicuous figure in American theatricals for many years, was born in England in 1793 and made his stage début in Manchester. Brought to this country by Mr. Holman, he made his first appearance in America at Charleston, S. C., November, 1816, as Belcour in " The West Indian." His career as a manager began the following year at Columbus, Ky. He also managed a theatre at Washington. In 1818, he built by subscription the theatre at Petersburg, Va., and that same year presented the first play seen in Richmond since the fatal fire. He ended his first New Orleans season in April, 1820, and then returned with his company to Petersburg. The following year, Caldwell returned to New Orleans with two big stars—Junius Brutus Booth and Thomas 'A. Cooper, and on May 29, 1822, laid the corner-stone of the first American theatre built in New Orleans. This house, known as the Camp Street Theatre, was opened January 1, 1824, with the comedy " Town and Country," the following players being in the cast: Messrs. J. H. Caldwell, Ed. Caldwell, Forrest, Garner, Ludlow, Gray, Russell, Scott, Higgins, McCafferty, Scholes, Mesdames Russell, Ludlow, Higgins, Mongin, Noke and Miss Jane Placide.

The new theatre was illuminated throughout with gas, being the first building lighted by such means in the city of New Orleans. In 1835 Caldwell built in New Orleans a more elaborate theatre which he called the St. Charles. More luxurious in its appointments than any theatre yet built in America, the St. Charles rivalled in size and importance the most famous playhouses of Europe. It was destroyed by fire in 1842 and the following year Caldwell retired from the stage. After filling several official positions in New Orleans, he went to New York at the outbreak of the Civil War and died there in 1863.

In 1843 the St. Charles was rebuilt and reopened under the management of Messrs. Ludlow and Smith with " The Honeymoon." The house remained New Orleans' most fashionable theatre for many years, nearly all the famous stars appearing on its boards. The old French Opera House, built early in the century, and still standing, is the last of New Orleans' earliest theatres. The Academy of Music and the Varieties were opened in the fifties. The latter house shared honors with the St. Charles for many years, and in the eighties superseded it in the public favor. The Tulane, which now plays all the first-class attractions, and the Crescent were erected in the nineties.

Mr. Ludlow, after closing in New Orleans in 1818, went to Natchez where he was taken very ill, and as a consequence the company disbanded and was dispersed. On his recovery, Ludlow joined a partnership with Alexander Cummings, whose wife had acted at the Park Theatre, New York, to organize a company and invade Alabama, still virgin territory as far as any theatrical troupe was concerned. The first place visited was Huntsville, then a town of twelve or fifteen hundred inhabitants. There was considerable difficulty in getting together a company. Although encouraging reports of profitable Western tours had reached the seaboard cities, actors could not be induced to join. When asked, they would exclaim: " I've no desire to be devoured by savages!" All Ludlow could muster was seven males and three females. He says:

> Our commencement at Huntsville was with considerable misgivings of success. First, because the town was very limited in point of population, and, secondly, because there did not appear much expression of a desire to witness theatricals. Both of these apprehensions disappeared, however, as we came to understand that the wealthiest and best-informed classes, those from whom we really obtained our principal support, resided not generally within the town limits, but from two to five miles around in the adjacent country, being mostly planters, and men of wealth and leisure. These would frequently come to town in their carriages and bring their families to witness our performances; and they soon began to consider theatrical amusements necessary to their pleasure. As our company was very small, and half of it entire novices, we were much troubled to find pieces we could place before the public with any probability of affording satisfaction; but, with some skill in managing on our part, and a large share of indulgence on the part of our auditors, we succeeded, I believe, in meeting their expectations. The opening play was Tobin's comedy " The Honeymoon," but cut down by me to three acts, and performed under the title of the " Duke's Marriage"; the first time, I believe, it was ever played under that name. The whole piece was not badly played, except that Mr. Flanagan made the Spanish count an Irish count. Our opening farce was Sam Foote's " Liar."

This was the first company of professional actors that ever performed in Alabama. In 1824 Mr. Ludlow went to Mobile and on December 24 opened the first theatre ever erected in that city. The bill was, as usual, Tobin's popular " Honeymoon," followed by the farce " The Liar." Regarding the theatre, which had been built by subscription, the manager says:

THE THEATRE IN AMERICA

The building was of brick, and erected on a part of the site of an old fort, built and occupied by Spaniards during the time when the country was a portion of the territory of Spain. The theatre stood on the northwest corner of Royal and Theatre Streets, the latter taking its name after the erection of the theatre. It had a front of about sixty feet on Royal Street, running back-west about one hundred and ten feet. It was arranged with a pit and two tiers of boxes, and would seat between six and seven hundred people. The centre of the upper tier was partitioned off for the use of the colored population; this was subdivided so as to accommodate a certain class of them known as "quadroons," who, having a portion of white blood in their veins, would not condescend to mix with those that had purely negro blood, and whom they looked upon as an inferior class.

Always on the lookout for new territory to conquer, Mr. Ludlow's attention after his first venture in Alabama, was attracted to St. Louis, Mo., then a town of some three or four thousand inhabitants. A friend told him that there had never been a dramatic company in St. Louis, that the people were fond of amusements, and that no doubt he would do well. Tempted by this glowing picture, Ludlow decided to embark on the adventure:

About the 20th of November we embarked with our luggage on a "keel-boat" for St. Louis. We were a week in getting to the Ohio River, including the delay of taking the iron-castings on board, and nearly two days from there to the Mississippi River. All of this from Nashville, so far, was down stream; but now came the tug. The remainder of the voyage was to be performed against the current of the Mississippi, at that season of the year equal to five miles an hour. In those early days, I think there were but two or three steamboats that ran to and from St. Louis, and one of these was called the "Missouri Packet," and she had passed down to New Orleans a long time before our arrival at the junction of the Ohio and Mississippi Rivers. The only method of ascending this rapid river by keel-boats was "cordelling," and this process was by putting out on shore a long, strong rope, which six or eight men would take on their shoulders, and by main strength pull the boat up against the current; opposed to this pulling, the captain of the boat would steer his craft so as to keep her from running into the river bank. It was very hard work and very slow proceeding, seldom accomplishing more than twenty or twenty-five miles a day. I confess I felt a little discouraged when I landed in St. Louis; it was not anything like as cleanly or as well built as any of the towns of the West or South that I had previously visited. The building occupied by us had been erected by means of subscriptions, expressly for a theatre; it was started by and intended for the use of an amateur society. It fronted east and stood about forty feet back from the west side of Main Street. We began our season about the middle of December, 1819, with " The Honeymoon." The cast included the following professionals: Messrs. Ludlow, Vos, Cargill, King, Hanna, Frethy, Dauberman, Flanagan, Mesdames Ludlow, Vos, Hanna, Miss Macaffrey.

This was the first dramatic performance by a professional company given in the city of St. Louis. Owing to lack of patronage, the season did not prove successful and Mr. Ludlow was forced to disband. But this initial effort, unsuccessful as it was, helped to give a stimulus to theatregoing and from that time on the drama began to prosper in St. Louis. In 1820 Collins and Jones took a company there, and seven years later J. H. Caldwell transformed the old Salt House building into a theatre and gave performances. But there was no theatre worthy of the name in St. Louis until 1837. Two years previously, Ludlow and Sol Smith started a public subscription to erect a temple of Thespis which should be a credit to the city. They succeeded in raising $65,000 and the theatre opened July 3, 1837, with " The Honeymoon." Later St. Louis theatres were the National, built in 1845, Bates Theatre (1851), afterwards St.

Louis and De Bar's Opera House; Olympic (1868);
Pope's Theatre (1879), later the Century (1896);
People's (1881), later Havlin's (1888); Grand Opera
House (1884). More modern houses are the American (1908); the Coliseum (1909), with a seating
capacity of nearly 10,000 used for conventions and
sometimes for grand opera, and the Shubert Memo-
rial Theatre (1910).

Among the historic playhouses of the West, the
Salt Lake Theatre, built by Brigham Young in 1862,
is one of the most famous.[2]

The Mormons have always been fond of theatricals, and the elders entertained so high an opinion of
the drama as an educational force that Joseph Smith,
the prophet, long before the exodus from Nauvoo in
the forties, encouraged the formation of a dramatic
company. In this early theatrical organization Brigham Young and other prominent Mormons occasionally acted, professional strength being infused by
Thomas A. Lyne, a favorite tragedian in Eastern
cities, who went from Philadelphia to join the
Nauvoo players. Hiram B. Clawson, who twenty
years later was joint manager with Joseph T. Caine
of the Salt Lake Theatre, made his first appearance as
an actor with this company in " Pizarro." In 1847
the Mormons left Nauvoo and, marching westward,
finally settled in the great valley.

Almost immediately after Brigham Young's followers started to build their " city of saints," dramatic performances were given at the " Bowery," a
small frame building situated on the site of the big

---

[2] For some of the data regarding the early beginnings of the Mormon
Players the author is indebted to an interesting little brochure by Horace
G. Whitney, entitled "The Drama in Utah."

Tabernacle, and here, in 1850, the famous Salt Lake Theatre stock company began its career with the drama " Robert Macaire," followed by a dancing interlude and a farce " The Dead Shot." Two years later, the players moved to larger quarters, a building known as Social Hall, where " The Lady of Lyons " was the opening attraction. This was Salt Lake City's principal place of amusement until 1861, when a rival organization, known as the Mechanics' Dramatic Association and headed by Henry Bowring and Phil Margetts, two comedians, gave performances in " Bowring's Theatre," which had so small an auditorium that Brigham Young, impressed by the lack of space, took steps to bring the rival organizations together, promising them a real theatre, and this led to the consolidation of the two companies and the erection of the Salt Lake Theatre.

Work on the new playhouse, which cost $100,000, was begun in 1861, while the Civil War was raging, and it was opened on March 6 of the following year with religious services followed by the play " The Pride of the Market," after which there was dancing. The players who took part included: John T. Caine, Henry Maiben, Jos Simmons, R. H. Parker, David McKenzie, H. B. Clawson, S. D. Sirrine, R. Matthews, Henry Snell, John B. Kelly, Mrs. Woodmansee, Mrs. Margaret G. Clawson, W. C. Dunbar, W. E. Bowring, W. H. Miles, Phil Margetts, Mrs. Bowring and Miss Maggie Thomas.

At first there was a ban on tragedy and melodrama, Brigham Young taking the ground that laughter, not tears, was the ideal amusement for the people, and the appearance of " Gentile " actors—

non-believers—was forbidden.[8] But in time these restrictions were removed and the most distinguished players appeared on the boards of the Salt Lake Theatre, among others George Pauncefort, Julia Dean Hayne, an immense favorite with Salt Lake City audiences, C. W. Couldock, James Stark, E. L. Davenport, John McCullough, James A. Herne and Lucille Western, Charles Wheatleigh, Lotta, Edwin Adams, Edwin Booth, Lawrence Barrett, Salvini, Ristori, Mary Anderson and Joseph Jefferson. Annie Asenath Adams was a popular member of the company in 1864 and her daughter, Maude Adams, began her successful career at this house in 1873.

A unique feature of the early American drama in the West, which first made its appearance about this time, was the river showboat, or floating theatre—a development from the itinerant players who, travelling on canal boats and flat bottoms, gave performances in the stuffy cabins at each settlement along the river banks they came to. Prominent among the players who adopted this novel form was the well known Chapman family. William Chapman, Sr., was born in England, and made his first appearance in America at the Bowery Theatre in " Othello " October 22, 1828. Shortly afterwards he organized a company consisting of members of his own family and others and started for Pittsburgh, where they acted in the dining room of the hotel. While in the Iron City, they had built for them a floating theatre. It was nothing but a large flat boat with a rude kind of

---

[8] Thomas A. Lyne, the tragedian, who returned to Salt Lake City in 1863 and played a long engagement there, appearing in such dramas as "Damon and Pythias," "Richelieu," "Othello," "Richard III," "William Tell," "Pizarro," etc., had joined the Mormon faith at the time of his visit to Nauvoo in the forties.

house erected upon it. Above the roof projected a
staff with flag attached, upon which was the word
" Theatre." Inside, hard board seats stretched from
one side of the boat to the other, while at the far end
was a little stage with muslin curtain and tallow
candles for foot lights. Chapman and his family
acted and lived in this boat and for years travelled
up and down the Ohio and Mississippi Rivers, visiting all the principal towns. At one settlement on the
Ohio where they stopped and performed, some young
men complained of the price of admission. Offended
because they could not get in to see the show for a
quarter of a dollar, the price being a half a dollar for
adults, they did not go away, but remained around on
the shore, in hopes of seeing or hearing something
without paying for it. Finding this could not be
accomplished, they took an occasion when the performance was proceeding quietly to cast the boat from
its moorings before the actors or audience were aware
of it. The current carried the boat out more than a
mile before it could be got to shore again and the
spectators had to trudge their way home as best they
could.

Even at the present day the river show boat can
be seen in all its splendor on the Monongahela and
Missouri Rivers. The modern floating theatre is, of
course, far superior to Chapman's rude craft. A
writer gives this interesting description of one of these
aquatic playhouses:

From $40,000 to $50,000 is not an unusual price for the finer
ones—a cost far exceeding that of many good city theatres. Often
designed after the plans of famous playhouses, such as the Black-
stone, of Chicago, these water auditoriums are scientifically built

and lavishly furnished. For instance, the " Golden Rod," a source of wonder to many a river boy, possesses an auditorium one hundred and sixty-two feet long and forty-six feet wide, with nineteen upholstered boxes and a seating capacity of fourteen hundred. Many a city of fifty thousand people cannot boast of such a stage—forty-six feet wide, twenty-four feet deep, with six elaborate drop curtains and numerous " set " pieces and many changes of scenery. Sometimes the handbills of these crafts proudly—and truthfully—announce a " family circle," with cushioned settees for five hundred, and a " dress circle," with a thousand armchairs, while steam heat in winter and cold-air blowers in summer make the audience forget the weather on shore. In the days immediately after the Civil War hundreds of gas jets and innumerable mirrors made the white walls of the boat glisten; but now a thousand electric lights glow within and without, and send their many colors shimmering far over the rippling waters. An inspection of one of the larger boats casts out all doubt as to the cost of building. For example, the " American Floating Theatre " finds necessary two steam engines, one gasoline engine, a thousand-pound ice plant, a steam laundry, an electric vacuum cleaning outfit, two large dynamos, electric fans, a well-equipped printing plant, a telephone system, a complete hot and cold water system, a thousand electric lights, a huge American flag composed of seven hundred and fifty colored incandescent globes, and, of course, the joy of every American boy, a huge calliope.[4]

There were no public amusements of any kind in Chicago until 1837 when Dean and McKinly of the Eagle Street Theatre, Buffalo, N. Y., applied to the city council for a permit " to open a theatre in some suitable building for a term of one or more months, as the business might warrant." That same year H. Isherwood and Alexander McKenzie turned the banquet hall of the historic Sauganash Hotel into a theatre. In a letter to the late J. H. McVicker, some interesting details are given by Isherwood regarding this pioneer venture:

[4] From an article by Carl Holliday in the *Theatre Magazine* for May, 1917.

THE DRAMA IN THE WEST

In 1837 I arrived in Chicago at night and was driven to a hotel in the pelting rain. The next morning we went out to take a view of the place. There was a plank wall in front of the building, and, to my astonishment, I saw a flock of quail on the plank. I returned to the hotel disappointed at what I saw of the town, and made up my mind that this was no place for a show. I told my landlord of my intention to return, and he gave me such a glowing account of what our success would be that he induced me to remain. At length some one hit upon a place that would do. It had been a rough tavern, with an extension of fifty feet in length added to it and stood at some distance out on the prairie, solitary and alone. I arranged with the owner and painted some pretty scenes. I then wrote to Mr. McKenzie, and he came from Buffalo with the company. It consisted of Messrs. Sankey, Childs, Wright, and others. A young Irishman who made one of the party became very unruly, and I was obliged to dismiss him. He said: "Where shall I go, with Lake Michigan roaring on one side and the bloody prairie wolves on the other?" I can only remember one play, "The Stranger." When the season was concluded, we took to the prairies, visiting the towns in the interior. Returning in the spring to Chicago, we fitted up a new place. It was on a street leading to the bridge. Joseph Jefferson and his wife, with young Joe, joined us there.

Joseph Jefferson has given us some idea of what Chicago looked like at that time. In 1838 the Western metropolis had just turned from an Indian village into a thriving little place, and his uncle had written to Jefferson, Sr., urging him to join in the management of the new theatre which was then being built there. Our Rip says:

I think the new theatre was an old one refitted. I know it was quite the pride of the city and the idol of the new managers, for it had one tier of boxes and a gallery at the back. I don't think that the seats of the dress circle were stuffed, but I am sure they were planed. I was the comic singer of the party, making myself useful in small parts and first villagers; now and then doing duty as a Roman senator at the back, wrapped in a clean hotel sheet, with my head peering over profiled banquet tables. I was just nine years old. I was found useful as Albert and Duke of York. In those days the audience used to throw money upon the stage, either for comic songs or for dances; and oh, how I used to lengthen out the verses! The stars during the season were Mrs. McClure, Dan Marble, and A. A. Adams. Some of the plays acted were " Lady of Lyons," " Stranger," " Rob Roy," " Damon and Pythias," " Wives as They Were, Maids as They Are," and " Sam Patch." The city at that time had about three to four thousand inhabitants. I can remember following my father along the shore when he went shooting on what is now Michigan Avenue.

Chicago did not boast of a theatre worthy of the name until late in the forties, when John B. Rice, later mayor of Chicago, and a successful theatrical manager, erected a frame building on Randolph Street, near Dearborn Street. This first theatre was opened on June 28, 1847. The population by this time had increased to 17,000 and Chicago was rapidly becoming one of the most important cities in the West. The first season stock production occupied the boards and the following year such prominent players as Dan Marble, Mrs. John Drew, James Murdoch, Eliza Logan, Julia Dean, Barney Williams and others played star engagements.

In 1850 the theatre was destroyed by fire, and Rice at once purchased ground on Dearborn Street and began to build the first brick theatre in Chicago. This new house was opened on February 3 of the following year. Some time before this a temporary stage had been fitted up in the Tremont House and here the Bateman children made their first appearance in Chicago, November 18, 1850. In September, 1854, the Metropolitan Hall was opened to the public. The following year Levi J. North opened on Monroe Street North's Amphitheatre, and C. R. Thorne, Sr., inaugurated the National Theatre with " The Hunchback." In 1857 James H. McVicker, a New York actor, who had made his début at the Chatham Theatre in that city as a low comedian, went to Chicago and began his long career as a successful theatre manager by building a $85,000 theatre on Madison Street. This was opened November 5, 1857, with " The Honeymoon."

California's first acquaintance with the English spoken drama came as the natural result of the rush for the gold fields in 1849. The first theatrical performance given by professional actors in the city of San Francisco took place in January, 1850, in Washington Hall, a two story wooden building situated in Washington Street. The bill was Sheridan Knowles' play " The Wife," and the company, under the management of Messrs. Atwater and Madison, included J. B. Atwater, H. F. Daly, J. H. McCabe and Mrs. Frank Ray. " It is recorded," says John P. Young,[5] " that although the attendance was good, the actors were poor and not worth the price of admission." This first attempt was presently followed by the opening of another place of amusement, named the Olympic, on Kearney Street, where an Australian company under the management of Messrs. Lowe and Long presented " Othello." A little later a French vaudeville troupe, under the direction of M. Gunter, opened a theatre on Montgomery Street. Four theatres were operating simultaneously prior to 1851.

San Francisco, at that time, had just emerged from the sleepy Spanish village into a hustling American

---

[5] History of San Francisco. By John P. Young.

city. Most of its buildings, constructed of wood and hastily put up, fell an easy prey to the devastating fires which occurred periodically, destroying houses almost as fast as they were built. The population had increased to 42,000—a rough and ready crowd of miners, speculators and adventurers from every part of the world. When Jenny Lind, the Swedish nightingale, made her first appearance in America in 1850 the singer created such a sensation that three San Francisco theatres were immediately named after her. The first Jenny Lind Theatre was opened in 1850. That building being wiped out in the fire of 1851, another Jenny Lind Theatre was erected, and this was afterwards converted into a town hall. In 1850 Mr. and Mrs. James Stark made their first appearance in San Francisco at the Kearney Street Theatre. Mr. Stark was a favorite tragedian in California and appeared in all the familiar tragic rôles. In 1856 Mrs. Stark was manager of the Union Theatre, San Francisco. In February, 1852, a company headed by Mr. and Mrs. Lewis Baker, two favorite players, opened with Sheridan Knowles' drama "The Hunchback." The play ran twenty-five nights to crowded houses and was such a success that the company was induced to make a tour of the camps in the mining regions where the rough miners, to show their appreciation, showered nuggets and coins on the stage.[6]

The drama having thus obtained a foothold, theatres sprang up on all sides. Owing to the high prices of admission charged—$3 orchestra, $2 first

---

[6] This practice kept up for some time in California and it is not recorded that it was anywhere regarded as an unwelcome innovation by the players.

balcony and $1 gallery—the local managers were able to offer more liberal terms to visiting stars than Eastern managers could afford, and actors from New York, Philadelphia and Boston, allured by fanciful stories of fabulous salaries to be earned in the new Eldorado, rushed to California.

Theatres built about this time were the Adelphi, Italian, National, Phoenix, Atheneum, Olympic, American, Lyceum. The early managers included: John S. Potter, Charles R. Thorne, Sr., Wesley Venua, Joseph Rowe, Daniel Wilmarth, Charles A. King, Samuel Colville, J. B. Booth, Jr., McKean Buchanan, George Ryer. Favorites among the players were James Stark, William Barry, Frank Lawlor, John Woodward, James H. Warwick, Elizabeth Jefferson, Edward N. Thayer, John Dunn, Dan Virgil Gates, Mrs. Judah, "the grand old woman of the Western stage," Mary Woodward and Marie Duret.

The Metropolitan, San Francisco's first brick theatre, was opened December 24, 1853, as a home for a stock company, a feature being made of star engagements. Many, if not all, of the leading players of the day trod its boards, among them being Edwin Booth, Edwin Adams, John Drew, Sr., James E. Murdoch, Edwin Forrest, Lola Montez, J. B. Booth, Jr., Matilda Heron, C. W. Couldock, Laura Keene, Lotta, Frank Mayo, Barney Williams, Adah Isaacs Menken, John Brougham, John T. Raymond, Mr. and Mrs. Charles Kean, Charlotte Thompson, J. W. Wallack, Jr., Charles Wheatleigh, William A. Mestayer, Julia Dean, John E. Owens, Kate Denin, Walter Montgomery, Edward A. Sothern, Barry

355

Sullivan, James O'Neill, Lawrence Barrett, John McCullough, James A. Herne, Frank S. Chanfrau, Ben de Bar, Charles Coghlan, Barton Hill, Adelaide Neilson, Dion Boucicault, Helena Modjeska and many others.

Owing to the polyglot population, grand opera early took a strong hold in San Francisco. All the best operas and concert singers were heard, performances being given in Italian, French and English. Extravagant prices were paid for seats, the scale being $5, $3 and $2. Among the operatic favorites were Mme. Anna Bishop, Signora Bianchi, Caroline Richings, Kate Hayes, Signora Garbatas, Signora Biscaccianti, Mme. Balili-Thorn and Miska Hamer.

In 1869 John McCullough built the California Theatre, and at this house, in partnership part of the time with Lawrence Barrett, McCullough achieved some of his greatest successes. It was at the California Theatre that he first acted Virginius.

www.ingramcontent.com/pod-product-compliance
Lightning Source LLC
Chambersburg PA
CBHW050905100426
42737CB00048B/3006